Christian Hermetic Astrology

A TRILOGY DEDICATED
TO A NEW STAR WISDOM
(ASTROSOPHY)

Hermetic Astrology Volume I
Astrology and Reincarnation
(1987)

Hermetic Astrology Volume II
Astrological Biography
(1989)

Christian Hermetic Astrology
The Star of the Magi and the Life of Christ
(1991)

Christian Hermetic Astrology

The Star of the Magi and the Life of Christ

ROBERT A. POWELL

. . . .

Then will appear the sign of the Son of man in heaven, and then all the tribes of the earth will mourn, and they will see the Son of man coming on the clouds of heaven with power and great glory.

—MATTHEW 24:30

Anthroposophic Press

Copyright © 1991 by Robert Powell

All rights reserved. No part of this publication may be reproduced or transmitted in any form or by any means, electronic or mechanical, including photocopying, recording, or any information storage or retrieval system, without permission in writing from the publisher.

ISBN 0-88010-461-9

Contents

Introduction 7
Opening Invocation 13

A Discourse of Hermes to

Tat: The Mystery of the Zodiac 15

Closing Invocation 26

Discourses of Hermes to

King Ammon:	The Star of the Magi	28
Asclepius:	The Journey of the Three Kings and the Flight of the Holy Family to Egypt	35
Tat:	The Adoration of the Shepherds	43
Asclepius:	The Two Became One	52
King Ammon:	The Start of Christ's Ministry	56
Tat:	The Temptations in the Wilderness	71
Asclepius:	The Wedding at Cana	82
King Ammon:	Jesus' First Visit to Jerusalem Since the Baptism	93
Tat:	The Conversation at Jacob's Well and the Healing of the Nobleman's Son	100
Asclepius:	The Sun Chronicle in the Life of the Messiah	106
King Ammon:	The Raising of the Youth of Nain and of the Daughter of Jairus	116

Tat:	The Ministry Up to the Beheading of John the Baptist	124
Asclepius:	The Miracles of the Lord	133
Tat:	The Transfiguration	143
Asclepius:	The Raising of Lazarus	155
King Ammon:	The Journey of Jesus Christ to the Pagans	169
Tat:	The Last Supper	178
Asclepius:	Gethsemane Night	205
King Ammon:	The Stages of the Passion	213
Tat:	The Mystery of Golgotha	226
King Ammon:	The Forty Days After the Mystery of Golgotha	236
Tat:	The Whitsun Mystery	258
Asclepius:	The Christ Impulse in History	271
King Ammon:	The Most Holy Trinosophia	283

Closing Invocation 298
Sun Chronicle 300
Bibliography 306

Introduction

What was "The Star of the Magi"—a comet, a new star, a spectacular planetary configuration, a supernatural appearance in the heavens! Who were the three wise men from the East, and what led them to Bethlehem?

In this book we will explore these questions with the awareness that the magi were the last true representatives of an age-old spiritual tradition, a tradition in which a living relationship to the starry heavens was cultivated. This 'living relationship with the starry heavens,' or star *wisdom* lived also in the temples of ancient Egypt and Mesopotamia and formed the central content of the priestly rites and mysteries celebrated there. The magi belonged to a spiritual tradition of star wisdom inaugurated by the great initiate Zoroaster in Babylon in the sixth century B.C. (Zoroaster was known to the Babylonian priesthood as *Zaratas*.) Pythagoras, from the Greek island of Samos, traveled to Babylon and was initiated there by Zoroaster. And it is thanks to Pythagoras that knowledge of the *harmonies of the spheres* has been transmitted down to us.

Zoroaster himself attained to a still higher level of initiation than that of *hearing the harmonies of spheres*, which he mediated to Pythagoras. He attained to the sublime experience of *standing before the throne of God*. This experience was attained also by the apostle John, who describes the throne of God in the opening verses of chapter four of the Book of Revelation. This is the experience of the "holy living creatures" attending the Lord God Almighty—those twelve holy creatures whose *forms* are revealed outwardly in the twelve zodiacal constellations.

On the basis of his experience of *standing before the throne of God,* Zoroaster was able to delineate for his pupils in the Babylonian priesthood the spheres of influence of the zodiacal constellations. Thus originated the earliest definition of the sidereal zodiac.[1] On the basis of this definition of the zodiac into twelve equal signs, the Babylonian priests were able to follow the movements of the Sun, Moon and planets against the background of the fixed stars. This was not just on the level of physical-astronomical observation, however; it also entailed *reading the occult script of the stars.*

Through the excavation and decipherment of cuneiform texts from Babylon, we have come to know something of the external side of this great spiritual tradition. We know, for instance, that the Babylonian priesthood, from the sixth century B.C. onwards, made extensive astronomical observations of the movements of the Sun, Moon and planets through the twelve stellar signs of the sidereal zodiac—recording their positions at the moment of a person's birth. All of this stemmed from the great impulse given by Zoroaster to the priestly caste of Babylon. But to what purpose was all this?

None of this can be understood without taking account of the spiritual side of the path inaugurated by Zoroaster—a path leading upward from the stage of *neophyte* and culminating—for his most advanced pupils—in the *hearing of*

---

1. See Robert Powell and Peter Treadgold, *The Sidereal Zodiac* (Tempe, AZ: American Federation of Astrologers, 1985), for a formal definition of the sidereal zodiac. See also Robert Powell, *The Zodiac: A Historical Survey* (San Diego, CA: Astro Computing Services, 1984).

INTRODUCTION

the spheres (as exemplified in the initiation of Pythagoras). There was then, an outer, more astronomical-astrological side of the tradition, which we know of from cuneiform sources; and there was also an inner, spiritual side to Zoroaster's teaching. And the three magi, who lived toward the end of the first century B.C., were the last representatives of this inner, spiritual side of the tradition. Indeed, it could be said that this tradition culminated with the magi and found its fulfillment in them, and thereafter disappeared. The magi—although they lived centuries later—were true spiritual pupils of Zoroaster and, as we shall see, they were the deeper reason for Zoroaster having inaugurated the tradition at all.

As representatives of this path of star wisdom, the magi were able to *read the occult script of the stars*. And thus, on the night of the birth of Jesus—it was Full Moon in the constellation of Virgo—they were able to *read* the deeper significance of this event. Thus, we could say, the overriding reason for the existence of this ancient stream of star wisdom was to help prepare the way for the coming of Christ Jesus. And just as the purpose of this ancient wisdom had to do with the first coming of Christ, so its resurrection now, in our time, is related to the second coming of Christ. How may this be understood?

Here, it may help to imagine a metamorphosis of the Horus cult celebrated by the Hermetic priests of Egypt. Instead of Horus, revered in ancient Egypt, it is Jesus Christ who now occupies the central place. And instead of bowing down to Horus in a temple, those who gaze up to the starry heavens and allow the impressions received there to echo on in their inner being, may do so in a spirit of bowing down to the majesty of Jesus Christ in his second coming, swathed in the cosmic aura of the Earth, as within a cradle at the center of the cosmos.

Christian Hermetic Astrology thus seeks in modern times to continue the stream of ancient star wisdom represented first by the priests of Hermes who celebrated the cult of Horus, and then later by Zarathustra (Zoroaster) and the three magi—this stream having passed through the *needle's eye* of Christianity. For almost 2000 years Christianity has ostensibly been asleep to the cosmic dimension of the life and deeds of Christ. Our own time, however, calls for a profound renewal of the Christian Mysteries, and an essential element of this renewal is the cultivation of a modern *path of the magi* leading to a *Christian* wisdom of the stars.

The form chosen to present this work will be recognized by some readers as having an historical prototype in the *Hermetica*, the collection of writings attributed to the Egyptian Sage Hermes Trismegistus.[1] The dialogue form

---

1. *Hermetica*, trans. Walter Scott, 4 vols. (London: 1924); reprinted by Hermes House (Boulder, CO: 1982). The *Hermetica* were written during the first three centuries A.D.—long after the time of Hermes Trismegistus. They were written in Greek by anonymous authors who obviously regarded Hermes with awe and reverence as the inaugurator of the Egyptian Mystery Wisdom tradition. In this way they contributed to the Hermetic tradition. Nonetheless, their contribution was to Hermeticism in its pre-Christian form, because they did not include any reference to Jesus Christ or to Christianity. Just as with the anonymous authors of the *Hermetica* who chose the literary form of the dialogue, the present author also looks to Hermes as the source of the tradition and has chosen the same literary form as his predecessors in order to contribute to this tradition. The difference in the case of the present author is his setting the dialogues in the Christian era looking back to the life of Jesus Christ. This standpoint is that of Christian Hermeticism—a modern Christian metamorphosis of ancient Hermeticism.

was also employed by Plato in his writings. This form is ideally suited to the presentation of deep and intimate spiritual truths—those requiring a "protective atmosphere," such as is provided in these dialogues by the participants themselves.

When, in the text of the dialogue, planetary positions for events in the life of Christ are discussed, the reader is encouraged to consult the Sun Chronicle at the end of the book for the *cosmic commemorations* related to these past events. The astronomical and astrological basis of these computations is described in my volumes I and II of *Hermetic Astrology* and *Chronicle of the Life of Christ* and *The Horoscopes of Jesus Christ and the Blessed Virgin Mary*.[1] I suggest that the reader who has earnest questions regarding the Sun Chronicle direct them, for the time being, directly to the author, via the publisher. The reader who would like to explore in more depth Christian Hermeticism, and the basis of Christian Hermetic Astrology, is also referred to the annotated bibliography at the end of this book.

Finally, the author would like to express his profound indebtedness to the work of Rudolf Steiner (1861-1925) and Anne Catherine Emmerich (1774-1824). I am especially indebted to them for bringing to my awareness many events in Christ's life not narrated by the Gospels—the authenticity of which I have been able to confirm through my independent research. In the following pages these two individuals are reverently referred to as the "initiate" and the "blessed seer."

---

1. Robert Powell, *Hermetic Astrology vol. 1: Astrology and Reincarnation* (Kinsau, Germany: Hermetika, 1987); *Hermetic Astrology vol. II: Astrological Biography* (Kinsau, Germany: Hermetika, 1989); *Chronicle of the Living Christ* (Hudson, New York: Anthroposophic Press, 1996).

The author would also encourage the meditative reader to take the time to read the Opening and Closing Invocations—(which for the sake of space have only been included before and after the first discourse)—prior to, and following each individual discourse.

OPENING INVOCATION

In the holy temple of the Sun, Hermes is standing at the altar in the East, Tat at the altar in the South, Asclepius at the altar in the West, and King Ammon at the altar in the North.

HERMES: Encircling spirits in the East, South, West and North—may thy wisdom, beauty, strength and righteousness bless and protect this gathering in the holy temple of the Sun.

(turning to the East): Holy Michael, thou Sun-radiant power whose rose-hued aura shines on high, bestow on us thy omniscient light from thine inexhaustible fount of wisdom.

(turning to the South): Holy Gabriel, thou glowing one clothed in silvery moonlight, breathing graciousness, fill us with the ineffable beauty of thy gentle loving piety and reverence.

(turning to the West): Holy Raphael, thou gold-gleaming tower of strength, empower us with the magnificent force of thy healing presence.

(turning to the North): Holy Uriel, thou blue radiance of shining glory, instill in us the inexpressible grandeur of thy awesome righteousness.

Michael, Gabriel, Raphael, Uriel—encircling spirits in the heights, servants of the sublime Sun Spirit—may thou protect, guide and bless all who meet together in the Name of Christ, and watch over us in our humble endeavor to serve His Holy Word.

A Discourse of Hermes to Tat

The Mystery of the Zodiac

HERMES: Here in the temple of the Sun, the mysteries of the past, present and future are revealed to the eye of the spirit. Let us raise up our hearts, in purity of mind and soul, in preparation for a holy discourse.

TAT: Thou, father, who dost behold the secrets of the universe, pray tell us of the animal circle which is called the zodiac.

HERMES: My son, it is good that we commence this discourse by contemplating the ineffable mystery of the all-embracing circle of stars, for this in turn will lead us to contemplate still more sublime cosmic mysteries. What is the zodiac? And how long has it existed? The zodiac is the circle of stars which embraces the movements of the Sun, Moon and planets. It is divided into twelve starry regions of space, each named in accordance with the animal or human figure corresponding to the cosmic power that radiates from that region. It has existed since time immemorial. But let me now refer to one, an Elder Brother of humanity, who more than any other mortal has been able to penetrate the mystery of the zodiac. I mean he who long ago bore the name Zarathustra. I look to him as a spiritual father; and from him I have learnt much concerning the zodiac and the mysteries of the stars. Long ago in ancient Persia Zarathustra was initiated by the sublime Being of the Sun, *Ahura Mazdao*, who elevated him to knowledge of the cosmos. Zarathustra was shown the mystery of the Father and the Son—the Father, *Zervana Akarana*, meaning "Infinite Time," and the Son, *Ahura Mazdao*, meaning "Aura of Light." He beheld the radiant "Aura of Light" surrounding and indwelling the Sun. And above and beyond the Sun, he beheld the mighty circle of stars, the zodiac, as the outer manifestation of Zervana Akarana, the Heavenly Father, father of both Ahura Mazdao and Ahriman, the Evil Twin. Already then in ancient Persia Zarathustra spoke of the four royal stars as the four "foundation stones" of the zodiac—*Aldebaran*, the Bull's eye, the central star of the Bull; *Regulus*, the Lion's heart, shining from the breast of the Lion; *Antares*, the red-glowing Scorpion's heart, the central star of the Scorpion; and bright *Fomalhaut* in the mouth of the Southern Fish, beneath the stream of water flowing from the urn of the Waterman. These four stars form a cross in cosmic space from the four signs of the zodiac—the Bull, the Lion, the Eagle (Scorpion) and the Man (Angel). And the cosmic vision of these four signs as the "pillars" of the universe was bestowed not only on Zarathustra, but later upon the prophet Ezekiel, and later still on St. John the Evangelist. In St. John's revelation, the Apocalypse, we hear how he beheld the throne of God, and on each side of the throne four Holy Beings—bearing the throne, as a chariot—the Bull, the Lion, the Eagle and the Man, each of them with wings, full of eyes, and singing day and night a song of praise to the Lord God Almighty, whom Zarathustra named Zervana Akarana.

THE MYSTERY OF THE ZODIAC

TAT: But why, father, only four Holy Beings? Do we not see twelve great Beings in the starry circle of the zodiac?

HERMES: Yes, my son, it is true that we see twelve Beings in the stars of the zodiac. But look more closely and you will see that the star signs of the Bull, the Lion, and the Scorpion—with their brightly shining stars Aldebaran, Regulus and Antares—stand forth from the other signs. And looking across to the Waterman, is it not an impressive sight to see bright Fomalhaut in the mouth of the fish into which the waters pour forth from his urn? So you see, my son, that in the circle of the zodiac, the four starry signs—the Bull, the Lion, the Eagle (Scorpion) and the Man (Waterman)—stand forth, and it is these four Holy Beings that first reveal themselves to the eye of the spirit when raised toward the realm of Zervana Akarana. So mighty do these four appear! They manifest themselves as the founding pillars, as it were, supporting the chariot of God. But when the eye of the spirit beholds more closely, these four Holy Beings appear flanked on each side. Looking to the Man, the Waterman—who is really an Angel, for he is winged—on one side he is flanked by the Holy Being that appears as a Goatfish, and on the other side are the two Fishes linked together by a cord, which is the outer aspect of the Holy Being who radiates forth from the star-sign of Pisces. If we look in the direction of the Man, therefore, we see that on the eastern side he is flanked by Pisces (the Fishes), and on the western side by Capricorn (the Goatfish). So it is with the Bull, who is flanked to the east by Gemini (the Twins), and to the west by Aries (the Ram); also with the Lion, to the east flanked by Virgo (the Virgin), and to the west by Cancer (the Crab); and with the Eagle or Scorpion, to the east flanked by Sagittarius (the Archer), and to the west by Libra (the Scales). The four Holy Beings in the visions of Ezekiel and St. John therefore represent the great circle of twelve Holy Beings who encircle the whole universe, indwelling the twelve star-signs of the zodiac. All twelve radiate forth from the various zodiacal signs, but these four stand forth as representatives. Just as the four directions—North, South, East, West—represent the main axes in space, so the four signs—Taurus, Leo, Scorpio, Aquarius—represent the main axes of the zodiac. They are called the *fixed* signs of the zodiac.

TAT: Pray tell us, father, is there a correspondence between the four fixed zodiacal signs and the four directions of space?

HERMES: If we follow the spiritual rays streaming from the twelve starry signs of the zodiac, then on the Earth the spatial directions allocated to them are continually changing. For example, at sunrise in spring it might be that Taurus is in the East, and then at sunset Scorpio would be in the East. To the eye of the spirit, however, when raised away from the Earth toward the realm of the zodiac, the zodiac is experienced to be at rest. Then we can discern the cosmic directions of space, which are referred to as North, South, East and West, although this is only by way of analogy with these names as they are applied on the Earth. And, indeed, the four fixed signs coincide on the archetypal level of the zodiac with these four cosmic directions. Archetypally, the axis Taurus-Scorpio coincides with East-West, and the axis Leo-Aquarius coincides with North-South. Here is yet a further reason why the four Holy Beings—Bull, Lion,

Eagle (Scorpion) and Man—are primary in the visions of Ezekiel and St. John, as they offer spiritual orientation in the four archetypal directions. Now it will be easy for you to understand that archetypally the axis East-West runs from the middle of Taurus to the middle of Scorpio, and the axis North-South passes from the middle of Leo to the middle of Aquarius. For this reason the stars Aldebaran, Regulus, Antares and Fomalhaut were called the *royal stars* by Zarathustra. Aldebaran, the Bull's eye, is the *watcher in the East;* and Antares, the Scorpion's heart, is the *watcher in the West.* Cosmically speaking, Aldebaran lies exactly due East, being in the very center of the sign of the Bull. Similarly, Antares is located exactly due West, being placed in the very middle of the sign of the Scorpion. Looking at the cosmic spatial North-South axis running from the middle of the stars of Leo to the middle of Aquarius, there is a bright star in the Lion which does not lie exactly on this axis, but is very close to it; this is Regulus, the Lion's heart, which is called the *watcher in the North.* Likewise, if we look at the stellar configuration of the Waterman, there is a bright star just beneath which is Fomalhaut, the Southern Fish, that lies close to the axis running through the center of Aquarius, so Fomalhaut is called the *watcher in the South.*

TAT: O father, can you tell us how the zodiac came to be defined by human beings?

HERMES: Yes, my son, listen carefully. The key to the mystery of the zodiac, as I said before, was revealed to Zarathustra. When he lived long ago in ancient Persia he was initiated by the Spirit of the Sun, Ahura Mazdao, and gained knowledge of the Heavenly Father, Zervana

Akarana, who is borne in his chariot by the twelve Holy Beings dwelling in the starry realms of the zodiac. At that time Zarathustra taught concerning the four royal zodiacal stars marking the four cosmic archetypal directions in space: Aldebaran, the watcher in the East; Regulus, the watcher in the North; Antares, the watcher in the West; and Fomalhaut, the watcher in the South. This teaching was the first fruit of Zarathustra's cosmic revelation of Zervana Akarana.

In a later age Zarathustra incarnated again, at the time of Cyrus the Great, and became known to the Greeks as Zoroaster. He was known to the Babylonians as Zaratas, and was acknowledged by the Chaldean priests and stargazers as a great teacher. And when Pythagoras visited Babylon, he was initiated by Zaratas and was cleansed of the impurities of his past life. Zaratas (Zoroaster) taught in Babylon concerning the cosmic mysteries. He foresaw that a new age was approaching in which human beings would no longer behold the Holy Beings of the cosmos, but only their outer revelation by way of the stars and planets. He foresaw, too, the necessity for a science of the cosmos, which would truly express the cosmic mysteries, even if the underlying reality would no longer be seen with the eye of the spirit. It was his task in Babylon to *translate* the cosmic mysteries into a scientific form. Part of Zoroaster's teaching was transmitted to Pythagoras, who took up this task and, after returning to Greece, sought to continue it. Zoroaster was the one who stood behind that which Pythagoras accomplished in the sphere of cosmic science. Similarly, the Chaldean priesthood and stargazers in Babylon took up the teachings of Zoroaster and began to lay the foundations of a cosmic science. The definition by the Babylonians of the zodiac represents one of the first fruits of this work. For the Babylonian zodiac is defined so that the two royal stars—Aldebaran and Antares—lie exactly in the middle of their respective signs. The Babylonians instituted the division of the circle of the zodiac into 360 degrees, which they divided into twelve signs, each 30 degrees long. The question for them was: How are the twelve signs related to the stars of the zodiac, these stars being the outer manifestation or "body" of the Holy Beings radiating from the twelve divisions of the zodiacal circle? Here Zoroaster's teaching concerning the cosmic mystery of the zodiac was able to help them. The Babylonian zodiac was defined so that Aldebaran lay exactly at the center of the sign of Taurus (15° Taurus) and Antares at the very middle of the sign of Scorpio (15° Scorpio). By measuring in degrees the distance of other stars around the zodiacal circle, their longitudes within the zodiacal signs were determined. For example, Regulus was found to be at 5° Leo, not far from the center of the Lion, and Fomalhaut at 9° Aquarius, close to the middle of Aquarius. The Babylonian zodiac was the first scientific definition of the zodiac, and served as the archetype for all other zodiacs that have since been defined. And the Babylonian zodiac corresponds to the cosmic reality of the twelve Holy Beings manifesting through the twelve stellar divisions of the zodiacal circle. The Babylonian zodiac, which arose through the inspiration and vision of Zoroaster, who lived in Babylon at the time of Cyrus the Great, gives an authentic representation of the spiritual reality underlying the encircling stars of the zodiac.

TAT: What was the fate of the Babylonian zodiac? And how was it applied in the cosmic science of the Chaldeans?

HERMES: My son, let me tell you something of the Chaldean science of the stars. Long ago the priests and stargazers of Babylon looked up to the heavenly world and read from the movements of the Sun, Moon and planets the intention of the Heavenly Beings. For long ages they kept records of the events that befell king and country, recorded in relation to the starry heavens. And when a configuration in the world of stars appeared that reminded them of an earlier one, they consulted the "omen records" to see what kind of event might recur. In this way the Chaldean priests and stargazers developed the art of prophecy. Now, when Zoroaster began his teaching activity in Babylon, he was aware that the time had come for a new art of prophecy—as a cosmic science—to be developed. He knew that a science of destiny relating to the individual human being had to come about. So the foundation was laid for individual astrology, whereby the omens, which had hitherto been applied generally to king and country, were applied on an individual basis to each person, in relation to the planetary configuration at the person's birth. For Zoroaster the incarnation of the soul into the body was something that he could behold. With the eye of the spirit he could follow the descent of the soul from cosmic heights down through the planetary spheres, eventually to reach the Earth. It was this vision of the voyage of the soul which gave birth to the casting of horoscopes, whereby originally both the moment of conception and the moment of birth were taken into consideration. The moment of conception was seen as an important step on the journey into incarnation, at which the impetus was given for the formation of the physical body. And the moment of birth was seen as the start of the unfolding of destiny on the Earth, to be fulfilled by the soul indwelling the physical body that was built up between conception and birth. The planetary configuration at birth conveys something of the secret of the soul's destiny—it was knowledge of this fact which gave rise to the practice of casting horoscopes, as developed originally in Babylon through Zoroaster's inspiration. Like Zoroaster, the initiated Chaldean priests and stargazers also had the faculty of beholding the voyage of the soul into incarnation, so that astrology was not an abstract pursuit based solely on computation, but was a living wisdom. It was this faculty that was all-important for the origins of astrology. Especially significant for the Chaldean priests and stargazers was the passage of the Moon around the zodiac. They regarded the Moon as the gateway or portal of entrance for the soul on the voyage into incarnation, and they could behold the "descent of the stork" at the moment of conception, descending from the direction of the Moon to unite with the seed of the embryo. And by focusing their spiritual gaze upon the Moon they could gain awareness of the moment of birth of the incarnating soul. Thus the Chaldean priests and stargazers devoted much attention to following spiritually the path of the Moon through the signs of the zodiac, and in this way were able to gain knowledge of the conception and birth of incarnating souls. Before his death, Zoroaster taught his disciples of the importance of continuing this spiritual practice. He spoke of a holy mystery concerning a great king who would be conceived in the womb of a virgin, and who would be born to save the world. He prophesied that this king would be persecuted and crucified to death, and that Heaven and Earth would mourn for his sake; that he would descend to the depths of the Earth and then be raised up to the heights, and would come again upon white clouds with his armies of light. When his disciples asked him who this king would be, Zoroaster replied, "I am he, and he is I; he is in me, and I am in him. When his time comes there will be signs in the heavens, and a star will arise which will lead those who follow it to his birth. Guard this secret, and when his birth comes let ambassadors follow the star, that they may bear gifts and offer worship to him." For this reason, that the future incarnation of this king would be recognized, Zoroaster instituted the cosmic science of astrology among the Chaldeans of Babylon, and it was from the descendants of the Chaldeans in Mesopotamia that the three kings came, following the star to the newborn child. This child was named Jesus, and was an incarnation of Zoroaster himself. This is one aspect of the holy mystery surrounding the birth of Jesus.

TAT: Thank you, O father, for this holy discourse on the zodiac, and concerning the origin of the science of astrology in Babylon.

HERMES: It is good, my son, that the way is now prepared for the next discourse concerning the star of the magi. The magi (kings) were spiritual descendants of Zoroaster. As practitioners of the Chaldean cosmic science, they knew of the prophecy of Zoroaster and were awaiting the incarnation of the great king. For their observations and calculations the three kings made use of the Babylonian zodiac; and that they were successful in finding the newborn king is a tribute to the fulfillment of the task set by Zoroaster centuries before. But shortly after the time of the three kings the Babylonian zodiac ceased to be used by astrologers in the West, and it was only very many centuries later that—as ordained by destiny—it was rediscovered. Such was the fate of this zodiac. There is much more to be said concerning the mystery of the zodiac, but this can only be the subject of a future discourse. Now, my son, it is good that we draw the present discourse to a close.

TAT: Indeed, O father, we are ready for the invocation to close this discourse.

CLOSING INVOCATION

HERMES: Encircling spirits in the North, West, South and East—servants of the sublime Sun Spirit CHRIST—in sacred devotion to the Holy Sacrifice on Golgotha we direct our will, feeling, thought and all our love toward thee for the fulfillment of the Great Work.

(turning to the North): Holy Uriel, thou who bears the memory of the Golden Age of Saturn, whence streams the foundation of human will, pray strengthen the will of all who humbly seek to unite themselves with Christ and His Mission.

(turning to the West): Holy Raphael, thou who embodies the power of the Age of the Sun, whence flows the spiritual stream underlying feeling, may thou imbue human feeling with never-ending devotion to the Christ Being and His Healing Work of Redemption.

(turning to the South): Holy Gabriel, thou who carries the spirit-light of the Age of the Moon, whence radiates the fount underlying the life of thought, help illumine our thinking that it be raised to knowledge of the cosmic mystery of the Logos who is the Salvation of humankind and the Earth.

CLOSING INVOCATION

(turning to the East):   Holy Michael, thou who guards the Evolution of the Earth, during which the Mystery of Golgotha took place, whence comes the inner spirit-birth of the true Self of the human being, may thy radiant Being guide this Self in freedom and love along the path of human existence which receives its meaning alone through Christ.

Encircling spirits of the North, West, South and East—hear our prayer!

TAT, ASCLEPIUS, KING AMMON: Christ graciously hear us!

HERMES: Go forth in peace!

A Discourse of Hermes to King Ammon

The Star of the Magi

OPENING INVOCATION

HERMES: Now that we are gathered together in the temple of the Sun, let us raise up our hearts, in purity of mind and soul, in preparation for a holy discourse.

KING AMMON: O thrice-greatest Hermes, tell us, pray, what was the star of the magi?

HERMES: King Ammon, mark my words closely, for we shall contemplate the star of the magi as a mystery which belongs to the sublime mysteries of the Holy Grail. In a mood of reverence and devotion, let us direct our spiritual gaze to the magi who were continuers of the Chaldean astrological tradition inaugurated in Babylon by Zoroaster in the sixth century B.C. Who were these three magi, these "kings" who came to worship the newborn child Jesus? They are attributed with the names Caspar, Melchior and Balthasar. However, these were not their real names; but this is not of importance for the present discourse. What is important is that they faithfully continued the practice of stargazing, as Zoroaster and the Chaldean priests and stargazers of Babylon had done for centuries before. What did this practice consist of? On the one hand it entailed the calculation of the movements of the Sun, Moon and planets against the background of the starry signs of the zodiac, so that important planetary configurations were known of in advance. These calculations, which were made in terms of the sidereal zodiac, were inscribed on cuneiform tablets. On the other hand, it involved the nightly contemplation of the heavens, where in a state of rapture the magi beheld in dreamlike consciousness pictures of events taking place or about to take place on the Earth. In this state of consciousness the magi were receptive to that which certain groupings of stars and planets spoke by way of pictures and images.

KING AMMON: O Hermes, is this to be understood as a revelation from the world of stars?

HERMES: Yes, King Ammon, it is indeed. Each planet and each group of stars is the outer manifestation of a Heavenly Being or an entire colony of Heavenly Beings. These Beings guide the destinies of humans and watch over all that takes place on the Earth. The magi sought to read the intentions of these Heavenly Beings by watching the changes taking place in the world of stars. They were watching especially for the coming of the great king, the soul of Zoroaster himself. And in the year 7 B.C. they became aware of Zoroaster's approaching incarnation by a conjunction between the planets Saturn and Jupiter in the star-sign Pisces. There were in fact three conjunctions between Jupiter and Saturn in Pisces in that year, but it was the first of these three conjunctions which heralded the approaching incarnation of the great teacher Zoroaster, whose name means "radiant star." This first conjunction took place on May 27 at 24° Pisces, beneath the Eastern Fish of the two Fishes. At that time the Sun was in the sign of Gemini, close to the feet of the Twins. Two days later the New Moon took place in Gemini, and on the evening of May 30 the thin new sickle crescent of the Moon became visible on the western horizon. The magi, as was their practice, followed the passage of the Moon through the signs of the zodiac, watching it grow as it waxed brighter each evening. Each night they saw the progress of the Moon: through the signs of Cancer, Leo and Virgo, gradually increasing its distance from the Sun in Gemini. The waxing Moon was visible to them during the first part of the night. Later in the night Saturn and Jupiter rose together across the eastern horizon—a magnificent sight—to stand high overhead by the time of sunrise. On the evening of June 6, the Moon had just overtaken the star Spica at 29° Virgo, the ear of corn held by the Virgin, and entered Libra. Westward of the Moon was Spica, and six degrees further westward from Spica was Mars, also in the Virgin. Mars was in opposition to the conjunction of Jupiter and Saturn in Pisces. The Moon was not yet full but was an impressive sight in the night sky; it disappeared from view during the early hours of the morning of June 7. The gaze of the magi shifted again to the planets Jupiter and Saturn, together high above in Pisces. With a sense of wonder they felt the presence of the soul of Zoroaster. And indeed on that very day, June 7 in 7 B.C., the incarnation of this kingly soul began. The moment of spiritual conception, beheld clairvoyantly as the "descent of the stork," took place in Bethlehem shortly before midday. In the hermetic chart for this moment Venus and Pluto were in conjunction with the Ascendant in the sign of Virgo (13° Virgo). It was a conception in the sign of the Virgin, with the Sun high above in the Twins (16° Gemini) and the Moon in the sign of the Balance (10° Libra). Geocentrically, Saturn and Jupiter were close to setting on the western horizon and were in opposition to Mars; Pluto was rising, and Uranus—in opposition to Pluto—had just set. In the hermetic chart Mars and Neptune were in conjunction in the claws of the Scorpion, and Mercury was also in the Scorpion, in conjunction with Antares, the Scorpion's heart (15° Scorpio). From this moment on there began the weaving of the web of destiny of the incarnating soul of Zoroaster, who was born in Bethlehem nine months later and received the name Jesus.

KING AMMON: Is it true to say, then, O Hermes, that the first conjunction between Jupiter and Saturn in 7 B.C., which heralded the conception of the incarnating soul of Zoroaster, was actually the star of the magi?

HERMES: In part, King Ammon, but there is more to be said concerning this, from which you will see that the revelation of the stars during the entire period from the conception in 7 B.C. to the birth in 6 B.C. may be called the star of the magi. But in so far as the beginning of Zoroaster's reincarnation was heralded by the first meeting in 7 B.C. between Jupiter and Saturn, this may be called the onset of the star of the magi, the commencement of the revelation of "radiant star" (Zoroaster) from the world of stars, announcing to the magi his incarnation. And the culmination of this revelation was the birth nine months later. How did the magi experience this? From the day of conception onwards they continued to follow the Moon's passage around the zodiac, and also the further conjunctions between Jupiter and Saturn—the second on September 29 and the third on December 3, 7 B.C., by which time some six months had elapsed from the conception. They beheld, too, the progress of Mars through the signs of the zodiac—from Virgo (at the time of conception), through Libra, Scorpio, Sagittarius and Capricorn, in steady pursuit of Jupiter and Saturn. During the last three months of the incarnation into the physical body, Mars proceeded through Aquarius and Pisces, overtaking Saturn on February 20, 6 B.C., at 25° Pisces. Now the magi knew that the birth was imminent. What an occurrence! Mars, Jupiter and Saturn in close proximity to one another! Now together, after having been placed with Mars in opposition to Jupiter and Saturn at the conception! By this time, as his birth was approaching, Jupiter had already separated from Saturn by several degrees, having entered the star-sign of Aries a week earlier, on February 13. After overtaking Saturn, Mars was placed between Saturn and Jupiter, and as the birth approached, the red planet drew ever closer to Jupiter, entering Aries on February 27. And on the very day of the birth—on March 5—Mars entered into conjunction with Jupiter in the Ram ($4\frac{1}{2}°$ Aries). This was the culmination of the star of the magi, which had started nine months earlier with the first conjunction between Jupiter and Saturn.

But let us now contemplate the speaking of the stars—and of "radiant star" (Zoroaster)—to the magi on this day, or rather on the evening of March 5, for the birth took place in Bethlehem almost exactly two hours after the Sun had set.

The Sun was in the middle of Pisces, and Saturn (in Pisces) and Mars and Jupiter (in Aries) had already set. It was the night of the Full Moon. The shining orb of the almost Full Moon shone above the eastern horizon from the middle of the Virgin. The Moon alone was visible in the night sky, for all other planets were below the horizon—except for Pluto, which was in conjunction with the Moon, but was not visible. In the East the star-sign of Libra was beginning to rise, and at the moment of the birth the Ascendant was at 10° Libra, exactly where the Moon had been at the conception nine months earlier. And the Full Moon was at 13° Virgo, which had been the place of the Ascendant at the conception. So the moment of the fulfillment of the hermetic rule had arrived, and the birth took place. From the womb of Mary, in her house in Bethlehem, the newborn child emerged to begin a new incarnation upon the Earth. And at this very moment the magi beheld an awe-inspiring vision in the heavens. They saw the Full Moon in the Virgin, whereby the Virgin appeared standing on the Moon. In her right hand she was holding a sheaf of wheat, at the tip of which was the ear of corn (Spica), and on her left side was a vine. Encircling the Moon they saw a magnificent halo, a rainbow of light, upon which the Virgin was enthroned. Issuing forth from the Virgin they beheld a chalice—the sacred vessel of the Grail—from which there arose a child. Above the child's head was a disc, like the Blessed Sacrament, from which rays of light streamed forth. The child was radiant with light, and proceeded from the Virgin towards them; and they knew that they were to follow it. And it was this child of radiant light, the incarnating soul of "radiant star" himself, which was the star that later guided them to the place of the birth. The entire experience of the birth of the child from the Virgin, on the night of the Full Moon in the Virgin, filled the three kings with inexpressible joy.

KING AMMON: O Hermes, this indeed was the star of the magi—"radiant star" (Zoroaster)!

HERMES: Yes, on the one hand, the inner reality of the star of the magi was the incarnation of "radiant star" (Zoroaster), descending from cosmic realms to be born on the Earth. On the other hand, the magi followed his descent between conception and birth in relation to the outwardly perceptible movements of the planets against the background of the starry signs. And here it was above all the conjunction in Pisces between Jupiter and Saturn which heralded his conception and dominated the night sky throughout the following nine months, and which culminated with Mars joining Saturn and Jupiter—the birth taking place on the very day of Mars' conjunction with Jupiter, in the evening, as the Full Moon rose in the Virgin. But more of this in the next discourse!

KING AMMON: Thank you, O Hermes, for this discourse on the star of the magi.

CLOSING INVOCATION

A Discourse of Hermes to Asclepius

The Journey of the Three Kings and the Flight of the Holy Family to Egypt

OPENING INVOCATION

HERMES: In the preceding discourse we raised our hearts and minds to contemplate the star of the magi, which belongs to the Mysteries of the Grail. The three magi were seekers for the Grail, watching for the incarnation of the great king, Zoroaster—not a king in the earthly realm, but in the kingdom of heaven: a great soul, a spiritual king, a master! The most important moments of conception and birth along the way of incarnation were revealed to the magi above all by way of their practice of following the passage of the Moon throughout the signs of the zodiac. At the moment of conception—clairvoyantly beheld as the "descent of the stork" from the Moon to the Earth—the waxing Moon was at 10° Libra. This was also the subsequent location of the Full Moon at the start of the Mystery of Golgotha, at the carrying of the cross up Mt. Calvary on Good Friday, April 3, A.D. 33. And at the birth, on the evening of the Full Moon in Virgo, the magi had the profound experience of beholding clairvoyantly the soul of "radiant star" (Zoroaster) issuing forth from the Moon and proceeding to the Earth. The Moon is therefore rightly named the "portal of the soul" on the passage of the soul into incarnation, and the experiences of the magi at these moments, in connection with the incarnation of "radiant star," were archetypal. They are the same for each incarnating soul, for every soul is a star!

ASCLEPIUS: O Hermes, can you reveal to us more of this Grail Mystery?

HERMES: Most honorable Asclepius, listen carefully. A great soul such as Zoroaster, who incarnated as Jesus, can be likened to a star of first magnitude, such as the star Sirius, which shines so brightly that it stands forth from the other stars in the firmament. At the birth of Jesus the magi beheld the radiant star of the soul, and it was this which went before them, guiding them to the place of birth. On the face of the Full Moon in Virgo the magi read the name written there and knew that it was their spiritual teacher whose birth they beheld. In his spirit they had continued the tradition of stargazing—a living astrology—which Zoroaster had inaugurated centuries earlier in Babylon. This great teacher summoned the three kings with his own being to the place of birth, going before them in shining starlike radiance. This was no outwardly perceptible star, and it was not visible to Herod and the others. Each incarnation of a great master follows the same archetype as that of Zoroaster. A star of first magnitude descends to the Earth, and at birth (or even earlier, at conception) the name of this *star* may be read by the eye of the spirit from the face of the Moon. This belongs to the Mysteries of the Holy Grail.

THE JOURNEY OF THE THREE KINGS

ASCLEPIUS: Pray tell us, O thrice greatest one, of the journey of the magi and of their encounter with Herod.

HERMES: Worthy Asclepius, it fills me with sadness to speak of Herod the Great. He was a king, an earthly king. But spiritually he was also a kingly soul—a bright star fallen from heaven! In his case we have a tragic warning of what may befall even a great soul when seized with the will to power. Thereby Herod opened himself to the powers of evil, and became an instrument in their endeavor to thwart the good. How he fell from lofty heights and degenerated! Thus he came to represent the lower self of human beings, open to the working of evil, in opposition to the true Self, the Christ Self. The lower self may indeed be *king* in the earthly world, but it is rightfully subject to the Self in the Kingdom of the Spirit, and sins when it sets itself against that Self. So it was with Herod, when he conceived of his evil plan to destroy the newborn child. The three kings (magi) came as representatives of the soul of humankind— of humankind's powers of thought, feeling and will—faced with the choice between serving the higher Self or collaborating with the lower self in pitting itself against the higher Self. The meeting with Herod represented a temptation for the three kings, a temptation which was of significance for humanity. But with the help of divine intervention the temptation was rendered impotent, and the three magi did not betray their spiritual king.

Having beheld the birth of Jesus from the sign of the Virgin on the night of the Full Moon in Virgo, the magi waited for further signs from the heavens and made plans to set off in order to pay homage to the newborn child. They waited nine more Full Moons—the Full Moons in

Libra, Scorpio, Sagittarius, Capricorn, Aquarius, Pisces, Aries, Taurus and Gemini—before setting out. It was the time of the Full Moon in Gemini, which took place on the night of November 25/26, 6 B.C., when the kings departed from Mesopotamia, setting out from a place on the Euphrates, some distance north of Babylon, on their camels. They made rapid progress across the desert, traveling mainly by night, in a straight line towards Judea. It was the soul of "radiant star" which guided them, going before them as a star of light. By the time of the next Full Moon—that in Cancer, on the night of December 25/26, 6 B.C.—they were approaching Jerusalem, but here they lost sight of their guiding star. It was Saturday evening, after the close of the Sabbath, on the night of the Full Moon, and Herod the Great had staged a banquet. When the kings arrived at his palace, Herod sent one of his courtiers to question them as to the purpose of their journey. When Herod heard that the magi had come to pay homage to a newborn king he became greatly distressed, and even though it was approaching midnight, he sent for the high priests and scribes. They told him of the prophecy of the prophet Micah: "But you, O Bethlehem, who are little among the clans of Judah, from you shall come forth one who is to be ruler in Israel!" Very early on the following morning Herod secretly summoned the three kings to his palace and asked them what they had seen. They reported to him what they had seen in the stars in the wake of the conjunction of Jupiter and Saturn—the birth of a child, a child that would be worshipped in adoration by all the peoples of the Earth. Herod then told them of the prophecy concerning Bethlehem. He requested that if the kings should find the child there, they should return to him and let him know, so that he also could go and pay homage to the newborn king. His real intention, however, was to have the kings imprisoned on their return to Jerusalem and to murder the child.

It was still not yet light as the three magi left Herod's palace on that Sunday morning. They proceeded from Jerusalem to Bethlehem, but stopped for several hours on the way in order to take refreshment and to feed and water their camels. At dusk they arrived in Bethlehem. Not long after the Sun had set, the full orb of the Moon rose in the East in the middle of Cancer. Suddenly they were filled with joy, for they saw above and surrounding a house in Bethlehem the glowing light of "radiant star" that had guided them on their journey. They went to the house, entered, and fell down in adoration before the child—now ten Full Moons old—who was sitting on his mother's lap. At the adoration of the magi, on the evening of December 26, 6 B.C., Saturn (2° Aries) and Jupiter (24° Aries) were high overhead in the Ram and Mars (13° Libra) was opposite in the sign of the Balance. The Sun (6° Capricorn) was in the horns of the Goat, and the Moon (15° Cancer) was opposite in the middle of the Crab. The three kings were in ecstasy, transfused by the light emanating from the child, which was no outwardly perceptible light, but was the Light of the World. They humbly knelt before the child and his mother, and offered up their prayers to the Lord who is eternal and is in all things. As they offered their gifts—gold, frankincense and myrrh—they said: "We have seen his star, and we have seen that he is king over all kings, and we have come to worship him and pay homage to him with our gifts." In their prayers they committed all to the child Jesus—themselves and their families, their lands, goods and possessions, everything that they owned. They besought the newborn king to accept not only their offerings but also their hearts and souls, that he might enlighten them and grant them peace. Filled with tender love and humility, they were blissfully happy at having now found the star whose coming their forefathers had waited for across the centuries.

On the next day, Monday, December 27, 6 B.C., the kings visited the child Jesus again. They were full of joy and happiness. They intended to leave on the morning of the following day and return to Jerusalem to tell Herod that they had found the child in Bethlehem. That evening they came to the house to say farewell, and brought more gifts with them. They stood in awe and gratitude before the child and his mother, and shed tears when the moment of parting came. At midnight that night an Angel appeared to them and warned them not to return to Jerusalem but to leave immediately and return home by another route. After warning the holy family, the kings left that night and went southward through the desert and along the shores of the Dead Sea, passing south thereof before turning northeast across the desert in the direction of Babylon.

ASCLEPIUS: O Hermes, what became of the holy family?

HERMES: The mother and father took the child Jesus, left their house in Bethlehem, and went to stay with relatives in Nazareth. When the three kings did not return to Jerusalem, Herod spread the rumor that they had been unsuccessful, that they had not found the child they had been seeking, and that on this account they had not returned to him. He wanted to give the impression that the whole matter was something of a hoax, in order to put a stop to the idea circulating that the Messiah had been born. But inwardly he was uneasy and disturbed. After some two months had elapsed, he was so plagued with the thought that the child had in fact been born, and that the magi had knowingly avoided informing him, that he resolved upon the murder of the children of Bethlehem. It was at this time that an Angel appeared one evening to the child's father, whose name was Joseph, and instructed him to flee with his family to Egypt. That very same night—it was the night of March 2/3, 5 B.C.—the holy family left Nazareth and set off for Egypt. The child Jesus was now almost exactly one year old. Subsequently the murder of the innocent children of Bethlehem took place, which marked the culmination of Herod's evil deeds. But before this abominable act took place, the holy family had already left Israel.

The holy family first went to Heliopolis (On) and stayed there for $1\frac{1}{2}$ years, then moved to Matarea, a small distance southeast of Heliopolis. They stayed on in Matarea almost five more years, in order to be sure that Herod and his successors had forgotten about the child of Bethlehem whom the three kings had visited. One night in the summer of A.D. 2 an Angel came to Joseph in a dream, saying that Herod was dead, that those who had sought the life of the child were no longer a threat, and that the holy family should return to Israel. The holy family then made their way back to Israel. Here again an Angel appeared to Joseph in a dream and told him to go to Nazareth, as Archelaus was now ruler over Judea in place of his father, Herod. When the holy family arrived in Nazareth it was September in the year A.D. 2 and Jesus was $7\frac{1}{2}$ years old.

ASCLEPIUS: Thank you, O Hermes, for this discourse on the adoration of the magi and the flight of the holy family to Egypt.

CLOSING INVOCATION

A Discourse of Hermes to Tat

The Adoration of the Shepherds

OPENING INVOCATION

TAT: In the two preceding discourses, O father, you have spoken of the star of the magi and of their journey to the child Jesus in Bethlehem; can you tell us also of the adoration of the shepherds?

HERMES: Yes, my beloved son, but first I must speak to you of a holy mystery which has remained concealed until the twentieth century. Here from the temple of the Sun, looking down upon the Earth, and upon the history of Christendom, two great seers stand out, who have beheld with the eye of the spirit the deeper mysteries surrounding the foundation of Christianity. The first seer bore the stigmata of Our Lord as a sign of her union with Him. She lived in Germany from 1774 to 1824, and was a nun in the Order of St. Augustine. This blessed seer received the stigmata on the afternoon of December 29, 1812, when the Sun ($15\frac{1}{2}°$ Sagittarius) was in the middle of the star-sign of the Archer in conjunction with Saturn (18° Sagittarius). For many years the blessed seer patiently bore the bleeding wounds of the Lord and waited for the coming of one whom she named the "pilgrim," who was destined to write down her words, bringing a new revelation of the Christ Mystery. After years of waiting the pilgrim finally came, and the revelation began. This seer was gifted with a power of vision surpassing all others before her in the history of Christianity, and beheld in precise detail the daily events in the life of Our Lord. For a period of 3½ years at the end of her life she revealed the day-by-day ministry and Passion of Jesus Christ. It was the time of a sublime revelation intended for the whole of Christendom. The cosmic indicator of this new revelation was the threefold conjunction between Uranus and Neptune in the star-sign of the Archer in 1821—on March 22 (11° Sagittarius), May 3 (11° Sagittarius) and December 3 (10° Sagittarius). But this new Christian revelation has had to wait until the next conjunction between Uranus and Neptune before becoming known as a historical fact—again a threefold conjunction in the star-sign of the Archer, in the year 1993: on February 2 (25° Sagittarius), August 19 (24° Sagittarius) and October 25 (24° Sagittarius).

Despite all that was revealed to the blessed seer, one deep mystery was not revealed to her. The time was not yet ripe that it should be unveiled, so this mystery was withheld from penetration by her spiritual gaze. This is the mystery surrounding the birth of two children, each of whom bore the name Jesus, both of whom grew up at the same time in Nazareth. The blessed seer came close, very close to this mystery, for with the eye of spirit she beheld the lineages of the two children, both belonging to the royal house of David, one extending back to David's son Nathan, the prophet, and the other reaching back to David's son Solomon, the king. She saw these two lineages proceeding from David, one to the right and the other to the left. The right line, the kingly line, passed by way of Solomon down to Jacob, the father of Joseph. Into this kingly lineage incarnated Zoroaster, who was born as Jesus, the son of Joseph of Bethlehem, and was visited by the three kings. His birth took place on the evening of the Full Moon in Virgo in the year 6 B.C. The left line, the prophetic line, the blessed seer saw proceed by way of Nathan down to Heli, later named Joachim, who was the father of Mary of Nazareth. She beheld with the eye of the spirit the crossing of the two lineages, the fruit of which was Jesus. For Mary married Joseph, and their child Jesus was the offspring of this union. This marriage, however, was the marriage of Mary of Nazareth to a man from Nazareth, Joseph the carpenter, not to Joseph of Bethlehem.

The mystery of two children with the name Jesus—one born from the line of Solomon and the other from the line of Nathan—remained concealed from the spiritual gaze of the blessed seer. However, this mystery was finally unveiled by an initiate who arose later in the history of Christendom, whose capacity of seership surpassed even that of the blessed seer. He lived from 1861 to 1925, and he began around the year 1900 to unveil the deeper mysteries concerning the foundation of Christianity.

Filled with the Holy Spirit, this initiate revealed the cosmic mystery of the seven days of creation, the human mystery of reincarnation, and the most sacred mystery of all: the Christ Mystery. As part of the unveiling of the Christ Mystery, the initiate revealed that it was Zoroaster who incarnated as Jesus in the line of Solomon—the same Zoroaster who had lived in Babylon under the name Zaratas, and who had lived on Earth earlier still, in the days of ancient Persia, with the name Zarathustra. But regarding Jesus who incarnated in the line of Nathan as the son of

Mary of Nazareth, the initiate beheld that this was not a case of reincarnation. Unlike Zoroaster, who had lived in many lives previously on the Earth, the child Jesus born as the son of Mary of Nazareth had never before been incarnated on the Earth. This was a pure soul, an immaculate soul, untainted by the consequences of the Fall—a soul straight from Paradise, so to speak. It was this child Jesus, born of Mary of Nazareth, who was visited by the shepherds on the morning after his birth.

TAT: When did his birth take place, O father?

HERMES: The Annunciation to Mary of Nazareth by the Angel Gabriel at the conception of the pure soul of Jesus took place on the same night on which the birth of "radiant star" had taken place four years earlier. The birth of Jesus of Nazareth took place nine months later. This was in the year 2 B.C., when Quirinius was governor of Syria. As the time of his birth drew near, Mary and her betrothed—whose name was Joseph, a carpenter in Nazareth—had to travel to Bethlehem, having been officially summoned there. In Bethlehem the only accommodation they could find was in a cave which was used as a stable, and it was here that Jesus of the line of Nathan was born. His birth took place shortly before midnight on the night of December 6/7 in the year 2 B.C. And just as the reincarnation of the kingly soul of Zoroaster was revealed to the three kings as they beheld the stars on the night of his birth when the Moon was full in Virgo in 6 B.C., so the birth of the pure soul of Jesus of the line of Nathan was made known to shepherds near Bethlehem, who were watching their flocks that night. An Angel appeared to them and announced the birth of the Messiah in the city of David, saying: "Glory to God on high, and peace on Earth to men of good will!" The shepherds gathered some presents together, and at dawn—it was Sunday, December 7—went down from their hill to the cave of the nativity. There they greeted Joseph of Nazareth and told him what the Angel had proclaimed to them that night. Joseph accepted the presents with humble gratitude and accompanied the shepherds into the cave itself, where Mary was sitting on the ground holding the child Jesus on her lap. The shepherds cast themselves down on their knees before Jesus and Mary, and wept for joy. For a time they remained speechless. Then they sang a Psalm and repeated the Angel's hymn of praise that they had heard that night on the hill. Weeping tears of joy they left the cave.

TAT: O father, having revealed to us the mystery of the star of the magi—the message of the heavens that culminated in the birth of "radiant star" in the royal line of Solomon—can you disclose the heavenly mystery surrounding the birth of the immaculate soul of the line of Nathan, who was visited by the shepherds?

HERMES: Yes, my son, with the help of the rule of Hermes it is possible to learn of the conception of this immaculate soul—truly an immaculate conception—by retracing the passage of the Moon through the signs of the zodiac. The blessed seer beheld the birth of this soul at around midnight following the Sabbath, at midnight from Saturday to Sunday, on the twelfth day of the month of Kislev. This means that the birth in fact took place in Bethlehem a little over half an hour before midnight on Saturday, December 6, 2 B.C. And the blessed seer beheld that from the

Christian Hermetic Astrology

birth to the Mystery of Golgotha 33 ⅓ years elapsed, which places the crucifixion at the beginning of April in A.D. 33. Here the vision of the blessed seer is in agreement with the seership of the initiate, who found with the eye of the spirit that the crucifixion took place on the afternoon of Friday, April 3, A.D. 33.

If the shepherds had done as the magi, if they had observed the stars on the night of the birth of the Messiah, what would they have seen? Saturn was bright in the night sky, high above Bethlehem at the time of the birth. It had just left the star-sign of the Bull and was entering the Twins (1° Gemini). At the moment of birth the star-sign of the Virgin was rising in the East; the Ascendant at the birth was 10½° Virgo. And Jupiter, too, was rising in the East, at 12½° Virgo. Over in the West the Moon—which was large, but not yet full—was on its way towards setting. It was in the Ram, at 10° Aries, close to where the Sun later stood at the crucifixion. As it was shortly before midnight, the Sun was at the deepest part of its passage beneath the Earth, and was in the middle of the star-sign of the Archer, at 16° Sagittarius. This, if you recall, my son, was the position of the Sun in the zodiac when the blessed seer received the stigmata on the afternoon of December 29 in the year 1812. A cosmic remembrance of the divine birth of the immaculate soul of Jesus takes place each year when the Sun is in the middle of the Archer, and it was at just this moment that the blessed seer received an imprint of the holy corporeality of Our Lord. Although the historical date of the divine birth was December 6, the cosmic remembrance—when the Sun is in the middle of Sagittarius—now takes place later. In 1812 this fell on December 29, but in the twentieth century the cosmic remembrance is more appropriately celebrated at midnight from December 31 to January 1. And it was at just this moment in time, from 1922 to 1923, that the *House of the Word*, designed by the initiate and sculpted in wood in dedication to the Advent of the Second Coming of the Lord, was tragically burnt down. This event in the life of the initiate parallels that of the receiving of the stigmata in the life of the blessed seer, but on a different level. Both events recall the night of the divine birth when the shepherds were watching their flocks on the hill near Bethlehem, and the Sun was in the middle of the star-sign of the Archer. That night, at the moment of the birth, only the Moon and Saturn were visible. But Jupiter was rising, so it too became visible a little later on. And somewhat later still, towards dawn, as the shepherds made their way down from the hill towards the cave of the nativity, Venus and Mars were visible together above the horizon in the East—in conjunction near the start of the star-sign of the Scorpion (3° Scorpio). This was, so to speak, *the star of the shepherds*, just as the star of the magi culminated with the conjunction between Mars and Jupiter on the day of the birth of "radiant star." In both cases the red planet Mars was involved, as the activator—with the magi: in conjunction with Jupiter, and with the shepherds: in conjunction with Venus. Jupiter, as the planet of wisdom, well symbolizes the birth of Zoroaster, the wisest of souls, and Venus, the planet of love, truly represents the birth of the pure soul of Jesus of Nazareth, whose nature was love through and through. Jupiter in conjunction with Mars signified the active wisdom of Zoroaster, whilst Venus in conjunction with Mars indicated the active love of the immaculate soul of Jesus of Nazareth. The proclamation of the Angel to the shepherds, "Peace on Earth to men of good will," brings to expression the star of the shepherds—the conjunction of Venus and Mars at the start of the sign of the Scorpion—shining above the eastern horizon as the shepherds made their way down from the hill to the cave of the nativity. As the Moon at the birth of Jesus of Nazareth was at 10° Aries, this was, according to the hermetic rule, rising at his conception nine months earlier. And as $12\frac{1}{2}°$ Virgo was rising at Jesus' birth, the Moon at conception was at $12\frac{1}{2}°$ Virgo or $12\frac{1}{2}°$ Pisces. The conception of the immaculate soul of Jesus—the event of the "descent of the stork"—in fact took place about one hour after sunrise (in Nazareth) on March 6 in the year 2 B.C., exactly four years after the birth of the kingly soul of Jesus of Bethlehem had taken place on the evening of March 5 in 6 B.C.. March 6 in 2 B.C. was the day of the New Moon in Pisces, and at the moment of the immaculate conception of Jesus of Nazareth the Moon was at $10\frac{1}{2}°$ Pisces and the Sun at 16° Pisces. The Ascendant, the degree of the zodiac rising in the East, was 10° Aries, and Venus at 15° Aries was about to rise—showing the strong imprint of Venus at the conception as well as at the birth of this paradisiacal soul. At the conception Mars and Saturn were in Taurus—Mars ($4\frac{1}{2}°$ Taurus) in conjunction with the Pleiades, and Saturn ($16\frac{1}{2}°$ Taurus) in conjunction with the Bull's eye, Aldebaran (15° Taurus). Moreover, Jupiter (4° Leo) was in conjunction with the Lion's heart, Regulus (5° Leo), and the invisible planet Uranus (24° Pisces) and Pluto (24° Virgo) were in opposition to one another, just as they had been in opposition at the conception of "radiant star" four years and nine months earlier.

Now, to draw this discourse to a close, my son, let us contemplate the star of the magi in relation to the star of the shepherds, looking especially at the position of the Sun in the zodiac at the conception and birth of the two Jesus children. We find three corners of a cross marked out in the heavens: the Sun (16° Gemini) at the conception of the elder Jesus was opposite the Sun (16° Sagittarius) at the birth of the younger Jesus. And the Sun (15½° Pisces) at the birth of the elder child was at the same position in the zodiac as the Sun (16° Pisces) at the conception of the younger child four years later. The fourth point of this cross is occupied by 16° Virgo, in the middle of the star sign of the Virgin, which was the location of the Sun on the night of September 7/8 in 21 B.C.—September 8 being the traditional birth date of Mary the mother of Jesus. It was on this night that Mary's birth took place.

Mary of Bethlehem, as representative of the sign of Virgo, was truly the Virgin Mary. The soul of "radiant star" represented the opposite sign, being born with the Sun in the middle of Pisces, whilst the immaculate soul of Jesus of Nazareth was born when the Sun was in the middle of Sagittarius the Archer. And as the soul of John the Baptist was born into the earthly realm six months before the birth of Jesus of Nazareth, the Sun was in the star-sign of Gemini the Twins at the birth of John. These four—Mary, John, and the two Jesus children—thus form a *human cross*, corresponding to the cosmic cross in the heavens whose axes extend from the middle of Gemini (John the Baptist) to the middle of Sagittarius (Jesus of Nazareth) and from the middle of Virgo (Virgin Mary) to the middle of Pisces (Jesus of Bethlehem, "radiant star").

TAT: Thank you, O father, for this discourse.

CLOSING INVOCATION

A Discourse of Hermes to Asclepius

The Two Became One

OPENING INVOCATION

ASCLEPIUS: O thrice-greatest one, what became of the two Jesus children?

HERMES: Let us contemplate again the two lineages, that of Solomon, culminating in the elder Jesus, the son of Joseph of Bethlehem; and that of Nathan, the younger Jesus, who was the son of Mary of Nazareth. The Solomon line is the kingly lineage and the Nathan line is the priestly lineage. The two Jesus children came into the world as representatives of the sacred posts—sacred in Israel—of king and priest. And John the Baptist filled the third post, that of prophet. For there are three sacred posts in Holy Israel: priest, king and prophet. But the two Jesus children became one, so that the posts of priest and king became united in one person. How did this happen?

The elder Jesus, the reincarnated Zoroaster, was four years and nine months older than the younger Jesus, the paradisiacal immaculate soul. One year after the birth of the elder Jesus the flight into Egypt took place, and then six of the first seven years of his life were spent in Egypt. He was 7½ years old when he and his family returned to Israel.

However, they did not return to their home in Bethlehem, but settled in Nazareth. This was in September A.D. 2. From the autumn of A.D. 2 onwards the two Jesus children both grew up in Nazareth. In December A.D. 2 the younger Jesus, who lived with his parents in Nazareth, turned three years old.

Now, it was the custom in Israel to journey to the temple in Jerusalem for the Feast of the Passover which takes place around Eastertime each year. At the Passover in A.D. 8, the younger Jesus, having attained the age of eight, for the first time accompanied his parents to Jerusalem. He did so again in A.D. 9 and in each subsequent year. He was a pure and loving child but did not yet display any sign of genius. After the end of the Feast of the Passover in A.D. 12, the 12-year-old Jesus parted company with his parents and set off on the return journey with other youths from Nazareth. But while still in Jerusalem, not far from the Mount of Olives, he took leave of his youthful friends, who thought that he was going to rejoin his parents. His parents, for their part, believed that he was with his young friends on their way back to Nazareth. It was at this moment in time that the two Jesus children became one. The decision on the part of the 12-year-old Jesus to separate from his parents and friends and return to Jerusalem came about through the union of the elder Jesus with him, an inner union whereby the soul of "radiant star" separated from his body and united with the immaculate soul to indwell the latter's body. This was the joining together of the two lineages in Jesus—the priestly line descending from Nathan and the kingly line from Solomon. Two months after this occurrence, the body of the elder Jesus—now just seventeen years old—having been vacated, was laid to rest.

This bodily death of the elder Jesus was simply an outer sign. The inner reality was his new life indwelling the body of the younger Jesus, in union with this immaculate soul, which was then imbued with the great wisdom of "radiant star." This union, which brought about a profound transformation in the 12-year-old Jesus, took place around April 3, A.D. 12, exactly twenty-one years prior to the crucifixion on April 3, A.D. 33, so that the Sun was at more or less the same place in the zodiac—close to 13° Aries—as it was later at the death on the cross. The sacrifice of "radiant star" in leaving his body to unite with the younger Jesus mirrored in advance—but on a lesser scale—the sacrificial death on Good Friday twenty-one years later.

The very next day the transformed 12-year-old Jesus went to one of the rabbinic schools in Jerusalem and discoursed with the doctors and scribes, astounding them—and also putting them to shame—with his questions and answers. The next day he repeated this at a second school, and on the morning of the third day again at a third school. By this time his parents, who had met up with the youths of Nazareth at a small village north of Jerusalem, had discovered his absence. They were greatly concerned for his safety and set off back to Jerusalem to search for him. On the afternoon of the third day since his transformation and separation from them, they finally found him. On this afternoon he was in the great hall of Solomon in the temple itself. There he sat upon a large chair surrounded by rabbis and many others who had gathered to listen to him and dispute with him. The doctors and scribes intended to humble the boy Jesus, who had embarrassed them with his profound knowledge during the past three days. They put one question after another to him, not only of a theological kind but also concerning nature, art and science. Jesus answered and taught. In reality the rabbis were confronted with the wisest of all souls—"radiant star"—whose wisdom had been accumulated through numerous incarnations upon the Earth. Jesus discoursed, with a facility beyond the reach of even the most learned rabbi, on astronomy, geometry, arithmetic, architecture, jurisprudence, medicine, agriculture and every subject which they put to him. And he showed himself to be profoundly knowledgeable on all matters to do with the Law and prophecies, the mysteries of the temple and the mission of Israel. In his listeners he evoked astonishment and wonder, but also rage on the part of the learned who, much to their chagrin, learned that the boy's knowledge far surpassed their own. After he had been teaching for some two hours, his parents entered the temple. They were quite awed and astonished at the remarkable transformation that had taken place in their son, for they saw that he had increased in wisdom and stature. Great was their joy at finding him, but they were also perplexed at his new-found independent spirit, and they reprimanded him for causing them so much sorrow and anxiety. Obediently he returned with them to Nazareth. From this time onwards he became a teacher among his companions, giving instruction when they walked or talked together.

ASCLEPIUS: In humble gratitude we have listened to this discourse, O father, and gained knowledge of how the two became one, how *wisdom united with love.*

CLOSING INVOCATION

A Discourse of Hermes to King Ammon

The Start of Christ's Ministry

OPENING INVOCATION

KING AMMON: We have learnt, O Hermes, how the two became one, how wisdom united with love when the immaculate soul, Jesus of Nazareth, attained the age of twelve. It is our ardent desire to learn now of the further course of the life of this One.

HERMES: Yes, King Ammon, in the preceding discourse mention was made of the three sacred posts of Israel—priest, king and prophet—and how the priestly Messiah and the kingly Messiah became one. Let us now look at the life of this One, and also at the life of the prophet, John the Baptist, who was born six months earlier than Jesus of Nazareth.

As customary, each year Jesus visited the temple in Jerusalem for the Feast of the Passover, which extends from Nisan 15 to Nisan 21 in the first month of the Jewish calendar. At around the start of the month of Nisan in A.D. 29, as Jesus was twenty-nine years of age, Joseph the carpenter died. Up until this time Jesus had helped Joseph in Nazareth and had become skilled in carpentry. The death of Joseph, however, signified a spiritual coming of age for Jesus, from which time onward he no longer worked as a carpenter. This

THE START OF CHRIST'S MINISTRY

coming of age corresponded with the completion of Saturn's first orbit around the zodiac since his birth. On the night of his birth, if the shepherds had looked up to the stars, they would have seen the Moon in Aries (10° Aries) in the sign of the Lamb, setting in the west; also, they would have beheld high above them the planet Saturn (1° Gemini) at the start of the sign of the Twins. At the death of Joseph, Saturn—looked at hermetically—was again at the start of the star-sign of the Twins (1° Gemini). This cosmic event bore tidings to Jesus, highlighted through a far-reaching stroke of destiny, the death of Joseph—tidings that Jesus was now to devote himself solely to the work of his Heavenly Father.

It was a solemn event for Jesus, shortly after the death of Joseph, for the first time to visit the temple in Jerusalem accompanied by Mary alone. In the temple, the house of his Heavenly Father, Jesus came to know that his mission was about to commence. At the very same time, around the last day of the Passover festival, the word of God came to John the Baptist, who was living in the wilderness. John then left the wilderness to take up his preaching mission, to prepare the way for the coming of the Messiah. This was towards the end of April A.D. 29. After Mary and Jesus returned to Nazareth, preparations began for a move to another place, not far from Capernaum. A wealthy friend of the holy family, a man called Levi, who lived in Capernaum, put a house belonging to him at the disposal of Jesus and Mary. Levi was well disposed towards Jesus and—seeing the persecutions that Jesus suffered in Nazareth at the hands of the Pharisees—provided him and Mary with this house, which was in a little village between Capernaum and Bethsaida. Here they could live without fear of disturbance, in a house large enough to accommodate small gatherings of Jesus' followers. The move here from Nazareth took place in the early part of May A.D. 29, about the time of Saturn's geocentric return to the star-sign of the Twins (1° Gemini), where it had been on the night of Jesus' birth.

This event—cosmically expressed by the return of Saturn—signified a radical change in Jesus' life, and not long afterwards he began his travels throughout the length and breadth of Palestine. He invariably returned though, to this home near Capernaum, where Mary remained most of the time. Capernaum and Bethsaida represented the central focus of Jesus' activity during the years of his ministry.

KING AMMON: Did this move to Capernaum in fact denote the commencement of the ministry, O Hermes?

HERMES: Most worthy King Ammon, the true beginning of the ministry was signified by the baptism in the Jordan, which followed some months later. But during these months intensive preparation was made by Jesus, including the start of his travels. The first long journey that he made was to the region of Hebron in Judea, to the place where John the Baptist had grown up. It was at the end of May A.D. 29 that Jesus set out on this journey. On the way he visited Lazarus in Bethany, who had already been acquainted with the holy family earlier, through their visits to Jerusalem, and had become a good friend of Jesus and Mary. At the same time as Jesus was away on this first long journey, during June A.D. 29, John the Baptist, having attained the age of thirty, began a journey through Samaria and Galilee, visiting Bethsaida, Capernaum, Tiberius, Nazareth, Jericho and other places as well. Everywhere he introduced himself as Zechariah's son, and spoke of himself as the forerunner

THE START OF CHRIST'S MINISTRY

of the Messiah. He made a second journey, visiting Bethsaida, Capernaum and Nazareth again, and then retired to a place on the Jordan, between Ainon and Salem, where he remained, teaching and baptizing. This was about three months prior to Jesus' baptism. After a time, he moved further south down the Jordan to a new place of baptism.

On his journey back to Galilee, Jesus visited those places that John the Baptist had recently passed through. Upon returning to the neighborhood of Capernaum, he paid a visit to the fishery of Peter, the later apostle, which was on the shore of the Sea of Galilee, not far from Bethsaida. Peter and his brother Andrew had already become disciples of John the Baptist by the time of this first contact with Jesus.

KING AMMON: Please tell us now, O Hermes, of the baptism in the Jordan.

HERMES: My dear King Ammon, from the age of twelve onwards, up to the time of the baptism, Jesus was a twofold human being; he was essentially the union of wisdom and love—of the wisdom of "radiant star" and the love of the immaculate paradisiacal soul of Jesus of Nazareth. On his travels through Palestine during June, July, August and September A.D. 29, leading up to the baptism, Jesus taught here and there, imparting his wisdom, and gained his first disciples. He preached repentance and advocated the baptism by John. He spoke, too, of his own forthcoming baptism, and declared that baptism, as the sign of the new covenant, would replace circumcision, the sign of the old covenant.

On the evening of Wednesday, September 21, he arrived again in Bethany, where he was greeted not only by Lazarus but also by other friends from Jerusalem—Nicodemus, John

Mark, and the aged Obed (a relative of the prophetess Anna). John Mark's mother, named Mary, and two other women from Jerusalem—Veronica and Susanna—were also there in Bethany as guests of Martha, the sister of Lazarus. On the next day Jesus' mother arrived at Lazarus' home, having traveled from Capernaum, and on that afternoon she and Jesus had a deep and spiritually profound conversation. At this moment in time Jesus was in a condition of "emptiness," having seen everywhere on his travels the dire need of human beings, especially the poor and the sick; and having witnessed the utter decadence of humankind's spiritual life. The wisdom-filled soul of "radiant star" saw that only a miracle could save humanity—a miracle that would entail sacrifice. During the course of the conversation with Mary it came to him like a flash of lightning that he should sacrifice himself and make way for the Sun Spirit CHRIST, whom he (Zarathustra) had known earlier as Ahura Mazdao, the "Aura of Light" of the Sun.

This conversation on the afternoon of Thursday, September 22, A.D. 29, signified the death of "radiant star," his withdrawal from the body of Jesus of Nazareth, which he had indwelt for almost 17½ years. This was the second death of "radiant star"—the first having taken place at the age of seventeen years and one month as the 12-year-old Jesus of Nazareth was visiting the temple in Jerusalem for the Passover in A.D. 12. Now, through the heart of Mary, as she and Jesus conversed together, the Presence of Christ made itself known, and the words resounded spiritually in the atmosphere: "Go to the place of baptism in the Jordan!" That very night, accompanied by Lazarus, Jesus made his way from Bethany towards the Jordan. But now Jesus had become an empty vessel—"radiant star" having

THE START OF CHRIST'S MINISTRY

offered himself up in the "sacrifice of death," meaning "withdrawal from the physical plane of existence."

As the first light of day was breaking—it was Friday, September 23—Jesus and Lazarus proceeded eastward towards the place of baptism. The waning crescent of the Moon was visible above the eastern horizon, approaching the middle of the star-sign of Leo. High above, Saturn was to be seen close to the center of the star-sign of the Twins.

When Jesus reached the place of baptism—on the west side of the Jordan, close to the village of Ono—a large crowd of people had already assembled to hear John the Baptist preach. John sensed Jesus' presence among the crowd, and this fired him with extraordinary zeal. He preached with great animation concerning the nearness of the Messiah, and then he began to baptize those who came forward. He had already baptized many people when Jesus came down to the baptismal pool. It was about ten o'clock that morning. John was assisted by Andrew, the later apostle, and by Saturnin, a young Greek of royal blood from the city of Patras, who later became one of Jesus' closest disciples. At the moment of baptism a voice of thunder spoke the words: "This is my beloved Son; today I have begotten thee!" Jesus became transparent with radiant light as the Sun Spirit CHRIST, the Son of God, united with him. At this moment the God-Man, Jesus Christ, was born, to begin his mission of salvation and redemption on the Earth. Into the vessel vacated by "radiant star," CHRIST—the Great Spirit of the Sun, known earlier as Ahura Mazdao—entered. This was the highest union in the history of humankind, between the Divine Word—the Logos—and the pure human soul Jesus of Nazareth. From this moment on God Himself, the Second Person of the Godhead, indwelt the body of Jesus—the Son of God had become a human being. This signified the start of the ministry.

KING AMMON: O Hermes, can you say more concerning the cosmic significance of the moment of the baptism?

HERMES: Indeed, King Ammon! As the baptism in the Jordan took place, the Sun had just entered the star-sign of the Balance. This was the point in time at which the Sun Spirit CHRIST transferred his place of abode from the Sun to the Earth. The transfer took place gradually, and only became complete at the Mystery of Golgotha, but the moment of baptism was decisive. It can be likened to the moment of conception in the incarnation of the soul. And whereas the soul is engaged between conception and birth in helping to build up its body, so from the moment of the baptism onwards throughout the ministry, the God-Man, Jesus Christ, was engaged in the building up of his resurrection body. From the resurrection onwards he indwelt this resurrection body, just as the human being indwells its body from the moment of birth onwards. The Mystery of Golgotha, extending from the crucifixion to the resurrection, signified the birth process of the Son of man, who emerged on Easter Sunday morning—newborn, newly arisen—in his resurrection body.

Counting the days, from the morning of the baptism on Friday, September 23, A.D. 29, to the morning of the resurrection on Sunday, April 5, A.D. 33, is 1290 days—this is the number of days referred to in the prophecy of Daniel, at the end of the Book of Daniel. The time of the building up of the resurrection body from the baptism to the resurrection lasted 1290 days. Following the resurrection, for forty days the Son of man manifested himself in his resurrection body to his apostles and disciples, before ascending to heaven. Then, ten days later, there came the descent of the Holy Spirit—sent by the Son of man—upon the apostles who were gathered together.

KING AMMON: And just as the movements of the Sun, Moon and stars through the star-signs are significant for the incarnating soul, is it true to say that the movements of the heavenly bodies during the ministry were of higher significance?

HERMES: Truly, King Ammon, this bears upon a cosmic mystery relating to the history of humankind since the Mystery of Golgotha! Without unveiling this mystery in full, it is possible nevertheless to approach it by way of analogy—through analogy with the incarnation of the soul. Conception is related to birth by the rule of Hermes, which is specified by the Moon's position in the zodiac at these times. And by following the passage of the Moon through the star-signs of the zodiac between conception and birth, the weaving of the destiny of the incarnating soul is revealed. This destiny is woven between conception and birth in such a way that it mirrors not only the passage of the Moon but also of the Sun and planets through the star-signs, especially in their conjunctions and oppositions with one another. The destiny thus woven begins to unfold from the moment of birth onwards according to a certain rhythm, unfolding in a sequence of 7-year periods.

By analogy, there took place a cosmic weaving of destiny between the baptism and the resurrection, the unfolding of which began after the Mystery of Golgotha. The rhythm underlying this unfolding, however, is not the 7-year period, but a much longer period. This comes to expression explicitly in the history of Christianity and implicitly in the history of humankind. For, since the Mystery of Golgotha, the rhythm of $33\frac{1}{3}$ years of the life of Jesus Christ has played an important role in world history and continues to do so.

Looking at the ministry of Jesus Christ, there took place on the one hand all the signs, miracles and other events leading up to the crucifixion, and on the other hand these events mirrored below the movements of the heavenly bodies above. The ministry—between the baptism and the Mystery of Golgotha—constituted the *embryonic period* of the Being of Christianity, the Being of the Sun Spirit Christ, who was born into the aura of the Earth at the resurrection. And just as we may come to an understanding of the life and destiny of the human being by referring to the cosmic events that took place between conception and birth, so the unfolding of the Being of Christianity may be comprehended by way of the cosmic events between the baptism and the Mystery of Golgotha, as well as the events of the ministry. These are of significance for the history of humankind and the Earth since the Mystery of Golgotha, because through the unfolding of the Christ Impulse a new Heaven and a new Earth are arising—the Heavenly Jerusalem, which is the goal towards which Christianity is evolving.

The path of evolution of Christianity is contained in seed form in the ministry of Jesus Christ, which may be looked at from an earthly perspective and a cosmic perspective, and these two perspectives apply to the course of history since the Mystery of Golgotha. The period of 1290 days extending from the baptism to the resurrection—looked at in terms of the ministry, and in relation to the corresponding movements of the heavenly bodies—holds the key to the historical events that have taken place on the Earth since the Mystery of Golgotha. In fact, a closer study of the correspondence between the ministry and the subsequent unfolding of the Christ Impulse reveals that Christianity is still at an early stage of development, and applying this correspondence in historical terms we are now living in the period of temptation, which began 28 ⅓ days after the baptism and lasted 40 days. The three temptations which presented themselves to Jesus Christ during the 40 days in the wilderness have also arisen historically, mirrored in the French Revolution, the Communist Revolution and the rise of National Socialism. But as well as taking on social forms, the three temptations also present themselves in an individual way to each person. The culmination of the period of temptation is signified by the simultaneous emergence of all three temptations combined, which historically betokens the meeting with Antichrist, a choice which each individual and humankind as a whole has to face—the choice between Christ and Antichrist.

KING AMMON: O Hermes, it would seem that the 1290 days between the baptism and the resurrection are all-important for the entire future.

HERMES: This is so, King Ammon. A study of the day-by-day events of the ministry in relation to the corresponding planetary, solar and lunar movements leads us into the realm of profound mysteries. Such a study entails an application of the hermetic axiom "as above, so below," applied to the life of Jesus Christ. This is the basis of Christian hermetic astrology. Obviously we cannot consider all the events of the ministry, but the most important events can be taken into consideration, in relation to the corresponding cosmic configurations.

KING AMMON: This being so, can we now return, O Hermes, to a consideration of the cosmic configuration of the baptism, which was the starting point of the ministry?

HERMES: This is a good point of departure, King Ammon. For, as the ministry contains in seed form the entire evolution of Christianity, so the baptism was the moment of the planting of this seed. And looking at the zodiacal position of the Sun at the moment of the baptism, it is striking that it had just entered the star-sign of Libra. This was Jesus' perspective from the Earth. But from the perspective of the Sun, which was that of the Sun Spirit Christ, the Earth had just entered the star-sign of Aries, and was at the beginning of a new orbit of the zodiac. Also, again viewed from the Sun, the planets Mercury and Saturn were exactly in conjunction at the feet of the Twins, in opposition to Pluto against the background of the Archer's bow. This hermetic conjunction of Mercury and Saturn is expressive of the voice of the Father, which resounded as thunder at the moment of baptism. For Mercury is the Messenger, and Saturn is the guardian of the portal to the Kingdom of the Father. And as they stood in opposition to Pluto, guardian of the portal to the Underworld, the Incarnation of Christ at the baptism also signified a confrontation with the powers of evil. This is apparent from the ensuing period of temptation, which was a time of direct conflict between Christ and the powers of evil, and which culminated on the day that the Sun became conjunct with Pluto. But before we proceed to look at the cosmic background to the period of temptation in the wilderness, let us contemplate further the cosmic configuration at the baptism.

The solar viewpoint is that of the Higher Self, in this case that of the Self of Selves, Christ; while the earthly perspective is that of the human self, in this case that of Jesus. These two perspectives hold good for the incarnation of _every human being. Moreover, the baptism may be viewed as the archetype for the *conception* of the incar_nating soul, and the Mystery of Golgotha as the archetype of the *birth*. For the birth of the soul into a physical body is simultaneously its death from the kingdom of the spirit—analogous to the death on the cross—but also contains the potential of resurrection, the overcoming of death.

The baptism was the moment of conception of the God-Man, Jesus Christ. So far we have looked at the solar perspective, which is included in the hermetic perspective. The hermetic viewpoint includes the solar perspective, but widens it, keeping the Earth at the center; and this presents a more complete expression of the spiritual standpoint. According to this hermetic perspective the Moon, which at the baptism was in the center of the star-sign Leo, was approaching conjunction with Mars, as from the solar point of view Mars was just past the center of Leo. This hermetic conjunction between the Moon and Mars was perceptible solely to the eye of the spirit. Seen from the Earth, from the standpoint of sensory perception, Mars was at the start of the star-sign of the Virgin, widely separated from the Moon in the middle of Leo.

KING AMMON: O Hermes, can you speak of the difference between a hermetic conjunction—for example, between Mars and the Moon—and a geocentric conjunction?

HERMES: Honorable King Ammon, listen closely, for this is a matter of profound significance. It concerns the different planes of existence. For human beings there are primarily three planes of existence to take into consideration: the physical plane, the astral plane, and the devachanic plane—although within the latter it is possible to distinguish between an upper devachan and a lower devachan, which makes four planes of existence. When incarnated upon the Earth, human beings dwell on the physical plane and their consciousness extends to this plane. The Earth is central as far as humans' consciousness is concerned when they are on the physical plane, and this is appropriately *called earthly consciousness.* In the period immediately preceding incarnation on the Earth, and also immediately succeeding it, the soul indwells the astral plane, in which the Moon is central. Here prevails *lunar consciousness.* Insofar as incarnated human beings are able to raise their consciousness beyond the earthly level to the astral plane, they are able to see by way of lunar consciousness beyond the physical appearance of things to behold a revelation of the inner nature or soul of things. For example, a conjunction between the Moon and Mars can be seen by way of the physical perception of earthly consciousness. But such a conjunction is a reality also on the astral plane, and its significance on the astral plane of existence can be grasped by way of lunar consciousness, which is the appropriate form of consciousness on this plane. A still higher form of consciousness is called for in order to grasp the significance of events on the devachanic plane of existence, the kingdom of heaven, into which the human being enters after death, after having traversed the astral plane. The Sun is the center of the lower devachanic plane, and the mode

THE START OF CHRIST'S MINISTRY

of consciousness intrinsic to this plane is *solar consciousness*, whereas on the upper devachanic plane it is *stellar consciousness*. With an understanding of the various planes of existence indwelt by the human being at different stages in time, it is possible now to answer your question, King Ammon. The three planes—physical, astral and devachanic—imply three different standpoints: earthly, lunar and solar. The hermetic perspective, which calls for the development of solar consciousness, refers to the devachanic plane. The hermetic conjunction in Leo between the Moon and Mars at the baptism related to the descent of the Logos from devachan, the Kingdom of the Sun. For, in the heavenly Sun kingdom, Mars is the planet of the Word. And Mars in Leo signifies the impulse of the Word to work right down into the realm of being—united with the Moon. The same conjunction—that between the Moon and Mars, let us say in Leo, if viewed from the geocentric perspective—relates no longer to devachan but to the astral plane. It is a matter of the same cosmic phenomenon, but in the one case—from the hermetic perspective—it is a reality on the devachanic plane, and in the other case (the geocentric perspective) it is an event on the astral plane. In the first instance it is a spiritual reality, and in the second a soul reality. The spiritual reality underlying the hermetic conjunction in Leo between the Moon and Mars at the baptism was the Incarnation of the Word. On the level of the soul, as indicated by the geocentric perspective, this same cosmic phenomenon would essentially refer to the soul's power of realization, the ability to bring impulses to realization.

But, in addition to the levels of the spirit and the soul, relating to the devachanic and astral planes of existence, there is the level of life, which is the deeper significance of the earthly plane. The Earth is the central point of reference for all living beings. Here is the Kingdom of the Mother—the Mother of everything living—in contrast to the heavenly Kingdom of the Father. With respect to their taking effect on the level of life, it is the spatial relationships of the planets to the Earth that have to be taken into consideration. Again, taking Mars as an example, Mars was high above the Earth, close to the Midheaven, at the moment of the baptism. Whereas Jupiter was deep below the Earth, and Venus was just above the Ascendant on the eastern horizon. These two axes—the vertical axis of the Midheaven, and the horizontal axis of the Ascendant—provide a frame of reference for the relationships of the Sun, Moon and planets to the Earth, how they manifest on the earthly plane, in the kingdom of life. The prominent positions of Mars and Venus at the baptism, considered from the earthly plane, point on the one hand to the tremendous life power of Jesus Christ in his daily preaching and on the other hand to the boundless compassion of his daily healing activity. Jupiter's prominence at the baptism, located at the deepest point below the Earth, was a *concealed prominence*, in that the wisdom, which on account of "radiant star" had been active up until the baptism, had now withdrawn, but was nevertheless still there working from hidden depths. This wisdom flowed from the depths into the public preaching and healing work of Jesus Christ.

KING AMMON: Thank you, O Hermes, for this discourse on the baptism and its cosmic significance.

CLOSING INVOCATION

A Discourse of Hermes to Tat

The Temptations in the Wilderness

OPENING INVOCATION

TAT: O father, can you now relate something of the temptations in the wilderness?

HERMES: My son, let us recall that the Sun stood in the first degree of the star-sign of Libra at the baptism. This was on the morning of Friday, September 23 A.D. 29. In fact, the entire ministry was expressive of the passage of the Sun through the twelve star-signs of the zodiac. This need not surprise us, for Christ came from the Sun. The life of Jesus Christ during the ministry, on his travels throughout Israel, harmonized closely with the Sun's course through the signs. The dates of entrance of the Sun into the zodiacal signs differ from age to age. In the twentieth century they are around the middle of each month, but at the time of Christ the dates of the Sun's entrance into the star-signs were approximately as follows:

Aries: March 20	*Leo:* July 23	*Sagittarius:* November 21
Taurus: April 20	*Virgo:* August 23	*Capricorn:* December 20
Gemini: May 21	*Libra:* September 22	*Aquarius:* January 19
Cancer: June 22	*Scorpio:* October 22	*Pisces:* February 18

What do we find when we follow the Sun's passage through the signs during the ministry? From the baptism to the Mystery of Golgotha the Sun passed 3 times around the zodiac. Starting out at 1° Libra at the baptism in A.D. 29, after almost three orbits of the zodiac the Sun was in Leo at the raising of Lazarus in A.D. 32. There then followed the passage of the Sun during the last part of the ministry through Virgo, Libra, Scorpio, Sagittarius, Capricorn, Aquarius and Pisces, with the triumphant entry of Jesus Christ into Jerusalem on the day of a total solar eclipse, as the Sun was about to enter the star-sign of Aries. At the Full Moon fifteen days later—there was a partial lunar eclipse—he was crucified on the cross at Golgotha, on Friday, April 3, A.D. 33, as the Sun was in the middle of the Ram, at 14° Aries. In order to look more closely at the path of the Sun during the ministry, let us return to the period immediately following the baptism. For the first four weeks after the baptism, as the Sun was passing through the star-sign of Libra, Jesus Christ remained primarily in Judea. But he made hardly any public appearances during this Libra period, as he intended to appear publicly only after a 40-day fast in the wilderness. Nevertheless, two of John the Baptist's disciples, Andrew and Saturnin, joined him after the baptism and through them he began baptizing. As instructed by John the Baptist, Andrew then went to Galilee to proclaim there that the baptism of the Messiah had taken place. During this time—Sun in Libra—the Lord retraced some parts of the way traveled by Joseph and Mary of Nazareth as they had made their way to Bethlehem, and he also visited the valley of the shepherds near Bethlehem.

At the start of the Sabbath on the evening of Friday, October 21, A.D. 29, Jesus began his 40-day fast in the

THE TEMPTATIONS IN THE WILDERNESS

wilderness, just as the Sun was about to enter the star-sign of Scorpio. Most of the forty days were spent in prayer and fasting in a small cave on Mt. Attarus, a wild and desolate mountain east of Callirrhoe. These forty days coincided with the Sun's passage through Scorpio and through the first ten degrees—the first decan—of the star-sign of Sagittarius. During this period he was subjected daily to temptation, but this culminated in three definite temptations towards the end of the forty days. Jesus Christ underwent these temptations—the confrontation with evil—on behalf of the whole of humankind, but especially for those who became his disciples and for the twelve who later became apostles. On Wednesday, November 30, when he had overcome the final temptation, the twelve Angels of the twelve apostles brought him heavenly nourishment. These twelve Angels were accompanied in turn by the seventy-two Angels of the seventy-two disciples. There took place a heavenly celebration of the Lord's triumphant victory over the power of evil, from which blessing and consolation radiated forth; and this was transmitted by the Angels to the apostles and disciples.

TAT: And what, O father, was the nature of this confrontation with evil?

HERMES: My son, the powers of evil arose from the abyss in an attempt to disrupt the mission of the Lord, to negate it from the outset. It was only by way of meeting with and overcoming the powers of evil that the mission of Jesus Christ could truly begin. In what did this mission consist? Through the words, miracles, and suffering and death of the Lord, seeds were sown on the Earth for the coming of the Kingdom, Power and Glory of the Heavenly Trinity. And the beasts of the abyss sought—and seek—to prevent this by revealing a false kingdom, a counterfeit power and an illusory glory. Above in the heights is the true Kingdom, the real Power, and the actual Glory of the Divine Trinity, and this is caricatured and falsely reflected in the depths, by the false kingdom, counterfeit power, and illusory glory of the beasts of the abyss. Historically the three temptations arose in the mass movements connected with the French Revolution, the Communist Revolution, and the Third Reich of National Socialism. In the case of the French Revolution it was the temptation of illusory glory ("glory to the Republic"); with the Communist Revolution it was counterfeit power ("*power to the people*"); and with National Socialism it was the false kingdom (*das dritte Reich*, "the third kingdom"). And as long as doubt, fear and hate exist within the individual, instead of the faith, hope and love of the Holy Trinity, the door is open within to the influence of the beasts of the abyss. Jesus Christ had to meet and overcome three definite temptations presented by the powers of evil, to set an example for humankind showing that it is possible to live on Earth solely through the faith, hope and love of the Divine Trinity, in bringing to realization the heavenly Kingdom, Power and Glory also here below on the Earth. The words, miracles and path of sacrifice of the Lord were a continuous revelation and manifestation, during the ministry, of the Kingdom, Power and Glory from above.

TAT: O father, what was the cosmic aspect of the period of temptation?

THE TEMPTATIONS IN THE WILDERNESS

HERMES: My son, the planet Saturn is the guardian of the portal to the Kingdom of the Father, and it was this planet which played a special role during the period of temptation. On the day after the baptism in the Jordan, Saturn began to move retrograde in the Twins. At the same time, the Moon's nodes were moving retrograde—the Ascending Node in Gemini the Twins and the Descending Node in Sagittarius the Archer—such that as the 40-day fast started, Saturn aligned exactly with the Moon's Ascending Node in the Twins. This signified that Saturn was acting with special strength, and it remained so throughout the forty days that during this time Saturn was aligned with the Moon's Ascending Node, both retrograding slowly toward the feet of the Twins. The Moon's Nodes are portals to the astral plane of existence, and so when a planet is aligned with the axis of the Moon's Nodes, it works in directly from the astral world with a much greater intensity than usual. The fact that Saturn was moving retrograde also points to a stronger-than-usual activity, for it is during the period of retrograde motion that the outer planets are most visible in the night sky, attaining their brightest when in opposition to the Sun. And Saturn reached opposition with the Sun on the afternoon of November 30, A.D. 29, which was the last day of the 40-day fast. On the afternoon of this day, after the Lord had overcome the final temptation, Saturn stood exactly opposite the Sun in the heavens. It was a cosmic sign of the victory of the Father, through the Son, over evil. And the Angels came to Jesus Christ to celebrate this triumph, the cosmic sign of this heavenly feast being a conjunction between the Moon and Jupiter at 29° Aquarius, which took place on the evening of November 30. The conjunction between Jupiter and the Moon then recurred one month later at the miraculous feast of the wedding at Cana, at which water was transformed into wine.

The Moon is the portal to the Kingdom of the Angels, and the heavenly sustenance which Jesus Christ received at the end of his 40-day fast was drawn by the Angels from the cosmic wisdom of Jupiter. Forty days previously, on October 21, the Moon had been in opposition to Jupiter—a cosmic sign of the start of the 40-day fast. And on the evening of October 21, as Jesus entered the wilderness, Jupiter began to move direct again, after a long period of retrograde motion. This was indicative of the higher wisdom underlying the step of embarking upon the 40-day fast in order to confront the powers of evil. For without this, the mission of Jesus Christ could not have been accomplished. The spiritual preparation for the path of suffering taken during the ministry was made during this 40-day fast. And through the confrontation with and overcoming of the powers of evil the way was cleared for the unfolding of his mission. The strength that was needed to embark on the 40-day fast was indicated cosmically by the hermetic conjunction between Mars and the Moon on the evening of October 21, A.D. 29, a recurrence of the hermetic conjunction from the day of the baptism one month previously. On the one hand, the culmination of the 40-day fast was signified cosmically by the opposition between Saturn (10° Gemini) and the Sun (10° Sagittarius), attained on the afternoon of the last day in the wilderness—this was the sign of the fulfillment of the will of the Father through the Son. On the other hand, the onslaught of daily temptations during the forty days reached a climax towards the end with the three temptations, when the beasts of the abyss rose with formidable strength. The cosmic sign of the last temptation was the conjunction between the Sun and Pluto at 9° Sagittarius on the evening of November 29, A.D. 29. This was preceded five days earlier, around midday on November 24, by a total eclipse of the Sun at 4° Sagittarius, which signified for Jesus Christ *the opening of the gates of hell,* leading to his meeting with the Prince of Darkness as the Sun stood close to Pluto. But this final temptation—the encounter with Satan himself—did not succeed, and the powers of evil were obliged to withdraw.

TAT: O father, profound is the mystery of the path taken by the Son of man. It would seem that every step he took was a fulfillment of the will of the Heavenly Father as reflected in the movements of the heavenly bodies above.

HERMES: Indeed, my son, it is so. "Thy will be done, as above in the heavens, so below on the Earth" is the key to the path of the Messiah, when viewed in relation to the correspondence between his earthly deeds and the parallel events taking place in the heavens above. This is the foundation of Christian hermetic astrology and is the ideal aspired to by all who seek to follow the path trodden by the Messiah.

TAT: In the previous discourse you spoke, O father, of the 1290 days of Christ's ministry as representing the embryonic period of the Being of Christianity. You referred to a cosmic mystery relating this embryonic period to the unfolding of the Christ Impulse since the Mystery of Golgotha. You said that this is analogous to the unfolding of an individual's destiny in 7-year periods, from birth through the course of life. Can you tell us more concerning this cosmic mystery?

HERMES: Yes, my son, listen carefully, for this mystery is of central importance in Christian hermetic astrology. It holds the key to the unfolding of history in terms of the Christ Impulse. Just as the human being's destiny is prepared during the embryonic period, whereby during each revolution of the Moon around the zodiac, destiny is prepared for seven years of life, so each day of Christ's ministry signified a kind of prefiguring of historical destiny for a certain period. This period is not the 7-year period, but a much longer one, connected with the planet Saturn. It is, in fact, the period of Saturn's revolution of the sidereal zodiac. This amounts to 29½ years. As I have already referred to in these discourses, Saturn is the portal to the Kingdom of the Father. And it is the will of the Father which comes to expression through the Son. In the words of Jesus Christ: "My Father is working still, and I am working." Thus, each day in the ministry of Jesus Christ becomes elaborated during the course of one revolution of Saturn around the zodiac, coming to expression in world history.

TAT: O father, can you give us an example of this?

HERMES: Let us consider again, my son, the temptations in the wilderness. The period of temptation started around 7 o'clock on the evening of the Sabbath, on October 21, A.D. 29, about one month after the baptism in the Jordan. In fact, about 28 ⅓ days had elapsed since the moment of the baptism. Multiplying by 29½—the period of Saturn—we arrive at 836 years, historically, corresponding to 28 ⅓ days in the life of Christ. Thus 836 years is the period that elapsed until the onset, historically, of the period of temptation. These 836 years have to be added to A.D. 33,

THE TEMPTATIONS IN THE WILDERNESS

when the Mystery of Golgotha took place. Thus we arrive at A.D. 869. In this year there began the period of temptation in the unfolding of the Christ Impulse historically.

TAT: And how long does the period of temptation last, looked at historically?

HERMES: Since the temptation in the wilderness lasted for forty days, the corresponding period lasts historically for forty revolutions of Saturn around the zodiac, signifying the coming to expression in history of the will of the Father through the Son. Multiplying Saturn's period of $29\frac{1}{2}$ years by forty, we arrive at 1180 years. Adding this to A.D. 869, the end of the period of temptation occurs historically shortly before the middle of the twenty-first century.

Although Jesus Christ was subjected to temptation throughout the entire forty days in the wilderness, the temptations gradually increased in intensity, building up towards the end of the forty days. Similarly, although the historical period of temptation began in A.D. 869, the climax is reached much later. I have already spoken of the French Revolution, the Communist Revolution, and the rise of National Socialism as historical manifestations of the three temptations—towards false glory, false power, and the false kingdom. But the real climax—the meeting with Antichrist signifies the emergence of all three temptations simultaneously, in the form of the temptation to replace the individual self of each human being with a false self.

TAT: Is it possible to date this fourth temptation historically?

HERMES: The climax of the temptations in the wilderness took place, as I said, at the conjunction of the Sun and Pluto at 9° Sagittarius during the last night of the Messiah's trials on Mt. Attarus. Approximately thirty-nine days had elapsed since the start of the temptation period. In terms of Saturn revolutions, this means thirty-nine Saturn periods of 29½ years, which amounts to some 1150 years. Added to A.D. 869, we arrive at A.D. 2019. In fact, in the year A.D. 2018 Saturn reaches 9° Sagittarius, crossing this point three times during the course of the year. Since Saturn is the bearer of cosmic memory, every time that Saturn reaches 9° Sagittarius—in the bow of the Archer—the climax of the temptations in the wilderness is remembered, cosmically speaking. In fact, just as the trials of the Messiah took place during the forty days of the Sun's passage through Scorpio and the first decan of Sagittarius, so the passage of Saturn through Scorpio and the first decan of Sagittarius remembers this cosmically. The arrival of Saturn at 9° Sagittarius in A.D. 2018 denotes the start of the fortieth day, historically, in the temptation period, which began with Saturn in Sagittarius in A.D. 869, and which ends with Saturn in Sagittarius in A.D. 2047, at the completion of Saturn's fortieth revolution of the zodiac since A.D. 869. But as well as Saturn's crossing 9° Sagittarius, also significant is its crossing of the opposite point, 10° Gemini, in the zodiac, where Saturn itself was located at the end of the Messiah's forty days in the wilderness. Here again the cosmic memory of this event—the triumph of Jesus Christ over the powers of evil—is recalled. Lastly, the passage of the outer planets—Uranus, Neptune and Pluto—across 9° Sagittarius is significant for a consideration of the end of the historical temptation period. The relevant dates are:

1986 (Neptune's crossing of 9° Sagittarius); 1989 (Uranus' passage across 9° Sagittarius), and 2010 (Pluto's transit of 9° Sagittarius). Obviously, this latter date is of quite special significance, as it recalls Pluto's actual position at the climax of the temptation period in the wilderness, when the Sun and Pluto were in conjunction at 9° Sagittarius. The buildup to Pluto's reaching 9° Sagittarius in A.D. 2010 begins with the entrance of Pluto into Scorpio in 1993, and its passage between 0° Scorpio (1993) and 9° Sagittarius (2010) mirrors the passage of the Sun through Scorpio and the first decan of Sagittarius during the forty days in the wilderness. However, just as Jesus Christ triumphed in the confrontation with evil and emerged victorious on the fortieth day—to be consoled by the heavenly nourishment of the Angels—so there is every hope that humankind as a whole will successfully navigate a course through the historical period of temptation. It is only after passing through this that the real unfolding of the Christ Impulse will come to manifestation. Then, for example, a historical mirroring of the miracle at the wedding at Cana will take place during the Aquarian age. In this way the unfolding of the Christ Impulse may be followed historically through 1290 Saturn revolutions corresponding to the 1290 days between the baptism and the resurrection.

CLOSING INVOCATION

A Discourse of Hermes to Asclepius

The Wedding at Cana

OPENING INVOCATION

ASCLEPIUS: O Hermes, can you relate the further course of the life of the Messiah after he left the wilderness?

HERMES: Noble Asclepius, immediately after leaving the wilderness Jesus Christ made his way to the Jordan, to the place where John was baptizing. As John caught sight of him on the opposite side of the river, he proclaimed to his listeners: "Behold the Lamb of God!" For the second time his two disciples, Andrew and Saturnin, left to join Jesus, this time to become Jesus' disciples.

At the time the Sun was in the second decan of Sagittarius, having traversed the whole of Scorpio and the first decan of Sagittarius during the forty days in the wilderness. As the Sun now passed through the second and third decans of Sagittarius, Jesus Christ preached in various places in Judea and healed the sick. Towards the end of the Sun's passage through Sagittarius, he made his way northward through Samaria to Galilee. On his way to Tarichea he encountered Andrew together with his brother Simon Peter, accompanied by John. Turning to Peter, Jesus said: "You are Simon, the son of Jonas; you shall be called Cephas."

THE WEDDING AT CANA

The Sun was at 29° Sagittarius and the Moon was in conjunction with Mars. On this very day—it was Monday, December 19—Mars entered the star-sign of Scorpio. And on the next day, as the Sun entered Capricorn, at the start of this period of his activity in Galilee, Jesus and his disciples were invited by a bridegroom to attend his forthcoming wedding in Cana.

Jesus Christ began his teaching activity in Galilee on the evening of the Sabbath—Friday, December 23—by preaching in the synagogue at Capernaum. Many friends and relatives of the Lord were in attendance, including the Blessed Virgin Mary. He taught there again on the following day, the day of the New Moon in Capricorn. After the close of the Sabbath, as was customary, Jesus and a group of his friends and disciples went for a walk in a valley near Capernaum. Among the people accompanying them was Philip, who, on account of his modesty and humility, hung back from the others. Jesus turned to him and said: "Follow me." At this time of Philip's summons to become a disciple, the Sun was in conjunction with Mercury, with Mercury between the Earth and the Sun. The call of Philip to become a disciple of the Lord was signified macrocosmically by the Messenger, Mercury, aligning with the Sun. Philip, in fact, became a disciple, and also acted as a messenger. For, on the following day, he sought out Nathanael Chased, who worked in the town of Gennabris, to tell him: "We have found him of whom Moses in the law and also the prophets wrote, Jesus of Nazareth, the son of Joseph." Nathanael replied: "Can anything good come from Nazareth?" But he was then persuaded by Philip to come and see for himself. By this time Jesus was already on his way to Cana. Philip and Nathanael caught up with him on the road. After a brief exchange of words, Nathanael exclaimed: "Rabbi, you are the Son of God! You are the King of Israel!" At this moment in time the Moon was in conjunction with Venus and Neptune, being between these two planets, close to the tail of the Goat. There took place a mystical illumination of Nathanael, whereby through the power of love he was able to behold the true being of the Lord, and this was signified in the heavens by the meeting between the Moon and Neptune and Venus.

ASCLEPIUS: Therefore, O Hermes, at the summons of Philip the Sun was in conjunction with Mercury, and at the illumination of Nathanael Chased, the Moon was in conjunction with Venus and Neptune?

HERMES: Every step in the unfolding of Christ's ministry perfectly mirrored the activity of the cosmos. There was a complete harmony between the events enacted on the Earth and the events in heaven. As the Son of God, and at the same time as the Perfect Man, the macrocosm itself came to expression in and through Jesus Christ. This is the goal, too, for every human being: to become one with, and a perfect expression of the macrocosm; to live on Earth in complete harmony with the cosmos. It is this sublimely harmonious condition that Jesus Christ brought to expression with the words: "I and the Father are one." Through bringing to realization the words, "Not I, but Christ in me," the human being, too, may become one with the Father in heaven. Human beings are then in a position to fulfill the words: "Thy will be done, as above in heaven, so also on the Earth." Every step taken by Jesus Christ, every action he performed, was a fulfillment of these words, and in complete freedom.

THE WEDDING AT CANA

ASCLEPIUS: What took place next, O Hermes?

HERMES: The illumination of Nathanael Chased at his meeting with Jesus Christ on the road to Cana took place on Sunday, December 25, A.D. 29. Afterwards they continued on their way and that evening they arrived in Cana. On the western horizon, shortly after sunset, the thin crescent of the New Moon was visible in conjunction with Venus, which, in turn, was close to Neptune. Higher up above the western horizon Jupiter could be seen near the start of the star-sign of Pisces, and above the eastern horizon Saturn was visible near the feet of the Twins. In Cana Jesus was received by the bridegroom, whose name was also Nathanael, and by the bride's mother and father, whose name was Israel, and also by the Blessed Virgin.

On the following day Jesus conversed mainly with those disciples who later became his apostles. On the evening of the day after this he taught in the synagogue concerning the significance of marriage, husband and wife, chastity and spiritual union, and subsequently addressed the bridal pair. On the morning of the third day the wedding took place in the synagogue at around nine o'clock. About one hundred guests were in attendance. Afterwards they made their way from the synagogue to the wedding banquet, at which Jesus had assumed the responsibility for providing the wine. It was towards midday that the miracle of the transformation of water into wine was fulfilled through the Lord. All present who drank the transformed water were filled with interior strength; they came to know inwardly the heavenly power of Jesus Christ and to acknowledge his divine mission. In their hearts they received faith, and they were united as a community. This was the first of his miracles. The octave of this first miracle took place at the last miracle, that of the Last Supper, at which, through the Holy Communion, the apostles were endowed with new spiritual strength for their mission.

At the wedding at Cana the community of Christ's disciples was born through the power of communion, in which they received heavenly sustenance by means of the consecrated water. Through consecrating it, Jesus Christ restored the water to the primal condition summarized in the words "And the Spirit of God moved over the face of the waters." The power of the Kingdom of the Angels—the Moon sphere being the Angelic realm—directly impregnated the water. The Moon was in conjunction with Jupiter, the planet of wisdom, as it had been one month earlier at the heavenly feast at the end of the period of temptation in the wilderness—the only difference being that in the course of this month Jupiter had moved from 29° Aquarius to 3° Pisces. This heavenly feast was repeated at the wedding at Cana, but this time not only Christ but also those of his disciples present received the Angelic blessing. However, it was not just the Angelic blessing with which the water became impregnated, but also—through the consecration—with the blessing of Christ himself. It was this that made the water taste like wine. For Christ brought the spiritual fire—the fire of cosmic love—into the wisdom-permeated water. Then it tasted like wine; and each one who drank it became inwardly fired with certainty as to the divine nature of Jesus Christ. It was a communion with Christ. This certainty, this faith, effected by the grace of the first miracle, balanced out, healed and compensated for the doubt that led to the original sin in Paradise. For in Paradise Eve listened to two contradictory voices—that of the Lord

THE WEDDING AT CANA

and that of Lucifer—and thus was filled with doubt. In this condition of doubt she ate from the Tree of Knowledge, and this led to the Fall. Doubt was the cause of the original sin, and the certainty of faith was the first sign of the grace that was bestowed by the Savior on his path of redeeming and overcoming the consequences of the Fall—the latter having arisen through the primal temptation in Paradise.

Christ as the Redeemer: this is the divine motivation underlying the Incarnation. And it is striking that at his first redeeming act—inspiring the certainty of faith through the communion of wine, which was actually transformed water—Venus was in conjunction with Neptune. For, at the baptism, which denoted the *conception* of the Sun Spirit Christ—the onset of the ministry—there had been a hermetic conjunction between Venus and Neptune. At the baptism, viewed from the solar perspective, Venus and Neptune were together again in the star-sign of Capricorn, indicating a meeting between the planet of love (Venus) and the planet of inspiration (Neptune). Three months later, at the wedding at Cana, Venus and Neptune were together in Capricorn—this time viewed from the earthly perspective. Here there was a bringing to realization on Earth, through the communion of the consecrated water, of the divine intention signified in the heavens at the start of the ministry.

Another point of relationship between the heavens at the baptism and at the wedding at Cana was that during the three days in Cana Mars—hermetically—was at the beginning of the star-sign of Libra. Mars thus recalled the memory of the position of the Sun at 1° Libra at the baptism. Mars, the Activator, called for the activation of the Christ Impulse—the Impulse of the Sun Spirit—which was realized through communion with Christ by way of the consecrated water at the wedding at Cana. As this communion took place, the star-sign of Aries the Ram (or Lamb) was rising in the East. It was this sign which at the Mystery of Golgotha became the *birth sign* of the Risen One, the *Lamb of God*, since at the resurrection the Sun was at $15\frac{1}{2}°$ Aries. And just as Mercury, hermetically speaking, had been prominent at the baptism—in hermetic conjunction with Saturn—so at the wedding at Cana there was a hermetic opposition between Mercury and Neptune. On both occasions the Messenger had a cosmic message to communicate.

ASCLEPIUS: And what took place after the wedding at Cana, O Hermes?

HERMES: Honorable Asclepius, at the wedding at Cana the Sun was in the first decan of the star-sign of Capricorn, at 8° Capricorn. Jesus Christ stayed in Cana for three more days, and celebrated the Sabbath there. Then he returned to Capernaum, where he remained—apart from a brief visit to Hanathon and Bethanat—while the Sun was in the second decan of Capricorn. During the early hours of Monday, January 9, A.D. 30, as the Sun entered the third decan of Capricorn, there took place a conjunction between Venus and the Sun, with Venus passing between the Earth and the Sun. This conjunction corresponded in the heavens with the meeting between Jesus Christ (Sun) and the Blessed Virgin Mary (Venus). Their conversation began on Sunday evening and continued until deep into the night (Monday morning). In the course of their conversation he told her that he would first journey to the place of baptism, then celebrate the Passover in Jerusalem, and afterwards summon his apostles and make his public appearance.

The journey to the place of baptism took some four days. Jesus was accompanied by eight disciples. He arrived on the morning of Friday, January 13, just as there was a conjunction between Neptune and the Sun at $24\frac{1}{2}°$ Capricorn. This cosmic event signified the continuation of John's baptizing activity by Jesus Christ (Sun), as a powerful source of inspiration (Neptune). Jesus himself, however, did not baptize, but through his disciples, initially Andrew and Saturnin. During the Sabbath, which he celebrated at the synagogue at Ono not far from the place of baptism, he proclaimed that he had come to continue the work begun by John the Baptist. John had by this time discontinued baptizing, although he still preached, speaking always of Jesus. He preached at a place on the east side of the Jordan some distance north of Ono, and those who came to be baptized he sent to Jesus. John also denounced Herod Antipas as an adulterer, thereby arousing the fury of Herodias. The baptism of Jesus differed from that of John in that John had baptized in the name of Yahweh, the Lord, whereas Jesus baptized in the name of the Father, the Son and the Holy Spirit. Jesus also healed the sick and cured the possessed.

ASCLEPIUS: Were these healings also miracles?

HERMES: Yes, Asclepius, almost everywhere he went on his travels Jesus Christ healed the sick miraculously simply by speaking some words or by laying on his hands. This was his work of redemption. Just as John the Baptist was so called because he baptized, Jesus Christ the Savior, which means Healer, was so called because he healed. A vast library of books would have to be written to describe all the miraculous healings of the Savior. The beloved disciple

John, the writer of the Gospel, refers to only seven healing miracles; however, each miracle represents a particular category of healing, and together they serve as seven archetypes for all of the healing miracles of the Lord. The first miracle described by John was that of the transformation of water into wine at the wedding at Cana at the end of A.D. 29, and the seventh miracle was the raising of Lazarus from the dead, which took place less than three years later in the summer of A.D. 32. But Lazarus was not the only person whom Jesus Christ called back from the dead. Nevertheless, as the raising of Lazarus was the most significant raising from the dead carried out by Jesus, it is this miracle which is referred to in the *Gospel of St. John*. It serves as an archetype for the other raisings from the dead, and thus represents this category of miracle.

ASCLEPIUS: Pray tell us, O Hermes, when the first raising from the dead took place?

HERMES: Indeed, Asclepius, it was shortly after the wedding at Cana. This wedding was celebrated on Wednesday, December 28, A.D. 29, when the Sun (8° Capricorn) was in the first decan of Capricorn. On the Sabbath day—Saturday, December 31—as he came out from the synagogue, some people cast themselves down before him and begged for help. A man had fallen from a tower and had broken his limbs and died. Jesus went up to the corpse and arranged the limbs, touching the broken places and then commanded the man to arise, which he did. It was the day of the hermetic conjunction between Mercury and Uranus in the Lion (7½° Leo), and the Sun (11° Capricorn) had just entered the second decan of Capricorn. The next

THE WEDDING AT CANA

raising from the dead followed several weeks after the wedding at Cana, when the sun was in Aquarius.

By the time the Sun entered Aquarius, on January 18/19, A.D. 30, Jesus had been at the place of baptism near Ono, and his disciples Andrew and Saturnin had already begun baptizing those who came there to receive baptism. They continued to baptize after the Lord departed for Ono. The Lord then went from place to place in the neighborhood preaching and healing. Jesus returned to Ono at the beginning of February, and on Thursday, February 2, A.D. 30, when the Sun (15° Aquarius) was in the middle of the star-sign of Aquarius, the disciples ceased their baptizing activity for the time being. Shortly after, together with the Lord, they made their way back towards Galilee. On the journey they passed through the town of Aruma, northwest of Jericho. Here Jesus received a message from the Essene Jairus that his daughter had just died after a lengthy illness. Jesus parted company from his disciples and went to the little town of Phasael where Jairus lived. Upon entering Jairus' house, he went up to the corpse, which was wrapped in a winding-sheet ready to be buried. Members of the family, shedding tears of grief, were gathered around. Jesus ordered the winding-sheet to be loosened. Then he took hold of the dead girl's hand and commanded her to rise. She raised herself up immediately and stood before him. She was about sixteen years old. It was Thursday, February 7, A.D. 30—the day of the Full Moon—when this took place. The Sun was at the end of the second decan of Aquarius, and the Full Moon was opposite in the star-sign of Leo, in which sign the Moon had been at the baptism in the Jordan. Just as Mercury and Saturn, viewed hermetically, had been in conjunction at the moment of the baptism, at this raising from the dead they were hermetically in opposition to one another, Mercury at 12° Sagittarius and Saturn at 12½° Gemini. This hermetic configuration indicates that this raising from the dead took place as a revelation of the cosmic power of the Sun Spirit Christ, who fulfilled the will of the Heavenly Father by descending from the Sun at the moment of the baptism to unite with the human being Jesus. Whereas the Father (Saturn guards the portal to the Father's Kingdom) was made manifest at the baptism by way of the voice of thunder that spoke the words, "This is my beloved Son; today I have begotten thee," here the Father was revealed through the raising from the dead, for death is a mystery of the Father. And just as later, at the crucifixion, the Moon was full, when Jesus Christ encountered and then overcame death, so at this raising from the dead the Moon was full, the Full Moon being an especially propitious time for the manifestation of the power of the divine-cosmic will. This raising from the dead preceded by some nine months the raising of the youth of Nain and by almost ten months the raising of Salome, the daughter of the chief rabbi of the synagogue at Capernaum, whose name was also Jairus. But this raising from the dead at the Full Moon in Leo did not become known outside of the small group of Phasael who witnessed it, as Jesus instructed them not to speak of it, and none of the disciples were present.

ASCLEPIUS: Thank you, O Hermes, for revealing in this discourse the cosmic nature of Christ, whose deeds on Earth truly reflect the divine will manifest in the movements of the heavenly bodies.

CLOSING INVOCATION

A Discourse of Hermes to King Ammon

Jesus' First Visit to Jerusalem Since the Baptism

OPENING INVOCATION

KING AMMON: O thrice-greatest one, pray reveal to us more concerning the cosmic mysteries that come to expression in the life of the Messiah.

HERMES: After the raising of the daughter of the Essene Jairus from the dead, Jesus returned to Capernaum. This raising from the dead, which took place as the Sun was at the end of the second decan of Aquarius, was kept secret by Jesus. But now, upon returning to Galilee, as the Sun was in the third decan of Aquarius, Jesus Christ began to come out much more openly to fulfill his mission. People came to Capernaum from all around to hear him preach, and everywhere he healed the sick and cast out demons from the possessed. So many came that he left Capernaum in order to escape the throng. He then traveled to Gennabris in Lower Galilee accompanied by seven of the future apostles: Andrew, Peter, James, John, Judas Thaddeus, Simon and James the Lesser. This first journey of the Lord with his future apostles then proceeded from

Gennabris through various towns in Lower Galilee. At this time the Sun entered the star-sign of Pisces. Everywhere he went the people thronged to hear him, and many proclaimed him to be a prophet sent by God.

Shortly after the Sun entered the second decan of Pisces, Jesus, who by this time had returned from Lower Galilee to Capernaum, set off on the journey to Jerusalem, in order to be there well in time for the Passover festival. This was his first visit to Jerusalem since the start of his ministry. He stayed at Lazarus' castle at Bethany, not far from Jerusalem. On the day after his arrival at Bethany, Jesus went with Lazarus to meet his Jerusalem disciples at the home of Mary Mark, which was located outside of the city wall opposite the Mount of Olives. On this day there was a hermetic conjunction between Mercury and Saturn in the middle of the star-sign of the Twins (14° Gemini), a repetition of this configuration from the day of the baptism in the Jordan. This was the second hermetic conjunction between Mercury and Saturn since the baptism, the first having coincided with the arrival of Jesus in Galilee, following the baptism. On the next day, Monday, March 20, A.D. 30—his first actual appearance in Jerusalem since the baptism—the Sun entered the star-sign of the Ram. Here again a perfect harmony between the Sun's path in the heavens and Jesus Christ's earthly path is revealed. For Jerusalem can be thought of as the "head" of Israel, and just as the human being's head corresponds to Aries, so Jerusalem corresponds to this zodiacal sign. It is no mere coincidence that the crucifixion, which took place when the Sun (14° Aries) was in the middle of Aries, occurred in Jerusalem on the hill of Golgotha, which means "the place of the skull."

FIRST VISIT TO JERUSALEM

On this day in Jerusalem Jesus walked the streets in his long white gown, the traditional garment of a prophet, but he did not teach. And on the next day when he remained in Bethany, there was a hermetic conjunction of Venus and Mars with Antares (15° Scorpio), the heart of the Scorpion. The previous hermetic conjunction between Venus and Mars had been in the middle of the Twins (17° Gemini) on May 9, A.D. 29, coinciding with the move of Jesus and Mary, after the death of Joseph, from Nazareth to their new home near Capernaum. After remaining another day in Bethany, Jesus went to Jerusalem again and visited the temple, but he did not begin to teach in the temple until almost a week later, on the evening of Wednesday, March 29, A.D. 30, on which there was a hermetic conjunction between Mercury and Uranus in the Lion ($8\frac{1}{2}°$ Leo), repeating the configuration at which Jesus had first raised someone from the dead. (This had been on December 31, A.D. 29, in Cana, when Mercury and Uranus had been hermetically in conjunction at $7\frac{1}{2}°$ Leo.) A week later, on the evening of Wednesday, April 5, A.D. 30, Jesus and his disciples celebrated the Feast of the Passover at Lazarus' home; on this evening there was a hermetic conjunction of Venus and Pluto in the Archer ($9\frac{1}{2}°$ Sagittarius). Early next morning Jesus and the disciples went to the temple in Jerusalem and drove out the vendors and money lenders. At this the Pharisees began to ask him what right he had to do such things. But their hostility grew even stronger on the next day when he healed about ten people in the forecourt of the temple. From this time onwards—the Sun was close to the middle of the Ram ($17\frac{1}{2}°$ Aries)—the Pharisees of Jerusalem began actively to direct a campaign against him, which lasted almost exactly three years, until they succeeded in having him crucified (Sun at 14° Aries, at the crucifixion in A.D. 33). A great commotion arose at the temple on account of the healings, but Jesus returned to Bethany and kept the Sabbath there with Lazarus.

KING AMMON: O Hermes, what steps did the Pharisees take against Jesus?

HERMES: After the close of the Sabbath a group of Pharisees went to the home of Mary Mark with the intention of taking Jesus into custody. But they found only the Blessed Virgin and some of the holy women there, whom they ordered to leave the city. Mary and the holy women went immediately to Bethany. There they found Martha together with her ill sister, Silent Mary. Silent Mary died that evening, Saturday, April 8, A.D. 30, in the presence of Mary, Mary Cleophas, Martha and others. She was gifted with clairvoyance and beheld in advance the coming persecution and trials of Jesus, which was more than she could bear. That same evening Nicodemus came from Jerusalem to Bethany and conversed with Jesus throughout the night—hermetically Mercury (22° Virgo) was opposite Jupiter (22° Pisces) and Venus (14½° Sagittarius) was opposite Saturn (14½° Gemini).

KING AMMON: It seems that the most significant events in the life of the Messiah were accompanied in the heavens primarily by hermetic planetary configurations.

HERMES: Indeed, King Ammon, for Christ, the Spirit of the Sun, it has always been the solar perspective that is all-important. For the human being Jesus, on the other hand, it is the Earth-centered geocentric perspective that has to be considered. From the moment of the baptism onwards, when Christ united with Jesus, the cosmic-solar perspective *as seen from the Earth*, that is, hermetically, became significant. For this reason both the hermetic and geocentric perspectives need to be taken into consideration when looking for the cosmic correspondences taking place in the unfolding of Jesus Christ's ministry. And throughout the ministry the cosmic configurations, according to the hermetic perspective, speak a definite language concerning events in the life of Christ. For example, the hermetic opposition between Venus and Saturn, referred to already, speaks of the death of Silent Mary, who died in the face of the burden of suffering that she beheld was in store for the Messiah. An arrow of grief pierced through her heart (Venus hermetically in Sagittarius) and she was called back to the realm of the Father (Saturn opposite in Gemini, guardian of the threshold to the Father). At the same time the hermetic opposition between Mercury and Jupiter speaks of the conversation that same night between Jesus Christ (representing the wisdom of Jupiter) and Nicodemus (representing the eagerness to learn of Mercury). This nightly conversation was in fact an initiation of Nicodemus. The task is to be able to read the language spoken by the movements of the heavenly bodies, to grasp their significance intuitively.

KING AMMON: O Hermes, at the time of the death of Silent Mary, and the nightly conversation between Nicodemus and Jesus, was the Sun still in Aries?

HERMES: Yes, King Ammon, on that night the Sun was at 19° Aries, close to the end of the second decan of Aries. Jesus remained hidden at Bethany for most of the time as the Sun traversed the third decan of Aries, but then he went to a place of baptism on the Jordan and—through Andrew, Saturnin, Peter and James—baptized there. During this time, as the Sun was in Taurus, large numbers of people came to be baptized by Jesus, and a dispute arose with some disciples of John the Baptist about the difference in purification of the two baptisms. John the Baptist, when he was asked about this, bore witness to Jesus saying: "He must increase, but I must decrease."

News of the large numbers of people asking to be baptized by Jesus reached the Pharisees in Jerusalem, who became alarmed and sent letters to the chief rabbis at all the synagogues throughout the land. They instructed that Jesus be delivered up and that his disciples should be seized and questioned.

About this time Jesus and the disciples left the place of baptism. He went through Samaria to West Galilee, and from there up to the boundaries of Tyre and Sidon, before returning to Capernaum. For the time being he did not appear so much publicly in synagogues, but rather taught privately at small gatherings.

As the Sun was in the third decan of Taurus, Herod, urged on by Herodias, seized John the Baptist and imprisoned him in his castle at Callirrhoe, but then freed him after about six weeks. However, on the night of July 17/18, when the Sun (25° Cancer) was in the third decan of Cancer in opposition to Neptune ($25\frac{1}{2}°$ Capricorn), Herod took John the Baptist into custody again, this time for good, subsequently imprisoning him at his castle in

Machaerus, where he was later beheaded. This imprisonment of John was a sign for Jesus to intensify his activity, and after a relatively quiet period since the Passover festival, he now resumed his public preaching and healing all the more powerfully.

KING AMMON: Thank you, O Hermes, for this account of Jesus' first visit to Jerusalem since the baptism.

CLOSING INVOCATION

A Discourse of Hermes to Tat

The Conversation at Jacob's Well and the Healing of the Nobleman's Son

OPENING INVOCATION

TAT: O father, pray speak of the course of Christ's ministry after the imprisonment of John the Baptist.

HERMES: My son, five days after the imprisonment of John the Baptist, on Sunday, July 23, A.D. 30, the Sun entered the star-sign of Leo. In ancient Egypt this event signified the start of a new year, for the cycle of decans worshipped by the Egyptians commenced here. Likewise in the life of the Messiah, whose mission is a work of love, who seeks only the kingdom of the heart, the entrance of the Sun into Leo indicated a new beginning in his ministry. For Christ himself is the Spirit of the Sun, and the zodiacal sign of Leo corresponds to the human heart, in which the Christ Impulse is implanted. The entrance of the Sun into Leo is a sign in the heavens for the igniting of the forces of the heart, the awakening of the Christ Impulse.

On this day in A.D. 30, as the Sun entered Leo, Jesus Christ announced to his disciples gathered together at Lazarus' castle in Bethany his intention henceforth to teach

THE CONVERSATION AT JACOB'S WELL

openly. Following this he and some of the disciples set off on the journey northward to Galilee. This time Jesus did not avoid Samaria by going round it. He entered Samaria and, accompanied by Andrew, James and Saturnin, made his way to Jacob's well, near Sychar. The Lord sent the three disciples into Sychar to buy food. He himself climbed the hill on which Jacob's well was located. A Samaritan woman, about thirty years old, whose name was Dina, climbed the hill to draw water from the well. It was about midday on Wednesday, July 26, A.D. 30. Close by the well she encountered Jesus sitting and waiting. He asked her for some water. She replied: "How is it that you, a Jew, ask a drink of me, a woman of Samaria?" Jesus answered: "If you knew the gift of God, and who it is that is saying to you, 'give me a drink,' you would have asked him, and he would have given you living water." As she handed him some water to drink, he said: "Everyone who drinks of this water will thirst again, but whoever drinks of the water that I shall give him will never thirst; the water that I shall give him will become a spring of water welling up to eternal life." She was struck by his words "living water" and had a presentiment that they signified the fulfillment of the promise concerning the coming of the Messiah.

In this conversation with Jesus Christ, Dina the Samaritan represented the entire Samaritan sect, separated from the true faith of Israel, from the fountain of living water. And Jesus at Jacob's well thirsted, that is, he thirsted after the chosen souls of Samaria, in order to refresh them with the living water from which they had cut themselves off. The Samaritans, through sin and self-will, had separated themselves from God's covenant with Jacob. But at Jacob's well Jesus Christ offered redemption to the believers among the souls of Samaria, to those who were awaiting the

Messiah. Dina represented these souls, for she was living in expectation of the Messiah, saying to Jesus: "I hope for, I believe in the coming of the Messiah. He will help us." And Jesus responded: "I am he, I who am now speaking to you." Dina, trembling with joy, gazed in amazement at the Lord. In that moment she received the living water of faith and her heart was filled to overflowing with love.

The Sun stood high in the heavens at 3° Leo, close to the star Regulus, the heart of the Lion. This was the macrocosmic symbol for the igniting of the Christ Impulse in Dina's heart. That which she had long prayed for, which had lived in her subconsciously, became raised to consciousness as she beheld the Messiah. This raising to consciousness of the subconscious was symbolized by the ascending Moon, which rose across the eastern horizon during the course of Dina's conversation with Jesus. The Moon was at First Quarter, at 3° Scorpio. Beneath the horizon Mars (28° Capricorn) and Neptune (25° Capricorn) were in conjunction in the star-sign of the Goat, symbolizing the rising from the depths of the Word (Mars) of Inspiration (Neptune), which converted Dina from her life of sin to become an ardent follower of Jesus Christ, who became the Sun of her life (Sun in opposition to the conjunction of Mars and Neptune). The hermetic opposition between Venus (7° Gemini) and Pluto (10° Sagittarius) indicates the evil passions (Venus opposite Pluto) which had beset her—although only about thirty years old, she had had five husbands in quick succession and was now living with a sixth man. But, as later with Mary Magdalena, Dina's love (Venus) became filled with new meaning and depth through her devotion to the Messiah. Her relationship to Jesus Christ, which began with the conversation at Jacob's well, is highlighted by the fact that

THE CONVERSATION AT JACOB'S WELL

the position of Venus hermetically at 7° Gemini was the same as the zodiacal location of the hermetic conjunction between Mercury and Saturn at the baptism in the Jordan.

TAT: The whole stellar configuration at the time of this conversation at Jacob's well speaks a sublime language!

HERMES: Yes, my son, without going into every detail, nevertheless a clear message is communicated by the stars. And this is so every step of the way along the path trodden by Jesus Christ. In terms of the stellar configuration, the conversation with Dina at Jacob's well was a prelude to the healing miracle which took place eight days later: that of the healing of the nobleman's son. On this day—Thursday, August 3, A.D. 30—Jesus was teaching at Cana in Galilee, when Selathiel came riding upon his mule to beg that his son Joel be healed. Joel, who was fourteen years old, had been adopted by the nobleman Zorobabel of Capernaum, in whose employ Selathiel was chief official. Joel had already lain sick with fever for fourteen days. No medicine was able to help him, and the boy constantly repeated: "Jesus, the prophet of Nazareth, alone can help me!" In desperation Selathiel rode to Cana to request that Jesus return with him to Capernaum to heal his son, who was now at the point of death. Filled with faith in his miraculous powers, Selathiel pleaded with Jesus: "Master, my son is in the agony of death! Come with me at once, he may perhaps already be dead!" Jesus answered: "Go, thy son liveth!" Selathiel asked: "Is that really true?" Jesus responded: "Believe me, in this very hour he has been cured." Selathiel believed him and, mounting his mule, hastened back to Capernaum. A couple of hours from Capernaum some of his servants met him and told him that the boy had suddenly been cured at the seventh hour, which was the very time at which Jesus had spoken to him.

TAT: O father, what took place here, that the boy was healed from a distance?

HERMES: My son, the boy's condition was a consequence of Selathiel's dependence on Zorobabel. In every family the self of the father works upon the physical condition of his children. And when the self, which is intrinsically of the nature of the Sun, becomes fixated on another human being in a condition of dependence, then it becomes a kind of satellite, becoming moonlike, and loses its true sunlike nature. This was the case in the relationship between Selathiel and Zorobabel, to the extent that Selathiel had given his son in adoption to Zorobabel. Selathiel wanted to please Zorobabel in his office of chief official, not just out of the will to serve, but because he desired to succeed. This desire had led him into a state of fixation in which he had become a kind of satellite of Zorobabel, and had more or less lost his true self. This condition worked back upon his son Joel, who eventually became feverishly ill. The faith of Selathiel in Jesus Christ was the starting point for the miracle of Joel's healing. Through this faith, Christ, the Spirit of the Sun, could radiate into the self of Selathiel to restore it to its true sunlike nature, and this in turn restored health to Selathiel's son. This was the deeper background to the miraculous healing of Joel.

TAT: And what, O father, was the cosmic background to this healing miracle?

THE CONVERSATION AT JACOB'S WELL

HERMES: My son, as at the conversation at Jacob's well, the Sun was in Leo, propitious for the igniting of faith in the heart as took place with Selathiel. Moreover, the Sun was in conjunction with Uranus, indicating the possibility for the radiating in of a spiritually awakening impulse, which in this case signified healing from a distance, by way of spiritual transmission, so to say. As eight days had elapsed since the conversation at Jacob's well, at which the Moon had been at First Quarter, it was now one day past Full Moon. The almost Full Moon was in the Waterman (25° Aquarius) opposite Leo, the star-sign of the Sun. And as the healing of Joel took place, the Moon was at the deepest point below the Earth, symbolizing the deeply subconscious nature of the forces at work here (how Joel's condition arose from the unhealthy dependence of Selathiel upon Zorobabel). That Joel was on the point of death is symbolized by the hermetic conjunction between Venus and Saturn in the Twins (19°/20° Gemini). And Mercury (15° Sagittarius), viewed hermetically, was more or less opposite in the heavens. This position of Mercury speaks of the boy's love for Jesus, for at the birth of the pure soul of Jesus of Nazareth, the Sun had been at 15° Sagittarius. The boy knew that Jesus alone could save him from death. And it was the power of Inspiration (Neptune) of the Word (Mars) which saved him, as Jesus spoke the words, "Go, thy son liveth!"—symbolized macrocosmically by the conjunction of Neptune and Mars in the Goat (25°/26° Capricorn).

TAT: Great indeed, O father, are the heavenly mysteries revealed in the life of Our Lord.

CLOSING INVOCATION

A Discourse of Hermes to Asclepius

The Sun Chronicle in the Life of the Messiah

OPENING INVOCATION

ASCLEPIUS: O Hermes, having described the main events from the baptism, coinciding with the Sun's entrance into the star-sign Libra, up to the healing of the nobleman's son, when the Sun entered the second decan of Leo, what was the further path of the ministry?

HERMES: Honorable Asclepius, let us follow the path of the Sun in the heavens further, and correspondingly the path of the Son of Man on Earth. After the healing of the adopted son of the nobleman Zorobabel, which was also the healing of the boy's father, Selathiel, Jesus proceeded to Capernaum, where he was festively received by Zorobabel. Zorobabel and his whole entourage of servants came to believe in Jesus on account of the miraculous healing of his adopted son Joel. The boy kneeled before Jesus, who laid his hand on the boy's head, and Jesus renamed him Jesse.

After teaching and healing in Capernaum and Sephoris, Jesus went to Nazareth. On the evening of the Sabbath, Friday, August 11, A.D. 30, he taught in the synagogue, reading from Chapter 61 of the book of Isaiah, "The Spirit of the Lord God is upon me, because the Lord has anointed me to bring good tidings to the afflicted, to proclaim the year of the Lord's favor," which he read and interpreted as if it referred to himself. On the next day he taught again in the synagogue, saying that there were many widows in Israel in the days of Elijah and comparing Nazareth with a leper who would not be healed. At this, the Pharisees were in an uproar. As Jesus was leaving the synagogue, about twenty Pharisees surrounded him and began to lead him towards the top of a hill, where they had the intention of pushing him off to his death. But Jesus managed to slip away unnoticed. It was already dark. This was the first serious attempt by the Pharisees to do away with Jesus Christ.

ASCLEPIUS: And what was the cosmic configuration at this event?

HERMES: The Sun was at the end of the second decan of the Lion (19½° Leo). That night the Moon was in conjunction with Saturn in the Twins (25° Gemini). And hermetically Mars (12½° Aquarius) was in opposition to Uranus (10° Leo). Jesus escaped the threat of death with the help of Angelic intervention, so that the Pharisees did not even notice that Jesus was no longer in their midst, until they reached the top of the hill.

After this, he left Nazareth and traveled to various towns in Galilee, teaching and healing as he went. Then he returned to Capernaum in time for the next Sabbath. There he healed many people and also drove out demons from the possessed. At about midday on Saturday, August 19, A.D. 30, he healed Peter's mother-in-law, who was seriously ill with a high fever. At the time the Sun was at 26° Leo, and hermetically Mercury (8½° Aquarius) was in opposition to Uranus (10° Leo).

So many miraculous healings were accomplished by Jesus Christ, everywhere he went: his fame as a prophet and healer spread far and wide. More and more people came to hear him or to be healed—so many, that he bestowed the gift of healing on the disciples Andrew, John and Judas Barsabbas, by laying his hands upon them, so that they could help him in his healing work. This took place as the Sun was entering the second decan of Virgo. Shortly after this, at about three o'clock on the afternoon of Monday, September 4, A.D. 30, Jesus healed Mara the Suphanite in Ainon, the town near which John the Baptist had begun his baptizing activity. Mara was a rich woman who, through repeated adultery, had become possessed by five demons. Jesus drove out the demons and forgave Mara her sins. She became, like Dina the Samaritan, one of his most devoted followers. It was Mara to whom Jesus later referred when he recounted the parable of the lost sheep. At Mara's healing the Sun was at 12° Virgo, the Moon (26° Aries) was hermetically in conjunction with Mercury (30° Aries), and there was also a hermetic conjunction between Uranus (10½° Leo) and Venus (12½° Leo).

Following the passage of the Sun further, it entered the star-sign of Libra on the evening of Friday, September 22, A.D. 30. At midday on the next day—Saturday, September 23, A.D. 30—Jesus raised a three-year-old child from the dead in the town of Gadara. The child, son of a heathen woman, had eaten some poisonous berries the day before, and—all attempts to help it having failed—now lay as if dead. Jesus breathed on the child and commanded two of his disciples, Judas Barsabbas and Nathanael the Bridegroom, to lay their hands on its head and bless it, at which the child was restored to life, completely healed. This took place exactly one year after the baptism in the Jordan, at which the Sun had stood at 1° Libra. This was, so to say, the first "birthday anniversary" of the ministry of Jesus Christ, one year after the baptism, the Sun having completed one orbit of the zodiac, having returned to 1° Libra in the sidereal zodiac.

Thirteen days later, on Friday, October 6, A.D. 30, as the Sun was at 14° Libra, Jesus healed the blind youth Manahem in the town of Correa. Lazarus was acquainted with Manahem, who had the gift of prophecy through inner vision (clairvoyance) and had been baptized by John the Baptist. To this inner vision came outer vision, bestowed upon him by Jesus. Thereafter Manahem became a faithful disciple of the Lord. At the time of this healing Venus (10° Libra) was opposite Jupiter (7° Aries), the Moon was hermetically in conjunction with Saturn (21½° Gemini), and Mercury (8° Libra) was hermetically in opposition to Jupiter (8° Aries).

ASCLEPIUS: The position of the Sun at 14° Libra also seems significant, as at the crucifixion two-and-a-half years later the Sun was exactly opposite in the zodiac at 14° Aries.

HERMES: Yes, Asclepius, here there was a prophetic shining in, as it were, of the Sun of righteousness, the Light of the World, who would be sacrificed on the hill of Golgotha. Manahem had been born blind and had in this way remained true to God's revelation, for he could see spiritually, clairvoyantly. Human souls living in paradise prior to the Fall saw spiritually, beholding the world as a revelation of God. But with the Fall a transformation of human seeing took place, whereby the eyes of human beings were opened, and henceforth they saw the "bare facts" of the world without the illumination of God. They no longer saw the world as an expression of God, which is spiritual seeing, but for its own sake, estranged from God, which is ordinary seeing. Manahem did not want to see this God-estranged world, and by being born blind he retained spiritual seeing. For, generally, either the external world is seen in an illusory way, which is the tendency of the left eye, or in a God-less way, which is the tendency of the right eye, or in the case of blindness the outer world is not seen at all, which gives the possibility of seeing with the *third eye*, the spiritual organ located in the region of the forehead between the right and left eye. Manahem's blindness meant he saw only with the *third eye*. On account of his faithfulness, Jesus Christ restored ordinary seeing to him. For, this is the ideal: to be able to see the outer world with ordinary seeing together with the spiritual seeing of the third eye, in the Light of God's revelation. This is *Christ seeing*, seeing by way of the Light of the World, beholding the outer world together with its archetypes, the revelation of the glory of God.

ASCLEPIUS: Is this, O Hermes, the basis of all true seership in the Christian tradition?

HERMES: Indeed, Asclepius, it arises through uniting with the Light of the World and thus seeing the world as it truly is, in its true light.

Following the Sun's passage through the zodiac further, on Tuesday, October 24, A.D. 30, the Sun entered Scorpio. The Sun was in conjunction with Venus, such that Venus was beyond the Sun, and on this day Venus and the Sun entered Scorpio together. It was on this very day that Judas Iscariot became a disciple of Jesus Christ. Judas was about twenty-five years old, and longed for fame and wealth. From all that he had heard concerning Jesus, he saw a possibility of his dreams being realized. The disciples were taken care of, and Lazarus—with all his wealth—supported Jesus. And Jesus was spoken of everywhere because of his miracles. Judas desired to become a disciple and share in Jesus' greatness, so he sought the acquaintance of several disciples and made himself generally useful. Judas traveled together with Bartholomew, Simon, Judas Thaddeus, and Philip to the town of Meroz, which Jesus was visiting. They arrived in Meroz on the evening of Monday, October 23, A.D. 30. Judas went to a home where he often stayed, and the other four went to the hostel where Jesus was staying. Simon, Thaddeus and Philip were already disciples, and that night Bartholomew also became a disciple, having already been inwardly called by the Lord. Bartholomew was a cousin of the brothers Simon and Thaddeus, and was also related to Philip. They spoke to Jesus concerning Judas, saying how much he desired to become a disciple. At this, Jesus sighed and was much downcast. On the next day, accompanied by the disciples, Jesus healed the sick in Meroz, and some time around midday or early afternoon Judas Iscariot came up to them. Bartholomew and Simon introduced Judas to Jesus, saying: "Master, this is Judas of whom we have spoken." Jesus was most friendly towards Judas, but was filled with an indescribable sorrow. Judas bowed and said: "Master, I pray that you may allow me to take part in your teaching." Jesus replied most gently the prophetic words: "You may take a place, unless you would prefer to leave it to another." Here Jesus was alluding prophetically to Judas' betrayal, forsaking his place among the Twelve, leaving it to Matthias.

Venus is the planet of desire, which can become transformed, however, to compassion, through union with the Christ-Sun. This is the transformation from passion to compassion (Venus ennobled by the Sun), which can even lead to self-sacrifice for the sake of higher ideals. Judas was filled with ignoble desire when he came to become a disciple of Jesus Christ. Bartholomew also was filled with desire, but his longing was for Christ and not for his own glory. Both became disciples of Jesus at the conjunction between Venus and the Sun, as the two planets were entering Scorpio. Bartholomew was the ninth disciple called of those who later became apostles. After him came Judas, whose desire might have become transformed, and a struggle did go on within him for some two years. However, on account of his desire for money, Judas was eventually led to betray Jesus to the Pharisees. Here was the "sting of the Scorpion" that Jesus took openly and willingly upon himself on the day he accepted Judas as a disciple. Judas represented the negative side of this cosmic configuration, whereas Bartholomew, who was a fine and noble soul, represented the positive side. Bartholomew later died a martyr's death in Abyssinia.

ASCLEPIUS: And how was it, O Hermes, that the next disciple of the Twelve was called?

HERMES: Asclepius, this took place just five days later, as the Sun was still in the first decan of the Scorpion (7° Scorpio). Jesus and his disciples were in Dothan, when Thomas approached the Lord and asked if he could become a disciple. Thomas was a twin; his twin brother, after the Lord's ascension, also became a Christian, and later traveled with the apostle Peter to Damascus. Their mother died in childbirth, and Thomas was the second-born of the twins. Even as a youth Thomas needed to have things proved to him, and this was so after the resurrection, that he doubted it had taken place, until it was proved to him by the unmistakable presence of the Risen One. This quality of mind on the part of Thomas was symbolized in the heavens by the hermetic conjunction between Mercury and Pluto in the Archer (10½° Sagittarius) on the morning that he became a disciple. But this very quality of doubt became transformed into the greatest faith, as shown by the miracles and conversions later accomplished by Thomas on his widespread travels. He traveled even as far as India, where he died the death of a martyr. The great courage of this apostle, who had to endure much on his many travels, is symbolized by the fact that Mars, hermetically, was entering Aries on the day of his becoming a disciple.

ASCLEPIUS: Pray speak further, O Hermes, concerning the Sun chronicle of Our Lord's ministry.

HERMES: Eight days after Thomas became a disciple, Jesus was in the town of Giscala, the birth place of Saul, who later became Paul. Saul having moved with his parents to Tarsus, the house in which he had been born was now occupied by a pagan officer named Achias, who was in command of pagan soldiers garrisoned in the town. He approached Jesus to beg that his 7-year-old son be healed. The boy was dumb and paralyzed, unable to move at all. Achias addressed Jesus with the words: "Lord, I believe that you are God's messenger, the fulfillment of the promise. I believe that you can help me, and I know that you said that those who believe in you are not strangers but your children. Lord, have mercy on my child." Jesus replied: "Your faith has saved you!" And he entered the house and healed the boy. The boy's name was Jephte, and he later became a zealous disciple of the apostle Thomas. Jesus told the disciples that the boy would later bear great fruit, as would another child who had been born in the same house.

At the time of this healing of Jephte, the Sun was in conjunction with Antares, the heart of the Scorpion (15° Scorpio) and the Moon was in conjunction with Regulus, the heart of the Lion (5° Leo). Hermetically, Venus was at $23\frac{1}{2}°$ Scorpio, transiting the axis of the Moon's nodes ($23\frac{1}{2}°$ Taurus), and Mercury (6° Capricorn) was square to Mars ($4\frac{1}{2}°$ Aries). Here there was a direct radiating in of the power of cosmic love (Venus) as Jesus restored speech (Mars) and movement (Mercury) to the boy, and the love was reciprocated by Jephte, by later becoming a disciple.

This healing of Jephte was a prelude to another healing miracle which took place a few days later, when Jesus arrived in Capernaum. There the Roman centurion Cornelius had a slave who was sick and at the point of death. Cornelius sent two Jewish elders to ask Jesus to come and heal his slave. Out of humility Cornelius himself did not come up to Jesus. When he saw Jesus coming, he fell down on his knees, and his messenger ran up to Jesus, saying: "The centurion bids me to say to you, 'Lord, I am not worthy to have you enter under my roof; speak but one word, and my servant shall be healed.'" At these words Jesus said to the crowd: "Truly, I say unto you, I have not found such faith in Israel!" Then addressing the centurion, he said:

"Go, and as you have believed, so be it!" Shortly after, the slave came running from the house, completely healed.

As this took place, the Sun was at the end of the second decan of the Scorpion (19° Scorpio). Whereas at Jephte's healing four days earlier Venus had been hermetically transiting the axis of the Moon's nodes, so now Venus was at $23\frac{1}{2}°$ Scorpio, exactly crossing the axis of the Moon's nodes ($23\frac{1}{2}°$ Taurus). In the former case, at the healing of Jephte, the cosmic aspect involving Venus had been on the devachanic plane; this had been a prelude to the same cosmic event now taking place on the astral plane, coinciding with the healing of the slave of Cornelius. In both cases it was a matter of healing on behalf of pagans (Achias and Cornelius) well-disposed towards the Jewish people, where Jesus showed his love to believers outside of the people of Israel, thus showing that he had come as the Savior also for the Gentiles. Both Achias and Cornelius subsequently were baptized, as were their entire households. The event that took place cosmically on the devachanic plane, coinciding with the healing of Jephte, showed its more spiritual nature in that Jephte later became a zealous disciple, for he had been touched in the core of his spirit by the love of the Messiah.

ASCLEPIUS: Thank you, O Hermes, for this account of the Sun chronicle in the life of the Savior, which you have described from the healing of the nobleman's son, when the Sun entered the second decan of Leo, to these two healings, that of the son of Achias and that of the slave of Cornelius, as the Sun was approaching the end of the second decan of Scorpio.

CLOSING INVOCATION

A Discourse of Hermes to King Ammon

The Raising of the Youth of Nain and of the Daughter of Jairus

OPENING INVOCATION

KING AMMON: With the entrance of the Sun into Scorpio the impulse of betrayal manifested itself in Judas Iscariot, who became a disciple at this time. But as the Sun was in Scorpio there was also the event of Thomas becoming a disciple and the healings directed to the Gentiles, which you described in the last discourse.

HERMES: More than this, King Ammon, the first conversion of Mary Magdalena took place as the Sun was at 17° Scorpio, when she was so deeply moved by Jesus that she anointed his head with costly ointment as he sat eating with the Pharisees as a guest of Simon Zabulon in Gabara. It is true that she returned to her life of debauchery not long after, but this conversion was the first step on her path towards becoming a devoted follower of Our Lord.

So we see that Scorpio has to do not only with betrayal (Judas Iscariot) and faith (Thomas), but also with debauchery and conversion from sin (Mary Magdalena). But Scorpio also has to do with life and death, as I shall now describe to you.

THE RAISING OF THE YOUTH OF NAIN

James the Elder's wife's sister, Maroni, was a rich widow living in the little town of Nain, south of Mt. Tabor. She was also distantly related to Peter, being the daughter of the brother of Peter's father-in-law. She had a 12-year-old son, later baptized Martialis, who was desperately ill, and so she came to see Jesus near Capernaum to beg him to come and heal her child, which the Lord promised to do. Three days later, accompanied by about thirty disciples, he came to Nain. It was around nine o'clock as he approached the town, on the morning of Monday, November 13, A.D. 30. At that moment a procession of mourning Jews came through the town gate bearing the coffin of the dead youth. Jesus went up to the coffin bearers and asked them to set the coffin on the ground, which they did. Turning to Maroni, who was weeping bitterly, Jesus said: "Woman, weep not!" Jesus took a little vessel of water and a twig of hyssop, saying to the bearers: "Open the coffin and loosen the bands!" Jesus looked up to heaven and spoke: "I praise thee, Lord of heaven and earth, that you have hidden all these things from the wise and understanding, and that you have revealed them to the simple-hearted. Yes, Father, for such was your gracious will. All things are delivered unto me by my Father; and no one knows the Son but the Father; and no one knows the Father but the Son and he to whom the Son chooses to reveal Him. Come to me, all who labor and are burdened, and I will vivify you. Take my yoke upon you, and learn from me; for I am gentle and humble of heart, and you will find rest for your souls; for my yoke is easy, and my burden is light." Jesus blessed the water, dipped the twig into it, and sprinkled first the crowd, then the dead youth, and with his hand made the sign of the cross over him, saying: "Arise!" At this Martialis sat up. He then stood, asking, "What is this? How did I come to be here?" Jesus took him by the hand, led him to his mother, and said: "Here you have your son back, but I shall demand him from you reborn in baptism."

At this raising from the dead both the Sun and the Moon were in Scorpio. It was shortly before New Moon. The Moon was at 12° Scorpio and the Sun at 22° Scorpio. Here the Sun was transiting the axis of the Moon's nodes (23½° Taurus), just as at the healing of Cornelius' slave Venus had been transiting this axis, and just as at the healing of Achias' son Venus had been hermetically transiting this axis. Now, at the raising of the youth of Nain, the full power of Christ, the Spirit of the Sun, worked in—overcoming death and raising the youth to new life. This overcoming of death was signified by the setting of Saturn, hermetically, on the western horizon at the very moment of the raising of Martialis from the dead. At this moment, too, Mercury was in conjunction with Pluto in the Archer (10° Sagittarius), symbolizing the ardent faith which Martialis later showed as a disciple.

KING AMMON: Was this not the same cosmic configuration—the conjunction of Mercury and Pluto in the Archer—as on the day that Thomas became a disciple?

HERMES: Indeed, King Ammon, with the exception that when Thomas became a disciple it was a hermetic conjunction between Mercury and Pluto in the Archer, signifying a cosmic event on the devachanic plane. This was on a more spiritual level—Thomas becoming a disciple of the Lord—whereas at the raising of the youth of Nain, the youth "became a disciple," but more on the level of the

THE RAISING OF THE YOUTH OF NAIN

soul. Only later, after his baptism, when he received the name Martialis, did this discipleship become raised to a more conscious level.

Five days after the raising of Martialis from the dead there took place the raising of Salome, the daughter of Jairus, head of the synagogue at Capernaum. Owing to circumstances which I shall describe, after the raising of Salome from the dead she died again, but was then raised from the dead for a second time. The first time was on the afternoon of Saturday, November 18, A.D. 30, before the close of the Sabbath. As Jesus was healing the sick in front of the synagogue, Jairus came up to him and begged him to come and heal his daughter. Accompanied by Peter, James and John, Jesus went with Jairus. Outside the house of Jairus mourners had gathered, for Salome had died. She was not more than twelve years old. Jesus went into the house, lifted up the corpse and breathed on it. He then laid the body down again, took hold of the girl's arm and said: "Maid, arise!" At this the girl sat up and her parents were filled with joy.

On this day the Sun was still in the third decan, close to the tail of the Scorpion (27° Scorpio). As at the raising of the youth of Nain, the Sun was still close to the axis of the Moon's nodes (23½° Taurus to 23½° Scorpio). The Moon, at the tail of the Goat (28° Capricorn), was in conjunction with Neptune (24° Capricorn). Hermetically, Venus (13° Sagittarius) was in conjunction with Pluto (11° Sagittarius), and Mars (11½° Aries) was in conjunction with Jupiter (12° Aries).

KING AMMON: Here again there was the overcoming of death—"the sting of the Scorpion"—as at the raising of the youth of Nain.

HERMES: Indeed, King Ammon, but the conjunction of the Moon and Neptune symbolized an element of deception. The parents of Salome, although they thanked Jesus for saving their daughter, took this act of grace most lightheartedly—even to the extent that the mother later spoke mockingly of Jesus to her daughter. The father, Jairus, was more concerned about maintaining his good standing amongst the Pharisees rather than paying any attention to Jesus and the disciples. Salome, of course, was influenced by the attitude of her parents. She, too, did not take to heart the grace of God that had saved her life. Already by the following Sabbath she fell ill again with fever. In the following days her parents watched the course of her illness with alarm, and inwardly it dawned on them that they had not shown proper respect for the healing miracle that had brought Salome back to life, that they had taken it quite lightheartedly and had made no effort to change their lives for the better. After a week of high fever, her parents saw death approaching once more. Salome's mother urged Jairus to go to Jesus again and beg for his help. This was at the onset of the next Sabbath, on Friday, December 1, A.D. 30. Jairus went to the synagogue in Capernaum to seek Jesus out. As Jesus was leaving the synagogue, Jairus approached him, cast himself down at his feet, and begged him to take pity on his daughter, who was now close to death again. Jesus promised that he would return with him. There was a large throng pressing around, among it a widowed heathen woman who had suffered a flow of blood for twelve years. Her name was Enue. She knelt down and leaned forward to touch the hem of Jesus' robe. She felt that she was healed instantly. Jesus asked: "Who touched me?" Peter replied: "You ask

THE RAISING OF THE YOUTH OF NAIN

who touched you; people are pressing in and thronging around you, as you see." But Jesus answered: "Someone touched me, for I felt a force issue forth from me." Enue then acknowledged what she had done, and begged Jesus to forgive her. Jesus said to her: "Be comforted, my daughter, your faith has healed you! Go in peace, and remain free from your affliction." Enue was in her thirties; she was tall, but very thin and pale. Her deceased Jewish husband had left her with a daughter, who was now looked after by her uncle.

Accompanied by Peter, James, Saturnin and Matthew, Jesus then continued on his way with Jairus. When they arrived at the latter's home, mourners were gathered outside. For Salome had died. On going into the house, Jesus broke off a twig in the garden and asked for a cup of water, which he blessed. The corpse of the girl was completely stiff. Jesus, whilst praying, dipped the twig into the water and sprinkled it onto the girl's body. He took her hand and said: "Maid, I say unto you, arise!" She opened her eyes, rose up, and went to her parents, who—sobbing tears of joy and relief—sank down at Jesus' feet. Jesus exhorted the parents to receive God's mercy thankfully, to completely renounce vanity and worldly pleasure, to do penance, and to beware of again compromising their daughter's life now restored for the second time. Salome herself was deeply moved and shed tears. Jesus told her that in the future she should no longer live according to the dictates of her flesh and blood, but that she should eat the Bread of Life—the Word of God—and she should repent, believe, pray, and do good deeds. Salome's parents became inwardly transformed and expressed their determination to change their ways.

KING AMMON: This was indeed an extraordinary grace, that the girl could be raised again from death.

HERMES: Honorable King Ammon, from this you may see how great is the mercy and compassion of Jesus Christ. In this example of Jairus' daughter is contained a teaching concerning the Second Coming of the Lord. Many are those who received the grace of Jesus Christ through his First Coming, but in later incarnations have forgotten it. Like Jairus and his wife, they have lived frivolous lives based on worldly concerns, even mocking the memory of the Holy One of Israel, the Savior of humankind. But misfortune is bound to strike whosoever turns away from the Source of all Goodness. And this is the situation in which many find themselves in their incarnations in the Age of the Second Coming. Salvation can be found only by turning to Jesus Christ, and as in the case of Jairus, a second opportunity will be given to all who sincerely seek him. And in the case of those who have missed the grace of Jesus Christ in their incarnations up until now, there is now another opportunity—as in the case of the pagan woman Enue—to seek out Jesus Christ and make contact with him. However great the throng, he notices each one, and his healing power of love and compassion goes forth to each who seeks it and needs it.

KING AMMON: And what, O Hermes, was the heavenly constellation at this time of the second raising of Jairus' daughter?

HERMES: The Sun was entering the second decan of the Archer and was in exact conjunction with Pluto

THE RAISING OF THE YOUTH OF NAIN

(10½° Sagittarius). Just one year previously, at the culmination of the three temptations in the wilderness, the Sun had been in conjunction with Pluto. Here it was a matter of wresting Salome's soul from the face of the underworld, which Christ was empowered to do, having triumphed over the underworld himself one year before. Mercury (25° Sagittarius) was in exact opposition to Saturn (25° Gemini), symbolizing the change in consciousness—the awakening of conscience that took place in Salome and her parents. Cosmically, what both these raisings from the dead have in common is that Mars was square (90°) to the Sun. Both times Salome was afflicted with fever (Mars) which led to her death, from which she was saved by Christ, the Spirit of the Sun. Also significant is that at all these raisings from the dead—that of the youth of Nain and the two times of the daughter of Jairus—Jupiter hermetically was close to that part of Aries at which the Sun stood at the crucifixion, indicating a radiating in in advance of the triumph of life over death.

KING AMMON: Thank you, O Hermes, for this profound discourse.

CLOSING INVOCATION

A Discourse of Hermes to Tat

The Ministry Up to the Beheading of John the Baptist

OPENING INVOCATION

TAT: O father, please tell us something of Jesus' relationship with the twelve disciples who became his apostles.

HERMES: As I have described to you, the calling of the eleventh disciple, Thomas, took place as the Sun was in the first decan of the Scorpion (7° Scorpio). Then came the calling of the twelfth disciple, Matthew, as the Sun was approaching the end of Scorpio, at the tail of the Scorpion (28½° Scorpio). All the time, on their travels together, when Jesus was not teaching publicly or healing, he gave instruction to the disciples. Not long after the calling of Matthew, when the Sun was in the first decan of the Archer (7½° Sagittarius), Jesus began the Sermon on the Mount, in which he taught concerning the Beatitudes. This extended over three days, and took place on the mountain ("Mount of Beatitudes") east of the town of Bethsaida-Julias, which was more or less due north of the northern end of the Sea of Galilee. Then he returned to Capernaum, and there occurred the second raising of the daughter of Jairus, of which I spoke in the last discourse. But Jesus came back to the Mount of Beatitudes on Monday, December 4, A.D. 30 (Sun at 13½° Sagittarius), and resumed his teaching there concerning the Beatitudes. Afterwards, it was late afternoon, Jesus bestowed his power upon the Twelve: the power to heal and to cast out demons in his name. He blessed them and said that he wanted to be with them always and to share everything with them. At the time of the bestowing of his power upon the disciples the Moon was in the middle of the Lion, where it had been at the time of the baptism (15° Leo), and it was in conjunction with the planet Uranus (14½° Leo). Also Venus and Mercury were in exact conjunction at 23½° Sagittarius. It was on the Mount of Beatitudes that the feeding of the five thousand took place some two months later, and about five months after this miraculous feeding Jesus Christ returned again to the Mount of Beatitudes and completed the Sermon on the Mount, in which he taught not only concerning the Beatitudes but also the Lord's Prayer.

As the Sun was approaching the end of the second decan of the Archer (19½° Sagittarius) Jesus went with the twelve apostles and about thirty disciples to a mountain near Hanathon, north of Capernaum. Here he addressed the apostles and disciples, saying that they should now go out into the world and teach and heal as he did. He said that John the Baptist would not live much longer, and that the apostles should baptize, heal by the laying on of hands, and cast out demons, and that the disciples should help them. He also gave detailed instructions as to how they should conduct themselves: that they should live frugally and not be a burden to anyone, that the apostles should go in pairs accompanied by several disciples; and he referred to other rules of conduct. He then sent out the six apostles Peter, James the Lesser, John, Philip, Thomas and Judas together with a number of disciples. All wept as they parted company and Jesus told them when and where they should all meet each other again. On this occasion Mercury and Saturn, viewed hermetically, were in conjunction in the Twins, Mercury at 27° Gemini and Saturn at 24° Gemini, recalling the hermetic conjunction between these two planets at the baptism. This was the fifth hermetic conjunction between Mercury and Saturn since the baptism.

Sixteen days later, on Tuesday, December 26, A.D. 30, Jesus taught on a hill near Azanath, north of Mt. Tabor and west of the Sea of Galilee. The Sun was in the first decan of the Goat (6° Capricorn). Lazarus' sister Martha managed to persuade her sister Mary Magdalena to attend this teaching. Seven weeks had elapsed since Magdalena's first conversion, when the Sun had been in the second decan of the Scorpion (17° Scorpio). During the seven weeks Magdalena had returned to her former life of sin, and the excess of her debauchery now surpassed by far her previous debauched way of life. Very reluctantly she came with Martha to Azanath, and now she sat on the hillside and listened to Jesus preach. Jesus spoke most powerfully, proclaiming woe upon Capernaum, Bethsaida and Chorazin. Every so often a child called out, "Jesus of Nazareth, most holy prophet, Son of David, Son of God!" including children who had never spoken before. Many people, also Magdalena, were deeply moved by this. At one point, with Magdalena in view, Jesus said that if a demon is cast out and the house is swept, then it will return with six others and cause more trouble than before. Magdalena was very shocked when she heard this. Then Jesus, addressing the entire gathering of people, offered to drive out the devil from those longing to be freed, but said those who wanted to remain bound to the devil should leave. A few people, including Magdalena, fell unconscious when they heard this. This was the start of the driving out of the seven demons that had taken possession of her since her relapse. At the end of this process of conversion, Jesus blessed her and spoke to her of the virtue of purity, recommending Magdalena to attach herself to the Blessed Virgin, who was completely pure, and who would advise and comfort her. Jesus said of Magdalena, "She was a great sinner, but she will also be an example to all penitents for all time."

TAT: What was the cosmic constellation at this second conversion of Mary Magdalena?

HERMES: Mercury was in conjunction with Pluto (12° Sagittarius) and in opposition to the Moon in Gemini. You may recall that on the morning that Thomas became a disciple of the Lord, Mercury and Pluto were hermetically in conjunction. This cosmic event, which as Thomas became a disciple was on the devachanic level, was repeated on the astral level as Magdalena became a disciple. Both Thomas and Magdalena were filled with great faith, but in Thomas' case this was more on the spiritual level—a consequence of his battle to overcome doubt—and in the case of Magdalena it was more on the level of the soul, as a consequence of her struggle to overcome temptation.

Mary Magdalena had to be freed from possession by evil, symbolized here by Pluto; for at the culmination of the temptation of the Lord in the wilderness, Pluto was in conjunction with the Sun, whilst here, with Magdalena, Pluto was in conjunction with Mercury. The opposition with the Moon points to this struggle for her soul; ultimately, the issue at stake was the *death* of her soul, which would have ensued if she had continued with her life of debauchery. But she overcame, and chose life for her soul, which became possible through Christ driving the demons out of her, and then blessing her. That the struggle was directed to her life of feeling, her passions, is indicated by the hermetic opposition between Venus (12½° Aquarius) and Uranus (12° Leo) as the process of conversion began, while she was listening to Jesus preach. Following this conversion, Mary Magdalena completely gave up her former way of life, and devoted herself—together with the other holy women around the Blessed Virgin—to serving Jesus Christ and the community of his disciples.

The second conversion of Magdalena took place just one week prior to the beheading of John the Baptist, which occurred at Herod's birthday celebration. The beheading took place at the instigation of Herod's wife, Herodias, and in her case we see the extent to which evil passions may drive someone. Herod's birthday was celebrated on the twentieth day of the month of Thebet in the Jewish calendar, which started on the evening of Wednesday, January 3, A.D. 31. The guests were already gathered at his palace at Machaerus when the celebration started that evening. Herod was thinking of setting John the Baptist free, for which his birthday presented an ideal occasion, but Herodias had quite different plans. She sent her daughter Salome to dance voluptuously before Herod, who became perfectly entranced, so that he said to Salome: "Ask of me what you will and I will give it to you. Yes, I swear it, even if you want half my kingdom, I will give it to you." Salome hastened to ask her mother what she should request of Herod, and Herodias told her to ask for the head of John the Baptist on a dish. Salome hurried back to Herod and said: "I will that you give to me at once the head of John on a dish!" Herod was as if struck down with shock, but Salome reminded him of his oath, and Herod commanded his servants that the terrible deed be done. So John the Baptist died that night.

The Sun was in the middle of the Goat ($14\frac{1}{2}°$ Capricorn) and the waning Moon (26° Virgo) was approaching the star Spica ("the ear of corn") in the Virgin (29° Virgo). The Moon was in opposition to Mars (25° Pisces), and Mars hermetically was at 7° Taurus in its node (7° Taurus), close to the Pleiades (5° Taurus). The whole deed was an evil inspiration of negative Mars spirits, opposed to the Word—the positive impulse of Mars—which John the Baptist had represented so powerfully. Also Mercury (20° Sagittarius) was in opposition to Saturn (22° Gemini), an indication that his death (Saturn symbolizing the Angel of death) was brought about by cunning (Herodias) and false movement (Salome), representing the negative side of Mercury.

TAT: Why was John not helped to escape, for he was only thirty-one years and seven months old when he was beheaded?

HERMES: My son, there is much to be learned from this ending to the life of John the Baptist. You ask why he was not helped to escape. Up to a certain age everyone is protected by his Angel, but beyond this age there must be the will to live, in order to continue to enjoy a certain measure of protection. In the case of John, he did not protect himself, and so he fell ultimately into the hands of the negative spiritual stream represented by Herod and Herodias. Someone who has a great mission—such as John—should not simply follow his destiny passively. Such a one must learn to will the future, otherwise the Angels and higher spiritual beings cannot help. They help up to a certain age, but then one must learn how to help and protect oneself. John the Baptist did not do this, and so he was delivered into captivity at the hands of the same spiritual stream with which he had had to do battle in his previous incarnation. This passive working of destiny, which took place without any resistance on his part, need not have been, if John had really willed to live further. But as far as he was concerned, he had already fulfilled his mission, having recognized and baptized the Messiah. He had said, with respect to the Messiah, "He must increase, and I must decrease." Here, already, he had renounced the deeper will to live. The Angels and higher spiritual beings, who had helped him up until the baptism, were obliged gradually to withdraw. Thus John the Baptist was already "spiritually beheaded" before he became actually beheaded. That the higher spiritual beings had withdrawn is revealed by the fact that when John was in prison he no longer knew with certainty that Jesus was the Messiah, and so he sent some of his disciples to ask him: "Are you the Christ?" That which previously, with the help of higher spiritual beings, he had known with certainty, he now began to doubt, as the protecting spiritual beings had withdrawn.

Here we can draw a great lesson, my son. If one does not keep alert, the powers of evil will always find a way to gain entrance. They seek continually for the weakest point, the point of attack. But if one remains alert and takes care, the powers of evil are unable to enter. A weak point presented itself in the case of John on account of his destiny in connection with Herod and Herodias, and this was used by evil beings, inspiring Herodias to urge Herod to take John into captivity. Herod did not take the evil inspiration into himself fully, as he wanted to set John free. But the powers of evil found an instrument in Herodias, and the diabolical plan was conceived, which led to John's death on the night of Herod's birthday.

The positive side of this event is that John's sacrifice helped to work against the forces of evil that had found a willing assistant in Herodias. For sacrifice always works in a redeeming way, working to break the power of evil. Moreover, John's mighty spirit lived on after the beheading, powerfully inspiring the apostles and disciples, becoming a kind of protecting spirit over the Twelve. On a deeper level it was this that John longed for, which is why he did not resist destiny but passively allowed it to work, leading to his death. And it is at this deeper level that the reason is also to be found as to why Jesus Christ did not help John to escape from captivity. John had to make way for Jesus in order for the latter to be able to completely fulfill his mission. John's continued physical presence would only have been a hindrance to many in taking up, fully and completely, Jesus' teaching and mission, whereas his spiritual presence worked as a powerful agent helping the disciples. Jesus knew this, and deep down so did John, which is why he spoke the words, "He must increase, and I must decrease." Understanding this, we can grasp that the beheading of John the Baptist, which took place just over fifteen months after the baptism, marked a decisive turning point in the ministry of Jesus Christ. From this point onwards a new level of working began in the life of the Messiah. The Twelve had been called together, the last four—Bartholomew, Judas, Thomas and Matthew—having become disciples as the Sun was in Scorpio; and now with the Sun in the middle of the star-sign of Capricorn, John was beheaded, so that from this moment onwards he was able to work as a kind of "inspiring Angel" of the Twelve.

TAT: Thank you, O Hermes, for this revelation of the being of John the Baptist in relation to Christ and the apostles.

CLOSING INVOCATION

A Discourse of Hermes to Asclepius

The Miracles of the Lord

OPENING INVOCATION

ASCLEPIUS: After the death of John the Baptist, what course did the ministry of Jesus Christ take?

HERMES: The death of John occurred as the Sun was in the middle of Capricorn. When the Sun was in Aquarius, the next sign, there took place three outstanding miracles: the healing of the man who had been paralyzed for thirty-eight years; the feeding of the five thousand; and the walking on the water. Let us now consider these miracles one by one.

The first took place on the day the Sun entered Aquarius, which was Friday, January 19, A.D. 31. On this day Jesus arrived in Jerusalem. After teaching in the temple that morning, and dining with the disciples at the house of Joanna Chuza, he and some of his disciples went to the pool of Bethesda. It was about three o'clock in the afternoon. Jesus began to heal the sick, and the disciples handed out bread and clothing. The sick gathered here at the pool of Bethesda, as its water had a special healing power on account of an Angel which periodically descended and set the water in motion. In earlier times many pious people had witnessed the descent of this Angel, but by the time of

Christ few saw it, although many could see the movement in the water brought about by the Angel. The water thus received a healing power which could be received by the first people to then immerse themselves in it. The paralyzed man, who had lain there for thirty-eight years, had no one to help him into the water. He had no alternative but to wait and pray that he would receive help. He lived from the scraps of food left over by the other sick people. Previously he had worked as a gardener. In his previous incarnation he had been ruled by his passions. In such a case this means that the human being then has no real control over his movements, and is capable of doing wrong through his uncontrolled movements, or even inflicting harm upon others. The karmic consequence of this in the case of the paralyzed man was his becoming lame, unable to move. He lost the ability to move, just as in his previous incarnation he had lost control over his movements. But whereas in the previous incarnation this lack of control had led to harm being inflicted upon others, now he became paralyzed and could do no one any harm. For thirty-eight years he had waited with great longing to be healed. It was this patient waiting in silent expectation which was heard by Jesus Christ, who—shortly after the Sabbath began—went up to him and asked him if he wanted to be healed. He answered that he had no one to help him down into the pool when the water was set in motion. Jesus addressed the man, saying that he should henceforth lead a pure life, for it was in punishment for sins of impurity that his sickness had come upon him. Jesus consoled him, telling him that God assists all who turn to him and repent. Then he said: "Arise! Take up thy bed, and walk!" The man arose, beside himself with joy, and Jesus instructed him to go and wash in the pool.

Then Jesus, accompanied by John, quietly left, and when the man was asked who had healed him, he did not know. It was only two months later, when he encountered Jesus teaching in the temple, that he went to inform the Pharisees that it was Jesus who had healed him.

ASCLEPIUS: And what was the cosmic configuration at the time he was healed?

HERMES: Mars (8° Aries) was in conjunction with Jupiter (7° Aries) and both planets, in turn, were in square to Mercury (11° Capricorn). This configuration speaks of the destiny of the paralyzed man. For, Mercury is the planet of movement, and Mars, which bestows the will and energy needed for movement, was held in check by Jupiter, the planet of wisdom. It was the higher wisdom of destiny which had led to his condition of lameness in order to make amends for the wrong done by way of his uncontrolled movements previously. And now it was a higher wisdom that Jesus Christ came to him and healed him, restoring will, energy and the power of movement to him.

Let us now turn to consider the next miracle, the feeding of the five thousand. Jesus left Jerusalem and made his way back to Galilee. After visiting Capernaum, he and the disciples went to the Mount of Beatitudes near Bethsaida-Julias. People knew in advance that he would teach there, and by the time Jesus arrived, on the morning of Monday, January 29, A.D. 31, already several thousand people had gathered. The crowd grew to be about five thousand strong by late afternoon. Jesus taught concerning the Beatitudes and also the Lord's Prayer. By about four o'clock in the afternoon many people, especially women and children, who had had nothing to eat, became hungry. When the apostles learned of this, they came to Jesus and asked him to stop teaching, so that the people could descend the mountain before nightfall in order to obtain food to eat. Jesus replied: "They don't need to go away on that account; give them something to eat!" Philip asked: "Shall we go and buy bread for a few hundred denarii and give it to them to eat?" Jesus answered: "See how much bread there is!" Someone had brought five loaves and two fishes, but Andrew said: "What is this for so many?" Jesus continued to teach the Lord's Prayer, speaking especially of the petition "Give us this day our daily bread." Then he said: "Let the people be seated, the most famished in groups of fifty and the others in groups of one hundred, and bring me all the baskets that are here." Jesus then began to cut the bread and fish with a knife, raising it up in his hands toward heaven and praying. He blessed it and began to break pieces off in strips, giving them to the disciples to be laid into the baskets and distributed to the people. As soon as the baskets were empty, they were brought back to be refilled. This lasted for about two hours. When all had eaten their fill, Jesus told the disciples to go around with the baskets and collect the scraps, that nothing be lost. They gathered twelve baskets full. The people were full of astonishment at this miracle and said to one another: "This is truly the Chosen One! He is the Prophet destined to come into the world! He is the Promised One!" By this time it was dusk, and Jesus sent the apostles and disciples away to return by boat to Bethsaida. He addressed the people concerning this merciful act of God and spoke a prayer of thanks. Then he left. A cry went up from the crowd: "He has given us bread! He is our king! We want to make him our king!" They hurried to find Jesus, but he had already disappeared from sight, and it was now dark.

ASCLEPIUS: O Hermes, did the heavenly configuration at this time have anything to do with the signs of Pisces and Virgo, as Pisces obviously signifies the two fishes and the Virgin holding the ear of corn clearly symbolizes the bread?

HERMES: Yes, indeed Asclepius! At the time of the feeding of the five thousand the Moon ($5\frac{1}{2}°$ Virgo) was in opposition to Venus ($4°$ Pisces). In the human being the forces corresponding to the Moon and Venus are those of reproduction and growth, and it is precisely those forces which Jesus Christ called upon in the multiplying of the loaves and fishes in his hands. The heavenly configuration corresponded exactly to the miracle that took place on the Earth below. At this moment in time the Sun was entering the second decan of Aquarius ($10\frac{1}{2}°$ Aquarius) and was in opposition to Uranus ($12\frac{1}{2}°$ Leo). Just over six months earlier Jesus Christ had been at Jacob's well and there, in the conversation with the Samaritan woman, Dina, she experienced inwardly the living water of faith; then the Sun ($2\frac{1}{2}°$ Leo) and Uranus ($9\frac{1}{2}°$ Leo) had been together in Leo. Now, at the feeding of the five thousand, the Sun and Uranus were in opposition, the Sun being in Aquarius, and the people experienced communion. If we contemplate these two experiences, we see something of the working of Christ in the opposite sign of the zodiac to that in which the Sun was placed. For the pouring out of the living water of faith is the gesture of the Waterman, Aquarius, in the heavens. And communion—at least the communion of bread—is experienced in the heart, the heart being the center in which the self of the human being resides. Here the zodiacal sign of Leo is significant, for the heart in the microcosm corresponds to Leo in the macrocosm.

ASCLEPIUS: But how may we understand this working of Christ from the opposite sign of the zodiac to that in which the Sun is placed?

HERMES: Asclepius, we must realize that the entire period from the baptism to the Mystery of Golgotha was the time of the Incarnation of the Sun Spirit Christ. And from the vantage point of the Sun, beholding the Earth, it is seen to be on the opposite side of the zodiac. When the Sun is in Leo, then the Earth is in Aquarius, as seen from the Sun, and vice versa.

ASCLEPIUS: You mentioned that the communion of bread is experienced in the heart. What about the fish?

HERMES: The communion of fish is something completely new that came with Christ. The communion of bread existed earlier; it was instituted at the time of Abraham by Melchizedek. Fish represents the moral element that Christ brought to the Earth, and this was new. For this reason the fish became a sign of Christianity. The five thousand were not yet ripe to experience the communion of fish, and so after the feeding nothing came back of the fish, whereas twelve baskets of bread were collected. The twelve baskets of bread represent the communion of the self with the twelve signs of the zodiac via the heart, corresponding macrocosmically to the passage of the Sun through the twelve signs of the zodiac. In the course of the Sun's passage through the twelve zodiacal signs, which takes exactly one year, nature passes through an entire cycle of growth and decay. During this time the grain of wheat grows to become corn, and this is made into bread. At the feeding of the five thousand Christ, the Spirit of the Sun, embodied the power of the Sun. The cycle of growth normally accomplished by the Sun in the course of one year was fulfilled by Christ in the space of a few moments, so that the bread multiplied in his hands.

However, the essence of this miracle was communion, through which hunger may be stilled even if only a small quantity of bread is consumed, as is the case with the Holy Sacrament. The five thousand experienced in their hearts oneness with the cosmic zodiacal world—cosmic communion, which was humanity's by nature in paradise, before the Fall. After the Fall the human self began to develop, cutting humans off from the cosmos, from the communion with the cosmic world that they had known in paradise. But Christ as the Self of selves, has the power to enter the human self, overcoming egotism and establishing a new communion with the cosmic world. This took place at the feeding of the five thousand, the communion of bread.

Only the disciples were ready to experience something of the communion of fish, and this took place the following night at the walking on the water. The fish are the symbol of the feet, for the feet in the microcosm corresponds to the zodiacal sign of Pisces in the macrocosm. The communion of fish is by way of the feet; it represents a communion with the interior of the Earth, with the Mother, Demeter, the Mother of all that lives on the Earth. After the crucifixion Jesus Christ descended to the Mother in the interior of the Earth, and was able to take up the force of spiritual warmth through his feet—this spiritual warmth being the special force bestowed by the Mother, the Mother of everything living. For the completion of the building up of his resurrection body Christ needed not only the spiritual light of the Father in heaven but also the spiritual warmth of the Mother in the interior of the Earth. The communion of fish—taking up the spiritual warmth of the Mother through the feet—can be accomplished only at a very high level of development, on the path towards resurrection. For, the powers of evil occupy the interior of the Earth and are placed between the Mother and humanity. And without having attained a high level of spiritual development, human beings run the risk of taking up forces of evil through their feet, if they are not sufficiently pure. They will then not be borne up by the good spiritual forces arising from the Mother below, but will sink down. This took place with Peter, who stepped out of the boat and tried to walk on the water towards Christ. But he was not completely pure, so he began to sink.

The experience of the disciples of Jesus Christ as he walked towards them on the water was that of the communion of fish, being borne up by the spiritual warmth forces arising from below, from the Mother, taken up through his feet into his resurrection body. It was an experience of Jesus Christ in his resurrection body, at that time only partially formed, just as the physical body is only partially formed halfway through the embryonic period.

It was a special moment in time in the ministry, when something of the impulse of resurrection—that of the Mystery of Golgotha—radiated in. For, at the walking on the water Mars was in the middle of the Ram (15° Aries), where the Sun was at the Mystery of Golgotha. In between the crucifixion and the resurrection there took place Christ's descent into the interior of the Earth to the Mother. In this time the Sun moved from 14° Aries to 15½° Aries. So Mars was placed in the Ram at this point in time, at the feeding of the five thousand and the walking on the water, where the Sun was later positioned at the descent into the Earth's interior. Thus something of this Mother force towards which Christ was striving with his whole Being—having come from the Kingdom of the Father with the aim of descending to the Realm of Mother—was able to be active in him already at the walking on the water. Hermetically, Mars was in the Bull (20° Taurus), in conjunction with the axis of the Moon's nodes (19½° Taurus), and so was working on a highly spiritual level, bestowing the cosmic energy of the Word, supporting Jesus Christ from above as he walked on the water. But there was also a connection between the heavenly configuration at the time of these two miracles and that at the descent from the Father at the moment of the baptism. At the baptism Mercury and Saturn were hermetically in conjunction, and at the feeding of the five thousand and the walking on the water Mercury (24°/25° Sagittarius) was hermetically in opposition to Saturn (26° Gemini). So Christ was borne by the power of light from the Father on high as well as by the spiritual warm from the Mother below.

The conjunction between Mercury and Neptune (27° Capricorn) at the feeding of the five thousand and the walking on the water symbolizes the tremendous power of inspiration that was at work, which brought Christ and the five thousand on the one hand, and Christ and the disciples on the other hand, very close together. But whereas in the case of the five thousand the inspiration worked upon them in such a way that they wanted to make Jesus their king, that is, an earthly king, it worked upon the disciples to initiate them into a revelation of Christ as king in a spiritual way—king over the cosmic forces from above, and over the elements below, in this case water. Here we see the two different tendencies inherent in Christianity: the great mass of believers being represented by the five thousand, and the spiritually striving being represented by the disciples. But Christ came for all. The communion of bread experienced by the five thousand foreshadowed the Holy Communion—that of bread and wine—inaugurated by Jesus Christ at the Last Supper, at which only the disciples were present. And if we truly grasp the mystery of the communion of bread, we can experience that this is the deeper meaning of our daily meditation on the passage of the Sun through the twelve star-signs of the zodiac during the course of the year. The content of this daily meditation may be summarized with the words, "Give us this day our daily bread"—meaning the spiritual-substantial bread of life of the Sun of righteousness, Jesus Christ, who said, "I AM the bread of life," and who brought these words to realization in the miracle of the feeding of the five thousand. This miracle and these words belong to the heart of our spiritual path of Christian hermetic astrology.

ASCLEPIUS: O Hermes, thank you for these words concerning the cosmic communion, which is an important and central mystery of Christian hermetic astrology.

CLOSING INVOCATION

A Discourse of Hermes to Tat

The Transfiguration

OPENING INVOCATION

TAT: What took place, O father, after the feeding of the five thousand?

HERMES: Jesus taught in Capernaum, proclaiming a great teaching concerning the Bread of Life. This was the teaching aspect of the miracle of the feeding of the five thousand. Afterwards he traveled northward in the direction of Ornithopolis, a town north of Tyre on the Mediterranean Sea. On the way he passed through Dan (Lais), west of Caesarea-Philippi in the northernmost part of Galilee. Here there took place a noteworthy healing miracle.

As was his custom, Jesus went from place to place healing the sick. On the afternoon of Monday, February 12, A.D. 31, he was busy healing the sick in the town of Dan. As he did so he was followed at a distance by a pagan woman from Ornithopolis, who kept calling out for help for her daughter: "Lord! Thou Son of David, have mercy on me! My daughter is tormented by an unclean spirit." The disciples asked Jesus if he would help her, but he said to them: "I have been sent only to the lost sheep of Israel." Eventually this Syrophoenecian woman came up to him and cast herself down at his feet, saying, "Lord, help me!" Jesus answered: "Let the children be fed first! It is not good to take bread from the children and cast it to the dogs." However, the woman pleaded with him: "Yes, Lord! For the dogs under the table also eat the children's crumbs which fall from the table of their master." The Lord then said: "Woman, great is your faith! On account of these words you shall be helped." He then asked her if she wanted to be healed herself, as she was crippled and bent over on one side. But she did not think herself to be worthy, and prayed solely for her daughter. Then Jesus placed one hand on her head and the other on her side, saying: "Rise up! Let it be unto you as you want it to be! The devil has gone out of your daughter." The woman raised herself upright, saying, "O Lord, I see my daughter lying peacefully in bed, now healthy." She was beside herself with joy.

TAT: So this was a twofold healing on behalf of the Gentiles.

HERMES: Indeed, my son. At this moment in time the Sun was in the sign of the Waterman (24½° Aquarius), as it had been at the feeding of the five thousand. But whereas at the feeding of the five thousand the Moon and Venus had been in opposition to one another, now they were in conjunction (20°/21° Pisces). At the same time, the conjunction of the Moon and Venus formed a square with Saturn (20½° Gemini). The Moon and Venus symbolized the mother and her daughter, and the relationship with Saturn indicated that it was the Father's will that they be healed together. Hermetically, Mercury (13° Aquarius) was opposite Uranus (13° Leo), which pointed to the nature of the conflict in the daughter, who was mentally (Mercury) plagued by an unclean spirit (opposition to Uranus).

The Syrophoenecian woman was a widow and was very rich. Her husband had died about five years previously, leaving her much wealth and property. She was highly thought of in Ornithopolis and did much to help the poor there. Her daughter was about twenty-four years old and after having had several lovers had become possessed by an evil spirit. From the time of this healing onwards, the Syrophoenecian woman did much to help and support the work of Jesus Christ and his disciples, and performed many charitable deeds for the Jewish people in and around Ornithopolis.

After visiting the home of the Syrophoenecian woman in Ornithopolis, Jesus then traveled back to Galilee. It was here, on a mountain northeast of the Mount of Beatitudes, that the feeding of the four thousand took place, which repeated the multiplying of bread and fish and the communion of bread as at the feeding of the five thousand. Here seven loaves of bread and seven fish were multiplied, and after the people had eaten to their fill, seven baskets full of bread were gathered. This took place at sunset on Thursday, March 15, A.D. 31. The Sun was at 25° Pisces, and that evening the crescent Moon was approaching conjunction with Mars (14° Taurus), which was crossing the axis of the Moon's nodes (15½° Taurus). Here at the feeding of the four thousand Mars was transiting the axis of the Moon's nodes, whereas at the feeding of the five thousand Mars hermetically was crossing the Moon's nodal axis.

Moreover, at the feeding of the four thousand there was a hermetic opposition between Mars (11½° Gemini) and Pluto (11½° Sagittarius). This was mirrored in a most powerful speech (Mars, the Word) at the time of this miracle.

On this occasion the words of Jesus Christ were most forceful and expressive. He spoke quite clearly of his being the Messiah and of the persecutions in store for him, leading up to his imprisonment. But on that day, he said, the mountains themselves would quake; and he pronounced woe upon Capernaum, Chorazin, and many other places in the region on account of having rejected salvation. On the day of his arrest they would become conscious of their having rejected him. He also spoke of the happiness of this region where he had broken the Bread of Life.

TAT: O father, what did it signify that seven baskets of bread were collected at the feeding of the four thousand, whilst twelve baskets were collected at the feeding of the five thousand?

HERMES: The twelve actually points to the communion of bread in connection with the cosmic realms of space, whilst the seven indicates the communion taking place in the course of time. Communion transcends space and time, but it may be approached in two different ways. It is the same communion, though. The macrocosmic side of the spatial aspect of communion is signified by the passage of the Sun through the twelve signs of the zodiac. This we discussed in the last discourse. The macrocosmic side of the temporal aspect of communion is not something visible, as it is temporal. It is bound up with the "seven days of existence," these being the seven pillars upon which the temple of creation is built. We are now in the fourth day of existence, three preceding days having already elapsed, and three days are to come. Each day of existence has a Christian aspect which solarizes the course of evolution, so that in the course of time each day takes on a solar aspect through Christ. Analogously, human beings live through seven planetary periods in the course of their lives; this is their astrological biography, so to say. One of these planetary periods—the middle part of life—belongs to the Sun. But to the extent that human beings take up the Christ Impulse, they bring the solar quality into the other planetary periods as well. The ideal is solarization—the Christianizing of all seven planetary periods—so that the whole of life is lived under the light of the Christ-Sun. Examples of this we find in the lives of some saintly people, such as the blessed seer, who from earliest childhood lived in the presence of Christ. Such cases of the Christianizing of life from childhood can only be explained by taking account of previous incarnations, in which already a certain degree of union with Christ had taken place. Union with Christ through all seven planetary periods of life would be the ultimate realization of communion in its temporal aspect, bound up with the mystery of seven. An image of this is given in the Revelation of St. John, in the Son of man who holds seven stars in his right hand. This would signify, in turn, union with Christ on all seven levels of the human being, for the seven planetary periods of life are periods during which different levels of the human being develop and unfold sequentially one after the other. The archetype of this sevenfold union is revealed to us in the transfiguration on Mt. Tabor, to which we shall now turn our attention. But before we come to the transfiguration, there is another important event we should consider, which took place just four days after the feeding of the four thousand.

TAT: What was this, O father?

HERMES: My son, it was the event of Peter receiving the keys of the kingdom of heaven. This took place at sunrise on Monday, March 19, A.D. 31, on a mountain southeast of Caesarea-Philippi, to which Jesus Christ had withdrawn with the disciples and the twelve apostles. The night before, when they came to this mountain, Jesus asked them to pray and to be ready for what he would communicate to them at dawn the next day; and then he withdrew to pray alone. At dawn he returned to them and they gathered around him. Jesus asked: "Who do men say that I am?" Some of the apostles and disciples repeated the various statements made by people, which they had heard here and there; some said that he was John the Baptist, others Elijah, and others took him to be the prophet Jeremiah arisen from the dead. Jesus then said: "And who do you say that I am?" At first no one answered. Then Peter took a step forward and affirmed boldly, as if speaking on behalf of all: "Thou are Christ, the Son of the living God!" Jesus replied: "Blessed are you, Simon, son of Jonas, because flesh and blood has not revealed this to you, but my Father who is in heaven! And this I say to you: You are a rock, and upon this rock I will build my church, and the gates of hell shall not prevail against it. And I will give you the keys of the kingdom of heaven. And whatsoever you shall bind upon earth, it shall be bound also in heaven; and whatsoever you shall loose upon earth, it shall be loosed also in heaven!"

These words were spoken just as the Sun was rising in the East. The Sun was right at the end of the star-sign of the Fishes (29° Pisces), about to enter Aries and start a new cycle through the twelve zodiacal signs. The Moon (19½° Gemini) was in conjunction with Saturn (21½° Gemini), and this reveals something of the mystery of this event. For Saturn is the guardian of the threshold to the Kingdom of the Father in heaven, and the Moon guards the gateway which leads—via the underworld—to the Realm of the Mother in the interior of the Earth. The keys to the kingdom of heaven signify the power, drawn from the Kingdom of the Father, to be able to hold in check the forces of the underworld arising through the gates of hell. Two keys laid one over the other form a cross, and it is precisely the sign of the cross to which the Father has lent power to banish the evil forces back into the underworld. This can only be achieved in purity and in faith, qualities which Peter had. But Peter was moved also by a zealous love for Jesus Christ and a deep sense of obedience to the Father. This was symbolized in the hermetic conjunction at this moment in time between Venus (25° Gemini) and Saturn (27½° Gemini).

TAT: But why did Jesus Christ choose only one of the circle of apostles? Why did he not take the entire circle of twelve to be the rock upon which he was to build his church?

HERMES: My son, here we are confronted with the mystery of unity. At a very high level of existence the twelve Holy Beings, whose outer nature manifests through the stars comprising the twelve signs of the zodiac, form a united circle. There, there is unity among the twelve, and this is the ideal. But humanity is a long, long way away from this high level of existence, and the reality is that when a great deal of spiritual presence is applied to a group of human beings, for example the group of twelve, the group will almost certainly split; the circle breaks at its weakest point. And this is not then like a rock, fixed and immovable. In the case of the circle of the twelve chosen disciples, the weakest point was Judas Iscariot. He left the circle on the night of the Last Supper, and at the point vacated by him the powers of evil were able to enter, and Jesus Christ was delivered up. It is sad but true, my son, that even a group or circle of noble and lofty human beings may split apart under great pressure. I am sure you have seen enough examples of this for yourself in all walks of human life. No, Christ could not build upon a council formed by the Twelve, but only upon one chosen from the Twelve who could speak in the name of the Twelve. This was Peter, who, as spokesman for that which the Twelve (with the exception of Judas) had recognized, was the *head* of the Twelve, just as John could be designated as the *heart*, as the apostle loved by Christ, who laid his head upon Christ's breast at the Last Supper and heard the beating of the Lord's heart.

Through Peter as the rock upon which he built his church, Jesus Christ adhered to the highest principle of unity—this is the Father principle. For, spiritually the unity of existence is given by the Father, who is the Father of all beings. And by becoming *father of the apostles,* Peter was placed in a position in the church analogous to the Father in existence. Thereby in its very foundation the church was given the Father principle of unity—in one who is the rock, the head of the church. On the spiritual plane of existence Christ himself is the head of the church. But he had to choose one human being to be head upon the Earth, for otherwise the community of his disciples would have split among themselves sooner or later after his death on the cross. This one human being was Peter. Before

THE TRANSFIGURATION

Peter's death, one human being had to be designated as his (Peter's) successor; and so on. Thus the Father principle of unity was established for the church through the ages.

The Son principle of unity is the ideal for the future. This is the principle of unity in the name of the Son: "When two or three are gathered together in my name, then am I in the midst of you." For example, the twelve signs of the zodiac are gathered in a circle around the Sun and form a unity, the zodiac. But this ideal of the Son principle of unity will be realized only when human beings have evolved to a level of union with Christ such that betrayal, as in the case of Judas leaving the circle of twelve, will no longer be possible. Only when each one in a group is so united with Christ, in his name, that there is complete unity on all levels, only then will the Son principle of unity be able to replace the Father principle.

As an example of this ideal actualized in the present, it is the Son principle of unity which holds in the Church of John, in contrast to the Father principle of unity prevailing in the Church of Peter. For, the Church of John is led by three individuals, united in Christ, none of whom acts as a personality, that is, in his own name. And just as the apostles John and Peter worked together in the service of Christ, so does the Church of John work together with the Church of Peter in the service of Christ. The Church of Peter has the task of leading human beings to the threshold of the spiritual world, and the Church of John has the task of leading them further, beyond the threshold. Both serve Christ, but on different levels. They only seem to be in conflict on account of their different principles of unity, but spiritually they are to work together, just as Peter and John worked together as apostles.

There are deep mysteries connected with the event of Peter receiving the keys of the kingdom of heaven which we cannot go into now, but which deserve meditation, as they relate to some of the profoundest aspects of Christianity. Now, however, let us direct our meditative enquiry to the event of the transfiguration.

TAT: What actually was this event, O father?

HERMES: My son, the transfiguration was a high point of the ministry, at which Christ fully revealed his divine nature to the disciples Peter, James and John, as a prelude to the Mystery of Golgotha. It was on the afternoon of Tuesday, April 3, A.D. 31, that Jesus Christ and the disciples reached the foot of Mt. Tabor. Sending off the other disciples to teach and heal, he proceeded to climb the mountain, accompanied by Peter, James and John. Upon reaching the summit Jesus told them that he would reveal to them who he was; they should behold him glorified, that their faith might remain strong when they would later see him humiliated, mistreated and condemned to die like a criminal. He began to instruct them concerning the Lord's Prayer and spoke of the mysteries of creation and redemption. He spoke so inspiringly that the three disciples were wholly transported by his words. The Sun set and it became dark, but the three did not notice it, so entranced were they by Jesus, whose whole appearance became brighter and brighter. He spoke further and shone with an ever-increasing transcendental splendor, becoming quite translucent. This glory reached its culmination at midnight—the shining of the midnight Christ-Sun—which was so intense that the apostles covered their heads and prostrated themselves on the ground. A shining pathway of light reached down from heaven upon Jesus Christ, comprising the different choirs of Angelic beings in descending order from heaven down to the Earth. Among the shining figures that approached Jesus in the light were Moses and Elijah, to whom Jesus spoke of the sufferings that he had endured up until now and would endure in the future, including his Passion, relating everything in detail. As this took place the disciples raised their heads and beheld Jesus in all his glory conversing with Moses and Elijah. As Jesus came to describe his exaltation on the cross, he spread out his arms as if to say: "So shall the Son of man be raised up." Peter, beside himself with joy at beholding the glory and majesty of Jesus Christ together with Moses and Elijah, exclaimed: "Master! It is good that we are here! Let us make three tabernacles, one for you, one for Moses and one for Elijah!" Returning to their normal waking state, Peter, James and John saw a stream of light descend from above upon Jesus and a sweet, whispering, sighing voice spoke the words: "This is my beloved Son in whom I am well pleased. Listen to him!" In fear and trembling they cast themselves upon the ground. Jesus went up to them, touched them and said: "Arise, and fear not!" Then they saw that he was alone, and together they descended the mountain. On the way Jesus told them that he had allowed them to behold the transfiguration of the Son of man in order to strengthen their faith, so that they would not waver when they would see him delivered up into the hands of evildoers, on account of the sins of the world. Then they and the other disciples would also witness the humiliating treatment to which he would be subjected, and at that time they would be able to strengthen the faith of the others. Jesus impressed upon them not to tell anyone what they had seen until after the rising of the Son of man from the dead.

At the culmination of the transfiguration—the shining of the midnight Christ-Sun—the Sun was in the middle of the Ram (14° Aries), exactly where it was located two years later at the crucifixion. In this sense the transfiguration was a prelude to the Mystery of Golgotha, at which the true Light of the World shone. The waning Moon, at 22° Capricorn, was hermetically in opposition to Venus (21° Cancer), signifying a revelation of divine love which penetrated the body of Jesus. This was the essence of the transfiguration: the divine I AM power of love, of the Being of Christ, completely irradiated the human form of Jesus, represented here by the Moon. The three disciples witnessed the Cosmic Christ. And just as Jesus Christ on Earth had twelve disciples, so gathered around the Cosmic Christ are twelve leaders of humanity, two of these being Moses and Elijah. These twelve leaders encircling Christ are the great teachers of humankind, who periodically incarnate upon the Earth in order to bring new spiritual impulses for the sake of humanity's evolution. Together they compose the "white lodge." It was into this sphere of the Christ-Sun surrounded by the teachers composing the white lodge that the three disciples gained a glimpse at the transfiguration.

TAT: Thank you, O father, for what you have revealed to us of these mysteries concerning the Messiah.

CLOSING INVOCATION

A Discourse of Hermes to Asclepius

The Raising of Lazarus

OPENING INVOCATION

ASCLEPIUS: O Hermes, following in time, after the transfiguration, which represented a high point in the ministry of Jesus Christ, what were the most important events that took place?

HERMES: Asclepius, the most important event of all was the raising of Lazarus from the dead. At the transfiguration the Lord showed himself in his divine glory to the three apostles, and at the raising of Lazarus he demonstrated his divine power on Earth. But before this miracle took place, as a prelude there was another raising from the dead six weeks prior to the raising of Lazarus. This took place in a shepherd village northwest of Jericho. Jesus was approached by a man from this village, whose daughter had died. She was about seven years old. The same disciples—Peter, James and John—who had been with him at the transfiguration were with him on this occasion. Jesus and the three disciples accompanied the man to his house, where the corpse of his daughter lay. Jesus placed one hand on the child's head and the other on its breast, and directed his prayers towards heaven. The child raised itself up, alive. This was on Thursday, June 12, A.D. 32. It was the day of the Full Moon, just as it had been Full Moon at the raising of the daughter of the Essene Jairus in the town of Phasael, which had taken place on Tuesday, February 7, A.D. 30. At the raising of the daughter of the Essene Jairus, the Sun had been at 20° Aquarius and the Full Moon had been opposite in Leo. Here at the raising of this little girl in the shepherd village northwest of Jericho, the Sun was at 21° Gemini and the Full Moon was opposite in Sagittarius. Hermetically, Neptune (29½° Capricorn) was in conjunction with Mars (1½° Aquarius), and Mars was exactly at its perihelion (2° Aquarius), it's closest approach to the Sun.

ASCLEPIUS: O thrice greatest one, why do you speak of this raising from the dead as a prelude to the raising of Lazarus?

HERMES: As I shall describe, there was a special stellar configuration at the raising of Lazarus, which allowed his soul to be called back into his body many days after he had died. This stellar configuration made the transition from the cosmic world back into the earthly world readily possible, despite the long period of time that he had been dead. It was the same at the raising of this little girl, although in her case she had been dead only three or four days. It was precisely the Full Moon—the alignment of the Sun, Earth and Moon—which facilitated the return of her soul from the cosmic world back into the earthly world. This alignment, which occurs at New Moon as well as at Full Moon, facilitates the incarnation of the soul, coming from the

THE RAISING OF LAZARUS

Moon sphere down to the Earth, whereby the Moon can be regarded as a kind of portal—a gateway from the cosmos to the earthly realm.

ASCLEPIUS: Now, O Hermes, perhaps you can describe the raising of Lazarus?

HERMES: So far I have described to you five of the seven miracles of the Gospel of St. John—the fifth being the walking on the water. The sixth miracle, that of the healing of the man born blind, took place in Jerusalem in the autumn of A.D. 31; I shall pass over this, having said much already in connection with the miracle of the healing of the blind youth Manahem. The seventh miracle, that of the raising of Lazarus from the dead, took place in Bethany almost one year later, in the summer of A.D. 32. This was the greatest of all the miracles wrought by Jesus Christ, and it was this that brought the Pharisees of Jerusalem to the resolve to have Jesus put to death.

ASCLEPIUS: Why, O Hermes, do you say that the raising of Lazarus was the greatest of all the miracles, for Jesus Christ had raised others from the dead already?

HERMES: Noble Asclepius, in order that you may grasp the full majesty of this miracle, I shall describe the sequence of events in detail. On Thursday, July 10, A.D. 32, Jesus and the apostles were in a small town near Samaria together with the Blessed Virgin, her elder sister Mary Heli, and the latter's daughter Mary Cleophas. A messenger came from Lazarus requesting the Lord to come to Bethany as Lazarus was very ill. The messenger and the three women remained in this town for the Sabbath, but Jesus went to another town to celebrate the Sabbath, where he remained teaching and healing for a few days. He then returned to where the holy women were waiting for him on Wednesday, July 16, A.D. 32, on which day news of Lazarus' death reached Jesus. However, Jesus said to the apostles simply: "Our friend Lazarus has fallen asleep, but I shall go to awaken him from sleep." Following this, Jesus and the apostles and the three holy women traveled to Ginea, where Lazarus had put a country house and estate at the disposal of Jesus and the disciples. Martha and Mary Magdalena, the sister of Lazarus, also traveled to the estate at Ginea, coming from Bethany, and arrived there on Friday, July 18, A.D. 32. That evening Jesus first went to celebrate the Sabbath in the synagogue of Ginea, before making his way to Lazarus' estate. When he arrived, Mary Magdalena went up to him and said that Lazarus had died, and she lamented the fact that Jesus had not been there to save his life. Jesus replied that it was not yet the right time, and that it was good that Lazarus had died. He added that Martha and Magdalena should let everything belonging to Lazarus remain in its place and that he would come in a few days. Jesus told the apostles: "Lazarus is dead; and for your sake I am glad that I was not there, so that you may believe. But let us go to him." After the Sabbath, Martha and Mary Magdalena returned to Bethany, and then Jesus and those accompanying him set out also. However, he stopped to teach on the way, which caused the apostles to become impatient, on account of the delay in reaching Bethany. Jesus did not show any signs of being in a hurry, and owing to the delay in the journey arising through his teaching, he did not arrive at Bethany until the Sun was setting on the evening of Friday,

THE RAISING OF LAZARUS

July 25, A.D. 32; the Sabbath was just beginning. Martha and Magdalena had arrived back at Bethany already four days earlier and had then buried Lazarus. When Jesus arrived, Magdalena cast herself down at his feet, weeping, and exclaimed: "Lord, if you had been here my brother would not have died!" Many of those present were weeping, and Jesus was deeply moved and wept also. Jesus and the apostles then took some refreshment, and he taught until late into the night concerning the mystery of death. The next morning Jesus and the apostles went to the crypt where Lazarus was buried. Many people were gathered around. When Jesus asked the apostles to lift the stone covering the grave containing Lazarus' corpse, Martha said: "Lord, by this time there will be an odor, for he has been buried four days." But the apostles lifted the stone, revealing the corpse embalmed and swathed in linen bands. Jesus raised his eyes to heaven and prayed aloud, calling in a loud voice: "Lazarus, come forth!" At this the corpse raised itself, and the apostles removed the linen bands swathed around the head. Lazarus appeared as if he had been woken from a deep sleep. Like a sleepwalker he went past Jesus out through the door of the crypt. At the sight of Lazarus, a shock went through the crowd. Then Jesus accompanied Lazarus back to the latter's house, where they were joined by the apostles. Lazarus knelt before the Lord, who laid his right hand upon Lazarus' head and breathed upon him seven times.

ASCLEPIUS: What did this signify, O Hermes?

HERMES: Through being breathed upon seven times, Lazarus received the seven gifts of the Holy Spirit, receiving them before the other apostles. By passing through death he had seen another world and come to know the mysteries of the Spirit, so he was spiritually mature in a way which the twelve disciples were not. He became initiated, and bore within him a great mystery. He had entered into the Kingdom of Light, the realm of the Father, and had returned to the Earth. This was a great initiation, out of which he received a new mission to be accomplished for the sake of the Earth. The tears wept by those who mourned for him were not only for his sake, but also for the sake of the Earth, which had been robbed of someone who had much to give. It was in the name of the Father that Jesus Christ called Lazarus back to the Earth. The combination of the tears being shed on Earth and the voice of spiritual thunder—the words "Lazarus, come forth" which resounded up into the heavenly world—called Lazarus back from the Kingdom of Light, to be reborn on the Earth with a new mission bestowed on him by Jesus Christ. He received the seven gifts of the Holy Spirit to help him accomplish this mission, but this refers to a mystery that can only be hinted at now. It is indicated in the fact that Lazarus became an apostle from this moment onwards by way of receiving the gifts of the Holy Spirit already, prior to the descent of the Holy Spirit at Whitsun. It was the descent of the Holy Spirit at Whitsun which transformed the disciples into apostles. But as Lazarus received the seven gifts of the Holy Spirit as part of his initiation by Christ, he became an apostle before the others.

ASCLEPIUS: Now I begin to see why this miracle ranks as the greatest of all the miracles fulfilled by the Lord.

THE RAISING OF LAZARUS

HERMES: Yes, Asclepius, there are profound mysteries underlying the solemn event of the raising of Lazarus from the dead. Lazarus chose the path leading to the Kingdom of Light. He lived so strongly for the Light, that he lost all connection with the Earth. He died. But this was for the glory of God, so that the Son of God could be glorified by means of it. And this glory was manifest as the Son of God called Lazarus back to the Earth from the Father's Kingdom. Into this glory radiated the Holy Spirit, who flows between the Father and the Son. Lazarus received the baptism of the Holy Spirit before any of the others.

In effect, Lazarus took the place of Judas Iscariot in the circle of twelve. Just as Lazarus lived solely for the Light, Judas lived for the darkness. At the time of the raising of Lazarus, Judas was already on the path leading to union with the Prince of Darkness. This union culminated at the Last Supper, when Judas went to betray the Lord. He went out and it was night; he went into the darkness, just as Lazarus went into the Light. The path of Judas, like that of Lazarus, led also to his death. But the death of Judas was not for the glory of God. It was a result of his dark path. He became smitten with fear and confusion that night—after the betrayal on the night of the Last Supper—when he realized what he had done. He had thought only of the money that he would receive for betraying the Lord, and had not thought of the consequences—that the Lord would be put to death. This became clear to him already that night, while it was still dark, before the Sun rose. He ran to the temple and tried to give the money back to the Pharisees. But they refused to accept it, as it was blood money. Casting the money onto the floor of the temple, Judas ran out into the field called Akeldama and—taking his girdle—hung himself from a tree; and he burst open in the middle and his bowels gushed out. He was driven to this death by Satan, the Prince of Darkness. He died on that Good Friday morning, around dawn, at which time the darkness began to give way to the light of day.

Judas left the circle of twelve, but his place had already been filled in advance by Lazarus. Both their destinies stood under the sign of death, the sign of the Scorpion in the circle of the twelve signs of the zodiac, whereby a correspondence exists between the twelve disciples and the twelve zodiacal signs. Judas' sign was that of the Scorpion; and from one point of view this was also the sign of Lazarus. But through the Christian initiation of Lazarus, a seed was sown for the transformation of this sign to become the sign of the Dove, the sign of the Holy Spirit. The two ways of dying—that of Lazarus leading into the Light, and that of Judas leading into the darkness—indicate the Eagle and the Scorpion, respectively. For the star-sign of the Scorpion was in earlier times seen as an Eagle. This was in ages long past, when human beings could still behold the world of the spirit with clairvoyance. But as this ancient clairvoyance faded, the sign of the Scorpion came to replace that of the Eagle. Instead of a clairvoyance that could fly high into spiritual realms—symbolized by the Eagle—humans became endowed with the faculty of thought and at the same time their perception of the external world was of a world more or less devoid of spirit. This new mode of consciousness was well symbolized by the Scorpion, representing death, for human beings could henceforth behold only the world in which death occurs; they could no longer see into the spiritual worlds of eternal life.

THE RAISING OF LAZARUS

Judas became possessed by Satan, the Lord of the world of death. He could think only of the money he would receive, money which belongs to the world of death and is of no value at all for the realm of the spirit. He stood under the sign of the Scorpion. Lazarus, on the other hand, lived solely for the Light of the spirit. He stood under the sign of the Eagle, and—dying—he ascended like an eagle ever higher into the Kingdom of Light. Called back by Jesus Christ, he came as a messenger of this world of spirit, this Kingdom of Light. Then he stood under the sign of the Dove, which is the symbol of the Holy Spirit. Here we see the metamorphosis of this zodiacal sign: from the Eagle to the Scorpion to the Dove. This is one of the more profound aspects of the raising of Lazarus from the dead.

ASCLEPIUS: Can you say more, O Hermes, concerning the mystery of this miracle?

HERMES: Indeed, Asclepius! Listen carefully to my words, for I shall now indicate a key to the meditative path of Christian hermetic astrology. At the raising of Lazarus, Jesus Christ spoke the words, "I am the resurrection and the life." These words belong to this miracle, just as the words "I am the light of the world" belong to the healing of the man born blind. Each of the seven miracles of the Gospel of St. John has a corresponding "I AM" saying. For example, "I am the good shepherd" belongs to the walking on the water; the good shepherd accompanied his disciples in the boat, symbolizing the boat of destiny sailing through cycles of time. It is evident that "I am the bread of life" belongs to the feeding of the five thousand. Further, "I am the door" is the saying corresponding to the healing of the paralyzed man, who had lain paralyzed for thirty-eight years; through sin he had become cut off from the flow of cosmic energy underlying all movement, but Jesus Christ came as the door opening it up to him again. Moreover, "I am the way, the truth, and the life" corresponds to the healing of the nobleman's son; through heredity (the sins of the fathers shall be visited upon their sons) the nobleman's son had become ill, whereby the harmony between body, soul and spirit had become seriously disturbed; Jesus Christ—the way (body), the truth (soul) and the life (spirit)—healed by restoring harmonious balance in the relationship between body, soul and spirit. Lastly, "I am the true vine" relates to the transformation of water into wine at the wedding at Cana; Jesus Christ is the wine and his disciples and followers are the grapes; they commune together in and through Christ so that, for example, through the sacrament of marriage the "water" of the routine of daily life becomes transformed into the "wine" of truly conjugal love.

Now, the "I AM" sayings and the healing miracles together comprise a sevenfold revelation of the I AM—this being the esoteric name of CHRIST—a revelation which can be likened to the seven prismatic colors stemming from the one source. The "I AM" sayings are a revelation of Christ, having their source on the plane of devachan; they are seven moral tones of existence, whereas the divine-magical healing miracles lead us to the astral plane of existence, where there are seven archetypal healing images. From a cosmic standpoint—this should be evident from the number seven—there is a correspondence with the planets; for meditative purposes this correspondence should be meditated upon in the order from above down, this being the stream of service signified by the image of the washing of the feet:

THE RAISING OF LAZARUS

Saturn: *I am the resurrection and the life*
Jupiter: *I am the light of the world*
Mars: *I am the good shepherd*
Sun: *I am the bread of life*
Mercury: *I am the door*
Venus: *I am the way, the truth and the life*
Moon: *I am the true vine*

ASCLEPIUS: What is the nature of this meditation, O Hermes?

HERMES: The fundamental hermetic axiom "as above, so below" points to a correspondence between the macrocosm and the microcosm. The "I AM" sayings and the corresponding seven healing miracles help us to find the way—through Christ—to a new relationship with the seven planets, which in turn are reflected within the human being. The "I AM" sayings are seven Christian mantrams and the healing miracles are seven Christian images which together bring about an inner transformation—a Christianization—when worked with meditatively.

ASCLEPIUS: Is there any particular time, cosmically speaking, at which this meditation is most effective?

HERMES: Yes, Asclepius! In order to communicate this, however, it is necessary to look at the cosmic configuration that prevailed at the raising of Lazarus. For there was a special cosmic configuration, and it was for this reason that Jesus Christ delayed coming to Bethany to raise Lazarus from the dead. Jesus had said to Mary Magdalena that it was not the right time. But what was the right time? The right time was approaching, but no one understood what it could be, for it was a mystery belonging to the world of stars. It was into this world that the soul of Lazarus had gone after leaving the body. And an appropriate time at which to call Lazarus back from that higher world, a time when, so to speak, a portal between the earthly world and the world of stars would be opened, was approaching. This was the New Moon, the astronomical conjunction between the Sun and the Moon. At the moment of the New Moon, the Sun, Moon and Earth are aligned, and then a soul indwelling the cosmic world can readily make the transition into the earthy realm. It was for this alignment that Jesus Christ waited. It came on the morning of Saturday, July 26, A.D. 32. On this morning, when he raised Lazarus from the dead, the Sun and Moon stood close together in the star-sign of Leo, in conjunction with the bright star Regulus, the Lion's heart, at 5° Leo. It was under this powerful configuration that Lazarus returned to the Earth, becoming endowed with new life—well signified by Leo, the zodiacal sign corresponding to the heart, the seat of life. At the same time, Venus and Uranus were in exact conjunction, also in the star-sign of the Lion, at 18° Leo. Here we have an indication of the role played by the love of Martha and Mary Magdalena for their brother Lazarus, a spiritual love (Venus conjunct Uranus) which reached out to Lazarus' heart (Leo) to call him back to the Earth through their tears of sorrow. But the most important aspect for us to note is the conjunction of the Sun and Moon, which takes place at New Moon. For, in meditating upon the "I AM' sayings—the highest of which is "I am the resurrection and the life"—at the New Moon, we effectively align ourselves with the cosmic remembrance of the raising of Lazarus, to which the saying "I am the resurrection and the life" corresponds. This cosmic memory is most powerful at the New Moon in Leo, especially the closer it falls to Regulus, the Lion's heart, but it is echoed to a certain extent with every New Moon. Therefore each New Moon recalls the raising of Lazarus, which was the crowning miracle of the seven miracles. And in so far as the seven miracles culminated in the raising of Lazarus, it represents the entire sequence of miracles—the entire sequence being recalled, together with the raising of Lazarus, at each New Moon, whereby the seven "I AM" sayings offer a mantric formula for focusing upon this cosmic memory or recollection.

Similarly, the occurrence of each Full Moon recalls the death on the cross. Again, this is most powerful at the Full Moon in Libra, as it was at the crucifixion on Good Friday, but is echoed to some extent with every Full Moon. And just as the seven "I AM" sayings comprise a Christian-hermetic meditation with a natural affinity to the New Moon, so the seven words from the cross belong to a Christian-hermetic meditation appropriate for the Full Moon—appropriate in the sense of the cosmic memory of the crucifixion prevailing at each Full Moon. Here the correspondence between the words from the cross and the planets is:

Saturn: *Father, into thy hands I commend my spirit*
Jupiter: *My God, my God, why has thou forsaken me?*
Mars: *I thirst*
Sun: *Today you will be with me in paradise*
Mercury: *Father, forgive them for they know not what they do*
Venus: *Woman behold thy son; son behold thy mother*
Moon: *It is fulfilled*

With these two Christian-hermetic meditations it is possible to find the light and warmth of the Christ Impulse. For Christ is the highest good and his divine light is revealed through the miraculous acts of healing to which the "I AM" sayings correspond. And Jesus is the highest human being, whose unfathomable depth of warmth of humanity is expressed through the words from the cross—even in the utmost agony, he comforted the repentant criminal on his right with the words, "Today you will be with me in paradise." Meditation on these words leads us closer to the profundity of the Christ Impulse. With these two Christian-hermetic meditations each month we may sanctify the astronomical occurrences of the New Moon and the Full Moon and draw nearer to finding the light and warmth of Jesus Christ.

ASCLEPIUS: Thank you, O Hermes, for describing the sanctification of the New Moon and the sanctification of the Full Moon, as the culmination to this discourse on the raising of Lazarus from the dead.

CLOSING INVOCATION

A Discourse of Hermes to King Ammon

The Journey of Jesus Christ to the Pagans

OPENING INVOCATION

KING AMMON: What took place, O Hermes, after the raising of Lazarus from the dead?

HERMES: When the news spread to Jerusalem that Jesus had brought Lazarus back from the dead, the Pharisees were thrown into a state of agitation. It became clear to them that if Jesus were to continue to work such signs and wonders, all the people would soon flock to him to become his followers. They resolved to seize him and have him put to death. Jesus, however, slipped away from Judea and traveled with his disciples up the east side of the Jordan to Galilee. Here he communicated to his disciples that he would retire into the desert for a time. He gave them instructions as to which towns they should visit in order to preach, baptize and heal, and which towns to avoid. He specified also when and where he would meet up with them again—during the second half of the month of Tebeth, at Jacob's well near Sychar. On Wednesday, August 6, A.D. 32 (it was the tenth day of the month of Ab in the Jewish calendar), Jesus parted company with the disciples, and set off on a journey eastward, taking with him only three shepherd youths—Eliud, Silas and Eremenzear—aged about sixteen to eighteen years. They traveled to Cedar, not far from the easternmost boundary of Israel, arriving there in time for the start of the Sabbath, and remaining for one month in the area around Cedar.

Here Jesus performed a further miracle of raising someone from the dead. This occurred at a place about one hour east of Sichar-Cedar, on Monday, September 1, A.D. 32. There a rich farmer—his name was Nazor—had died suddenly whilst working in the fields. Jesus was invited to attend the burial, and when he arrived Nazor's corpse had already been prepared for the grave. Jesus said to those present that if they believed in his teaching and would follow him, he would bring the dead person back to life, provided they would keep silent about it. For, he said, Nazor's soul had not yet been judged, and it remained still close to the place in the fields where he had fallen dead. Together with the accompanying people, Jesus then went to this place. There he prayed and called Nazor back into his body. Turning to the people, he said: "When we return, Nazor will be alive and sitting upright!" They made their way back to the house where they found Nazor swathed in linen bands sitting upright in his coffin.

KING AMMON: Was there also a special heavenly constellation at this raising from the dead, as there had been at the raising of Lazarus?

HERMES: At the raising of Lazarus there was a conjunction of the Sun and Moon; it was New Moon. Here, at the raising of Nazor from the dead, the Moon was at first quarter. That is, the Sun was at 9° Virgo and the Moon was at about 9° Sagittarius. On this day—Monday, September 1, A.D. 32—Mercury was behind the Sun, in exact conjunction with the Sun at 9° Virgo. And Mars, at 18° Aries, was aligned with the axis of the Moon's nodes (17° Aries). The conjunction of Mercury with the Sun was propitious for a healing miracle—Mercury being associated with healing. And the alignment of Mars with the axis of the Moon's nodes signified a powerful working in of this planet, the planet of the Word, through the power of which Jesus Christ called Nazor back into his body.

After the raising of Nazor from the dead, Jesus returned to Cedar, where he taught for another week. On the morning of Tuesday, September 9, A.D. 32, he and his three traveling companions then set off on a long journey through the desert. They made their way to the place where the three kings had set up their tents after returning from Bethlehem. By now only two of the kings remained alive—Mensor, who had borne gold, and Theokeno, who had borne frankincense. The third king, Sair, who had borne myrrh had died about nine years previously. Just as the kings had been warned in a dream not to return to Herod, so on their way back across the desert in the direction of Babylon they had been instructed to settle down at this place and live there in their tents, and wait for the King of the Jews to visit them. It was a place in pleasant surroundings not far from the westernmost boundary of Chaldea. When Jesus arrived, the two kings could hardly believe that he was the child they had visited so many years ago. By now they were both very old, and Theokeno was bedridden. Jesus told them that he had come into the world not only for the Jews but also for the pagans—for all who believed in him. When the kings said that they would like to accompany Jesus back to Israel, he said that this was not necessary, for his kingdom is not of this world. Jesus added that they would only be outraged and deeply shaken in their faith if they were to see how he would be mistreated by the Jews. He said that three years after returning to his Father in heaven, he would send his chosen disciples to them (referring to the visit of the apostles Thomas and Judas Thaddeus, who came and baptized the kings three years after the ascension).

On the day on which Jesus arrived—it was Sunday, September 21, A.D. 32—Venus (11° Sagittarius) and Jupiter (11° Gemini) stood hermetically in opposition to one another, just as they had done at the conception of the child Jesus whom the kings had visited in Bethlehem. At this conception, moreover, Venus had been hermetically in conjunction with Pluto, which also was the case when Jesus arrived, Pluto (hermetically) having stood at 14½° Sagittarius. Therefore the same hermetic configuration of Pluto in conjunction with Venus in opposition to Jupiter prevailed when Jesus arrived to visit the kings as at the time of the conception when the kings had begun to pay attention to the star of the magi (the heavenly configuration indicating the Incarnation, primarily the conjunction of Jupiter and Saturn in Pisces in 7 B.C.). Here we see an example of cosmic sympathy manifesting in the recurrence of a cosmic configuration, which was mirrored on Earth below in the bond of human sympathy that brought the kings together with Jesus and then prevailed again when Jesus came to visit the kings.

KING AMMON: What, O Hermes, was the deeper reason for Jesus' visit to the kings, considering that it was such a great distance for him to travel from Israel to Chaldea?

HERMES: The starting point of this series of discourses was concerned with the star of the magi, which heralded the Incarnation of the Messiah, and it is good that we now contemplate the magi themselves, for here we shall find an answer to your question, King Ammon. But to begin with I would like to draw your attention to the prophecy of Balaam: "The oracle of Balaam, the son of Beor, the oracle of the man whose eye is opened, the oracle of him who hears the words of God, and knows the knowledge of the Most High, who sees the vision of the Almighty, falling down, but having his eyes uncovered: I see him, but know not; I behold him, but not nigh: a star shall come forth out of Jacob."

This prophecy, which was made many centuries before the coming of Christ, refers to a deep mystery connected with the star of the magi. The star was both an outer phenomenon, visible in the heavens, and an inner phenomenon: namely, the incarnation of "radiant star," Zoroaster. Zoroaster, as I described in an earlier discourse, lived in Babylon in the sixth century B.C. and founded there the Chaldean science of the stars. The magi were spiritual descendants of the followers of Zoroaster. The name "magi" comes from the Persian *Maghush*, which means mighty or illumined. In the earlier discourse I referred to the names Caspar, Melchior, Balthasar, which are the traditional names for the three kings. Caspar means *he goes with love, joyfully on his way*; Melchior means *gold king* and can also be interpreted *he goes gently, with flattery*; Balthasar signifies *he takes hold of his will, swiftly and powerfully*. However, their actual names were Mensor (Melchior), Theokeno (Caspar) and Sair (Balthasar). These names signify: Mensor—*sublime helper;* Theokeno—*born of God;* Sair—*avenger.* From the traditional names it can be seen that the three kings represent intelligence (wisdom is symbolized by gold), love (frankincense stands for reverence and devotion), and will (myrrh indicates repentance and the power of sacrifice of the will). By bringing their gifts of gold, frankincense and myrrh they showed that it is into the service of the true self, represented by Jesus Christ, that the human faculties of intelligence, love and will should be placed. The three kings had been pupils of Zoroaster in their previous incarnations and each had developed especially in a particular direction. In their previous incarnations, one was renowned as a spiritual teacher in ancient Greece; the second was famed for his reverence and piety as a mighty Persian king; and the third was a great prophet who is remembered for his acts of repentance on behalf of the people of Israel. These three reincarnated as Mensor, Theokeno and Sair, and when they went to visit their reincarnated teacher, "radiant star," each bore a gift corresponding to the quality he had developed in the previous incarnation, and offered it up to the Messiah, symbolized by the presentation of his gift.

After being warned in a dream not to return to Herod, the kings were then instructed to settle at a place not far from the westernmost borders of Chaldea and wait for the King of the Jews. Having offered up to the Lord gold, frankincense and myrrh, signifying that they placed at his disposal their highly developed faculties of intelligence, love and will, they settled down and waited. And the visit of Jesus to them, after so many years, signified his return with the spiritually transformed gifts, now to bestow these upon the kings. For, that which is offered up to God will always be returned, albeit metamorphosed into a new form. The noble intelligence, reverent piety and powerful will that were offered up by the three magi, becoming placed in the service of the Messiah for the fulfillment of his mission, were now returned on a spiritual level, having been Christianized and ennobled. It did not matter that the third king, Sair, had already died, because the gifts brought by Jesus to bestow on the kings were of a purely spiritual nature. They were bestowed as seed impulses to be taken up in subsequent incarnations by all who connect themselves with the Christian stream of spirituality concerned with ennobling intelligence, feeling and will.

KING AMMON: Thrice greatest one, what became of the three kings?

HERMES: Like others who came into connection with the Messiah, these individuals have reincarnated again several times since the Mystery of Golgotha. Without discussing these incarnations in detail, their incarnations in the eighth/ninth centuries A.D. point to a connection with the spiritual stream of the Holy Grail, which was founded by Titurel, a contemporary of Charlemagne.

KING AMMON: And what took place, O Hermes, after Jesus parted company with the two surviving kings?

HERMES: Jesus and his three young traveling companions made their way to Ur, the town where Abraham grew up. Then they crossed the Arabian desert and went to Egypt. There they visited Heliopolis, the town to which the Holy Family had fled with the child Jesus of Bethlehem ("radiant star") when he was one year old. From Egypt, Jesus and the three young shepherds returned to Israel and met up again with the disciples, as arranged, at Jacob's well near Sychar.

This journey made by Jesus Christ towards the end of his ministry had a twofold aim: on the one hand to visit the pagans, especially the three kings, to show that he had come not just for the people of Israel but also for the sake of all who believe in him; and on the other hand to retrace the path of Israel taken across the centuries. This path started in Ur, the town of Abraham, and led to Egypt, where the people of Israel remained until the Exodus. On this journey Jesus Christ took into himself the entire history of the people of Israel and bore this within him as he returned to Israel for the last three months of his ministry, leading up to the death on the cross. The Messiah was the very reason for the existence of the people of Israel, and it was as the quintessential fulfillment of the entire history of this people that he stood before Pontius Pilate and was sentenced to death. As he stood there, Jesus Christ consciously bore the cross of destiny of his people, and of the whole of humankind.

It was on Tebeth 22, around dawn on January 13, A.D. 33, that Jesus and his three young traveling companions arrived at Jacob's well upon their return from the journey to the pagans. There they were met by Peter, Andrew, John, James and Philip, who greeted Jesus with tears of joy, having not seen him for some 5½ months. Jesus had commanded the three young shepherds not to say anything about where they had been, for he knew that it would be difficult for his disciples to accept that he had been to the pagans. So nothing became known historically of this journey to the three kings, to Ur and to Heliopolis.

KING AMMON: Thank you, O Hermes, for this discourse on this hidden aspect of the ministry.

CLOSING INVOCATION

A Discourse of Hermes to Tat

The Last Supper

OPENING INVOCATION

TAT: O father, what took place after Jesus returned to Israel, after the reunion with the disciples?

HERMES: At the time of the reunion with the disciples at Jacob's well, on January 13, A.D. 33, the Sun was in the third decan of Capricorn (24° Capricorn), and Mercury was hermetically in conjunction with Neptune at 0° Aquarius. It was an inspiring moment in time for the disciples, but also filled with foreboding, for Jesus was now preparing to take the final steps on his path of suffering. Something of the approaching trials was revealed in the hermetic position of Pluto, at 15° Sagittarius, reaching 15½° Sagittarius by the time of the crucifixion, transiting the place of the Sun at the birth of Jesus of Nazareth (15½° Sagittarius). Jesus remained in Samaria until the Sun reached the end of Capricorn. But as the Sun entered Aquarius, on January 18, A.D. 33, he left Sychar and traveled in the direction of Jericho. During the time the Sun was traversing Aquarius, he taught and healed in and around Jericho, then visited Capernaum and Nazareth for the last time, and from Galilee he journeyed to Bethany.

THE LAST SUPPER

But it was not until the Sun entered Pisces that he went to Jerusalem. He then visited the temple in Jerusalem on the evening of Thursday, February 19, A.D. 33, as the Sun was at 2° Pisces. There now began his last period of teaching, leading up to his persecution and death.

TAT: O father, what took place in this last period of time in Jerusalem?

HERMES: The triumphant entry of Jesus into Jerusalem took place on Thursday, March 19, A.D. 33. This was fifteen days prior to the crucifixion. However, this event is traditionally celebrated on Palm Sunday, five days before Good Friday. The day that Jesus chose for his triumphant entry into Jerusalem was that of an eclipse of the Sun. On the afternoon of March 19, A.D. 33, the Sun (29° Pisces) and Moon (29° Pisces) were aligned with the axis of the Moon's nodes ($7\frac{1}{2}°$ Aries), thus fulfilling the conditions for an eclipse. The visible Sun in the heavens receded, as it were, to make way for the Sun of righteousness, the Light of the World, the true King of the World, who in humility rode into the city of Jerusalem on a donkey.

TAT: Was the eclipse visible in Jerusalem?

HERMES: My son, no matter from what place on Earth an eclipse of the Sun is visible, when the eclipse is taking place the entire aura of the Earth is affected in such a way that a purification process takes place. The Sun is then able to spiritually absorb the impurities owing to sin that are present in the Earth's aura. And in the case of the Messiah, his triumphant entry into Jerusalem on this day was an expression of his resolve—as the Spiritual Sun—to take the burden of humankind's sin upon himself. This resolve, which was made at the time of the New Moon (Sun conjunct Moon), was fulfilled at the Full Moon on Good Friday, fifteen days later.

TAT: O father, what was the cosmic configuration at the time of the crucifixion?

HERMES: My son, it was the Full Moon, the opposition of the Sun and Moon, with the Sun at 14° Aries and the Moon opposite at 12° Libra. But before we look at the events on Good Friday more closely, let us consider the four days leading up to the death on the cross.

On the Tuesday prior to Good Friday, Jesus taught for the last time at the temple in Jerusalem. Here he was able to teach undisturbed, as no Pharisees were present on this occasion. He spoke of truth and the fulfillment of his teaching. The time of fulfillment had now arrived. It was not sufficient simply to believe; faith must also be fulfilled. He had taught only the truth; in the name of the Father he had spoken of the Father and His Kingdom. And now his teaching would be fulfilled in that he would ascend to the Father; he would show the way to the Father. But as he was now going to leave them—his apostles and disciples—he would bestow on them his power and authority. Although he would ascend to the Father, he assured them that he would unite himself inwardly with them in a union that would last until the end of time. They would become united as members in one body. That evening, as he left the temple, he said that he would not enter the temple again in his physical body. The apostles and disciples wept, and Jesus wept too. He then returned to Lazarus in Bethany.

THE LAST SUPPER

On the Wednesday before Good Friday, Jesus remained in Bethany. He taught the disciples and Lazarus and the holy women. That evening all went to the inn of Simon in Bethany, who, although a Pharisee, had become a disciple of the Lord and had been healed of leprosy. Here there took place a banquet for all of the apostles and disciples and holy women. Jesus taught during the meal. After they had eaten, he continued to teach. As he spoke, Mary Magdalena came up to him and washed his feet and anointed him with costly ointments, which provoked some disturbance among the disciples. Especially Judas Iscariot took exception to this act, complaining that it was a waste of money which could better have been given to the poor. Now he grew firm in his resolve to betray the Lord. Afterwards, he went to the Pharisees in Jerusalem and agreed to deliver Jesus up to them in return for payment. As this took place—it was the evening of Wednesday, April 1, A.D. 33—there was a striking configuration in which Mercury (17° Pisces) was in square to both Jupiter (17° Gemini) and Pluto (17° Sagittarius), the latter two planets being in opposition to one another. The opposition between Jupiter and Pluto became exact some 18 hours after the crucifixion, at the time of the descent into hell. On the Wednesday evening, at the time of Judas' betrayal, Mercury acted as a *go-between* and this was mirrored on Earth by the action of Judas Iscariot, who—under the inspiration of the Prince of Darkness—acted so as to deliver the Messiah into the hands of the Pharisees.

But the decisive step followed on the evening of the next day, Maundy Thursday. This was at the Last Supper, when Judas left the circle of twelve gathered around Jesus Christ.

TAT: Can you tell us, O father, concerning this?

HERMES: The Last Supper took place on the evening of Thursday, April 2, A.D. 33, at the Coenaculum in Jerusalem. The Coenaculum, situated on the south side of Mt. Zion, belonged to Nicodemus and Joseph of Arimathea, and was used as a hostel by disciples of Jesus when visiting Jerusalem. The Last Supper was the celebration by Jesus and the apostles of the Feast of the Passover one day earlier than it is usually celebrated. For, at sunset on that Thursday evening, Nisan 14 started, known as "the day of preparation" for the Passover, whereas the Feast of the Passover was always celebrated on the evening upon which Nisan 15 begins.

When Jesus was later brought before the high priest Caiaphas, one of the charges made against him was that he and his disciples had eaten the Passover lamb already on Nisan 14. However, Nicodemus and Joseph of Arimathea were able to show from scrolls that according to an old regulation the men of Galilee were allowed to eat the Passover meal one evening earlier. One reason for this right of the Galileans was that otherwise, in the case of large numbers of people in the temple, the Passover meal would not be able to be concluded at the time stipulated by the Law.

Early on the morning of Maundy Thursday, Jesus sent Peter and John from Bethany into Jerusalem in order to make preparation for the Passover meal in the Coenaculum. Four lambs were brought from the market place to the Coenaculum and three were slain at the temple in preparation for the meal that evening. Peter and John then went to the home of Veronica, where she gave them the sacred cup that was used by the Lord at the institution of the Holy Sacrament. This cup was the same as that of Melchizedek when he instituted the sacrifice of bread and wine with Abraham. From Abraham the sacred vessel was handed down to Moses, and later it became part of the treasures of the temple. Through divine dispensation it was sold to Veronica and thus it came into the possession of the community of Jesus' disciples in Jerusalem.

Around midday, after taking leave of his mother in Bethany, Jesus and the remaining nine apostles made their way from Bethany to Jerusalem. Judas had already gone to Jerusalem under the pretext that he had various things to attend to, whereas in fact he went to the Pharisees in order to make the final arrangements for the betrayal that night. As Jesus went, he taught the apostles; they made their way to various places around Jerusalem: the Mount of Olives, the Valley of Josaphat, and Mt. Calvary.

When all the arrangements for the Passover feast had been made, Peter and John went to the Valley of Josaphat and fetched the Lord and the nine apostles. At the Coenaculum they met up with all the other disciples who had come. Judas arrived only shortly before the meal began, after the lamb had been slain. Three of the four lambs had already been slaughtered in the temple and brought to the Coenaculum. The fourth lamb, which was eaten by the Lord and the twelve apostles, was slain in the forecourt of the Coenaculum, according to precise indications given by Jesus. He explained that this ceremony, instituted by Moses, would be fulfilled on the next day, when he himself would be the Passover lamb. He said, "A new era and a new sacrifice is to begin, which will last until the end of the world." With these words he was referring to the beginning of the Christian era, the era of redemption, and to the institution of the Holy Sacrament, which he inaugurated that evening as his last act of redemption prior to his death on the cross. The Last Supper was a Holy Mystery celebrated by Jesus Christ to inaugurate the new sacrifice for the new era then beginning. And his death on the cross was the fulfillment of this sacrifice, making it his Eternal Covenant with the Earth and humankind.

After the lamb had been sacrificed and roasted together with the other three lambs, Jesus and the twelve apostles sat at a table in the central hall of the Coenaculum. Adjoining the central hall were two adjacent halls. Nathanael and twelve of the older disciples sat at a table in one of the adjacent halls, and Heliachim and the remaining twelve disciples sat at a table in the other adjacent hall. The Blessed Virgin Mary and the holy women ate their lamb in a building adjoining the Coenaculum.

For Christian hermetic astrology it is of particular interest to note the order in which Jesus and the apostles sat at their table, as the Last Supper was the enactment of a cosmic mystery. As we shall see, in the light of the hermetic axiom, "As above, so below," every detail is of significance. Jesus sat between Peter and John, with Peter to his left and John to his right. To the right of John sat his elder brother James, and to the left of Peter sat his elder brother Andrew, who was the oldest of the apostles. To Andrew's left sat Judas Thaddeus, then Simon, then Matthew. Judas Thaddeus, Simon and James the Lesser were the three sons of Mary Cleophas through her marriage with Alpheus, whose son Matthew from his first marriage became the half-brother of Thaddeus, Simon and James the Lesser. Mary Cleophas was the daughter of Mary Heli, the elder sister (by some nineteen years) of the Blessed Virgin Mary. Thus, Thaddeus, Simon and James the Lesser were nephews of Jesus, as also was Matthew by virtue of his father's marriage to Mary Cleophas. To the left of Matthew sat Philip.

Proceeding around the table in the other direction: on the right of James sat James the Lesser, then Bartholomew, then Thomas, then—completing the circle—Judas Iscariot. Leaving Jesus, as the thirteenth, out of account, the twelve apostles may be placed in correspondence with the twelve signs of the zodiac. Starting with Andrew, the oldest of the apostles and the first of the twelve to have become a disciple, Andrew obviously corresponds with the sign of Aries. This fits astrologically with Andrew's temperament: he was enthusiastic, fiery, hardworking, energetic, faithful, persevering, generous, honest and sincere. From the beginning he was extremely zealous in spreading the teaching of the Lord.

Next to Andrew, Peter corresponds with the sign of Taurus. Peter was by nature shy and sensitive, and he was deeply attached to his business as a fisherman. But the experience of the miraculous haul of fish, followed by the conversation with the Lord in which Jesus said to him, "Fear not, from now on you will be a fisher of men," freed him of all earthly cares. Peter developed a boundless faith in the Messiah, exemplified in his attempt at walking on the water. This faith made him worthy to become the *rock* upon which Christ chose to build his church. This quality of rocklike firmness, which is able to support tremendous pressure, is indicated in the zodiac by the star cluster of the Pleiades in the neck of the Bull, this cluster of stars being known as the *foundation stone*.

To the right of Peter, John corresponds to the next sign, that of Gemini. John and James were the sons of Mary Salome, who was a cousin of Mary of Nazareth, so that John and James were also related to Jesus. John's character was childlike, loving and open, and he was full of admiration for the Lord; moreover, he was amiable, but very sensitive. On the occasion that Jesus taught for the last time at the temple, Jesus gave John the task of writing down his teaching. Here there is a clear correspondence with the sign of Gemini.

Next in the sequence came John's elder brother, James, who corresponds with the sign of Cancer. James was pale and earnest, but also of cheerful disposition. He was fond of putting questions to the Lord. Peter, John and James—representing the signs Taurus, Gemini and Cancer—were the disciples who accompanied Jesus at the time of the transfiguration. At this event Jesus himself represented the cosmic power of the sign of Aries, the Mystical Lamb, whose radiance shone with the glory of the midnight Sun. On Mt. Tabor, Jesus was revealed to Peter, John and James in his cosmic majesty. After the Last Supper, in the Garden of Gethsemane, it was again Peter, John and James who witnessed the trial and suffering of Jesus as he sweated blood. Here they beheld the Lamb, about to be sacrificed, in his purely human nature. Just as Peter embodied especially the virtue of faith, so John was filled essentially with love and James with hope. It was as representatives of faith, hope and love that Peter, James and John accompanied Jesus Christ at the transfiguration and on the night of Gethsemane, that they could bring to expression these virtues on behalf of the other apostles, having experienced at first hand the cosmic and human sides of the Lamb of God.

To the right of James sat James the Lesser, the younger brother of Simon and Judas Thaddeus. He represented the sign of Leo. James the Lesser was of a pious nature. In appearance he was handsome and bore a striking similarity to Jesus. However, he is not to be confused with James the so-called *brother of the Lord*, who was the son of Mary Heli, the elder sister of Mary of Nazareth, and who was therefore a cousin of Jesus.

To the right of James the Lesser sat Bartholomew, who was very refined in comparison with the other apostles. He was handsome and capable, elegant and noble, but also very modest. He was quick to take action, when called for. Before he became a disciple, he had worked as a scribe in the town of Dabbeseth. Bartholomew corresponds with the sign of Virgo.

Next to him sat Thomas, known as *the twin*, as he had been born with a twin brother. His mother had died in giving birth to the twin brothers, but their father had remarried and they had been brought up very strictly by their stepmother. Thomas was about three years older than Jesus. Through his father's business he had often come into connection with foreigners and foreign languages. His strict upbringing had led him to become self-willed and obstinate, always wanting to have things proven to him and to know the reason for things. He had studied at the school of the Pharisees, and enjoyed disputes, thinking things through for himself. This is typical of the "weighing up" associated with Libra.

To the right of Thomas sat Judas Iscariot, corresponding to the sign of Scorpio. Judas' mother had been a dancer and a singer, who wrote songs and verses and sang them, accompanied by the harp, which she played herself. She also taught other women to dance. While separated from her husband, she had had a relationship with a soldier, resulting in the conception of Judas. After his birth, she had given him into the care of some rich, childless people, and he had received a good education. However, on account of his bad behavior as a boy, he was sent back to his mother, but was then cursed by his mother's husband. After his mother's death, he had lived mainly with his uncle Simon in Iscariot and worked for him. Judas dressed finely, but he lacked firmness of character. He was very friendly, but often he had a dark and sad expression on his face, to do with his avarice and secret jealously. He was talkative and ready to help others, liking to make himself important. Secretly he longed for fame, honor and money. He learned arithmetic and trading, in connection with his work on behalf of his uncle. At the time he became a disciple he was about twenty-five years old, some six years younger than Jesus. He conceived of Jesus' kingdom as an earthly one, and was attracted to enter Jesus' service in order to secure a position of fame and honor in this earthly kingdom. As a disciple he was especially concerned with the finances, and it was this preoccupation which led him eventually to betray Jesus. As mentioned in the discourse on the raising of Lazarus, Jesus bestowed the seven gifts of the Holy Spirit upon Lazarus, thus making him an apostle—preparing him to take the place of Judas in the circle of the twelve. In Lazarus and Judas the two extremes of the sign of Scorpio are evident: the striving towards the light (the Eagle, or the Dove of the Holy Spirit), and the tendency towards darkness (the Scorpion).

To the right of Judas Iscariot sat Philip, corresponding to the sign of Sagittarius. Prior to becoming a disciple, Philip had worked as a scribe in Bethsaida. He became a disciple through Andrew. He was fine in his manners and very polite.

To Philip's right sat Matthew, the stepson of Mary Cleophas. Much to the dismay of his family, he became a publican, for it was considered a disreputable profession to collect taxes. His name was Levi, but when he became a disciple, Jesus bestowed on him the name Matthew. Matthew corresponds with the sign of Capricorn.

Next to Matthew sat Simon, the second son of Mary Cleophas. Before he became a disciple, Simon had worked as an arbitrator and scribe at the court of justice in Tiberias. Through his forceful manner he became known as *the zealot*. Simon corresponds with the sign of Aquarius.

Lastly, next to Simon sat his elder brother, Judas Thaddeus. Like Andrew, Peter, John, James and James the Lesser, before becoming a disciple of the Lord, Thaddeus had worked as a fisherman at Peter's fishery near Bethsaida. But his activity had not been limited simply to fishing; he had also been active as a tradesman, buying and selling in connection with Peter's business. He was capable and experienced in dealing with people he did not know. Thaddeus, as the last in the circle, corresponds with the sign of Pisces.

TAT: O father, why is it that the order in which the apostles sat at the Last Supper corresponds with the circle of the twelve signs of the zodiac?

HERMES: My son, the Last Supper was the enactment of a Holy Mystery of eternal significance, and every detail enacted has a higher meaning. The order in which the apostles sat at the table was not arbitrary, but mirrored exactly the higher reality of twelvefoldness which in the cosmos is the zodiac. Many have sensed this, and on the basis of considering the order of the apostles as painted by Leonardo da Vinci in his portrayal of the Last Supper, attempts have been made to place the apostles in correspondence with the twelve zodiacal signs. This approach is correct, but leads to a false correspondence, as Leonardo did not portray the order of the apostles correctly. Leonardo painted the Last Supper out of a profound inspiration, and it is quite evident that he had a deeply intuitive experience of this event, as his portrayal of the order of the apostles bears a certain degree of similarity with the actual order. For example, he painted the apostles Philip, Matthew, Simon and Thaddeus together, although with Thaddeus between Matthew and Simon. Also, he showed Bartholomew and James the Lesser together, and Andrew, Peter, John and James together, although with Judas Iscariot placed between them. However, he depicted Jesus as sitting between John and James instead of between Peter and John. It is only on the basis of the actual order of the apostles at the Last Supper that the true correspondence with the signs of the zodiac emerges.

TAT: What is the significance of Jesus' position between Peter and John?

HERMES: My son, in a cosmic sense Jesus Christ should be conceived of at the center of the circle of apostles, like the Sun in the middle of the zodiac. But in an earthly sense he took his place at the table together with the twelve apostles at the Last Supper, and so it is a question as to why he sat between Peter and John. In terms of the correspondence of this position with the zodiacal signs, that is, between Taurus and Gemini, there is no special significance to this, for, as is evident, the Spiritual Sun, Jesus Christ, belongs at the center—not between any two signs. But in a human sense there is a profound meaning to the fact that the Lord was seated between Peter and John. For these two apostles were chosen by Jesus Christ—Peter as the head of the exoteric church and John as the guiding individual of the esoteric church. In a higher sense the church is indivisible, as there is only one Christ, and all are united in him. But the church has an earthly aspect and a supersensible aspect. The latter is revealed to the human being after death, or—in the case of initiation—already during earthly life. The threshold between the earthly (exoteric) and the supersensible (esoteric) church is crossed at death, or by way of initiation. The Church of Peter has the task of leading human beings to the threshold, and the Church of John guides human beings after they have crossed the threshold. The Church of Peter unites human beings on the earthly side of the threshold, whereas the Church of John is the all embracing stream of esoteric Christianity which stands behind the Church of Peter. The Church of John has the task of uniting those human beings who are on the spiritual side of the threshold or who are seeking to cross the threshold from the earthly side. Both streams—that of the Church of Peter and that of the Church of John—lead back to the same founder, Jesus Christ. Peter and John work together, united in Christ. Jesus Christ unites the two—the earthly and the supersensible churches—as indicated by the fact of being seated between Peter and John at the Last Supper. Thus both participate in the central mystery ritual of Christianity, the Holy Sacrament of communion, celebrated in the exoteric church as the Mass and in the esoteric church as the Grail Mystery.

TAT: O father, can you say more concerning this mystery?

HERMES: My son, it is possible to grasp something of the deeper significance of the mystery of the Last Supper when we contemplate the goal towards which Christ is seeking to lead humankind through this mystery. This is the heavenly city, the New Jerusalem, which is to arise on the one hand through the descent of the Spirit from heaven and on the other hand by the raising up and transformation of the Earth from below. The stream of descent from above, from the Kingdom of Light of the Father meets the stream of ascent from below, from the Kingdom of the Mother; these two streams meet in the middle, the Kingdom of the Son, which is the Kingdom of the Heart. The New Jerusalem will be the new paradise, the Kingdom of the Heart, of which Jesus Christ spoke in his words from the cross: "Today you will be with me in paradise." The old paradise disappeared after the Fall, and the new paradise is in the process of coming into being through Christ. The sacrament of Holy Communion instituted by Jesus Christ at the Last Supper is the holy ritual, given by the Lord, through the enactment of which—until the end of time—the new paradise is to be attained. At the Last Supper the apostles were called to Eternal Being, to unite with the Spirit Sun of existence through communion; but Judas rejected this call. However, his place in the circle of twelve was already filled spiritually in advance by Lazarus. Twelve apostles around the Spirit Sun—this is the foundation stone of the New Jerusalem, the Kingdom of the Heart. For the heart—seen as a spiritual organ—has a twelvefold structure, like a lotus flower with twelve petals. This same structure was manifest at the Last Supper and again at Whitsun (Pentecost), when the Twelve were gathered together around the Blessed Virgin Mary. In both cases the cosmic archetype is the twelvefold structure of the New Jerusalem, the Kingdom of the Heart, but at the Last Supper the Spirit Sun, Jesus Christ, shone at the center and at Whitsun it was the Spirit Moon, Mary Sophia. At Pentecost Mary Sophia reflected the Holy Spirit in the midst of the apostles. The New Jerusalem will require no external Sun and Moon, but will be illumined by the Spirit Sun and the Spirit Moon. And this heavenly city will have a twelvefold structure comprising the twelve *spiritual families* of the twelve apostles. For, the twelve apostles can be regarded as the *spiritual fathers* of twelve groupings among Christian humankind, just as the twelve sons of Jacob were the patriarchs of the twelve tribes of Israel. The correspondence between the twelve apostles and the twelve signs of the zodiac indicates something of the nature of the twelve spiritual families of Christian humankind who will compose the new chosen people, Eternal Israel, indwelling the New Jerusalem. For example, the spiritual family of Andrew—corresponding to Aries—will comprise those ardent and fiery Christians who, like Andrew, are zealous in their devotion to Jesus Christ. And the spiritual family of Peter—corresponding to Taurus—will be made up of those whose faith in the Lord, like that of Peter, is boundless and unshakable.

TAT: O father, what of the mystery of communion itself?

HERMES: My son, Holy Communion signifies a consecration of the human being as a preparation to enter the Kingdom of the Heart, the holy city of New Jerusalem. Each time that the human being receives the sacrament through Holy Communion, or through interior grace, the archetype of the Last Supper is evoked through the celebration of this holy ritual. But what took place at the Last Supper? First there was the Feast of the Passover, at which the lamb was consumed by Christ and the apostles. This took place exactly in accordance with the institution of the Passover by Moses, and was celebrated by Jesus Christ as a sign and symbol of that which was to be fulfilled on the following day through his death on the cross: the Sacrifice of the Lamb of God. Then Jesus washed the feet of the twelve apostles, which was a preparation for the communion about to occur. For, the washing of the feet was an act of spiritual absolution, a purification from sin, through which the feet could then be placed upon the Earth in a pure way. Then came the institution of the Holy Sacrament. After the table had been cleared, Peter and John fetched the holy chalice which was covered with a white cloth, and placed it on the table before Jesus, where also there was a jug of water, a jug of wine, and a dish containing bread. The doors were closed, and the mystery began. Jesus spoke a prayer, and then removed the cloth from the sacred chalice. He blessed the bread and, holding the dish in his hands, raised it up, looking up to heaven, and prayed and gave thanks. Setting the dish down, he covered it, and took the holy chalice, into which—after receiving the Lord's blessing—Peter poured the wine and John poured water. Jesus blessed the sacred vessel and raised it up, again looking up to heaven, and prayed and gave thanks before he set it down. All the while Jesus' mood grew more and more intense, filled with warmth and love. He said that he wanted now to give them everything that was his, his very being, and it was as if he poured himself out in love, becoming radiantly transparent, as he broke the bread for them. He prayed, and the words issuing from his lips streamed like rays of fiery light into the apostles, with the exception of Judas. As he handed them the bread, he passed his right hand over it in a gesture of blessing, broke it and said, "Take it and eat it; this is my body, that is given to you." A radiance issued forth from him and accompanied the bread itself into the mouth of each apostle receiving it. Each became inwardly radiant, the only exception being Judas. Peter was the first to receive it, then John, and then Judas, to whom Jesus said quietly: "What you are going to do, do quickly." After each of the twelve apostles had received the bread, Jesus took the holy chalice, raised it, gave thanks and spoke the words: "Drink of it, all of you; this is my blood, the blood of the new covenant, which is shed for the forgiveness of sins." Holding the sacred vessel, Jesus let Peter and John drink from it, and then set it down. John, using a small spoon, ladled the consecrated wine from the chalice into beakers, which were passed on to the remaining apostles. Directly after receiving the wine, without saying a word of thanks, Judas left the Coenaculum. It was night. He ran through the darkness on his way to fulfill the act of betrayal. Jesus, however, gave instruction to the remaining eleven apostles. He instructed them to continue to celebrate the ritual of the Holy Sacrament, to do this in remembrance of him until the end of the world. He also taught them concerning the priesthood, how to anoint with consecrated oil, and how to consecrate the oil. Jesus then anointed Peter and John in turn, first laying his hands on their shoulders, then on the head, lastly making the sign of the cross on the head. Jesus thus consecrated Peter and John as the first bishops of the church. Andrew, James, James the Lesser and Bartholomew also received a consecration from the Lord, becoming the first priests. Through the sublime act of consecration with oil, Jesus transmitted something of supernatural essence to the apostles. He said that they would all receive the Holy Spirit and that after this they would be able to consecrate the bread and wine themselves and anoint the other apostles. Following this, Jesus taught at length, interspersing his teaching with several prayers. He was filled with love and the power of the spirit. At the end of the evening, after singing together a hymn of praise, Jesus and the apostles left the Coenaculum and went to the Mount of Olives.

TAT: O father, how may we understand the significance of the consecrated bread and wine of the Holy Communion?

HERMES: My son, deep mysteries are connected with this. For, the bread symbolizes the body of Christ and the wine his blood. Let us consider what took place at the Mystery of Golgotha. As Jesus Christ hung from the cross, his blood flowed down upon the Earth, consecrating the Earth from above. This is a movement from above to below, from the Kingdom of Heaven down towards the Earth, bearing the Light of the Father Kingdom down to humankind and the Earth. In the human being the blood bears the imprint of the self, the spirit, and in the case of Jesus Christ, his blood bore the Cosmic Self, THE SOLAR LOGOS, the Light of the World. On the other hand, the body of Christ, after it was taken down from the cross, was laid in the grave. The body was thus implanted into the Earth. With the descent into hell, Jesus Christ descended to the Kingdom of the Mother, and with the resurrection he rose again from the Kingdom of the Mother to the Earth's surface. The movement of Christ's body, seen in this light, is essentially an ascending one: from the Kingdom of the Mother below directed above to humankind on the Earth. It is the power of resurrection which is at work here, and this is symbolized by the bread. Bread is made from wheat, and the growth of wheat is a striving upwards towards the Sun. It is the Sun Power of Resurrection, the movement of the resurrection body from below to above, which is symbolized by the bread. In the Holy Communion these two directions of movement—from above to below, symbolized by the wine, and from below to above, symbolized by the bread—meet and interpenetrate in the heart. The washing of the feet of the apostles prior to the Holy Communion was to purify the relationship between their feet and the Earth, so that they could receive in a pure way something of the warmth from the Kingdom of the Mother radiating up from below. It was this warmth which bore up the resurrection body on its path of ascent. At the Last Supper, as they received the consecrated bread and wine, the apostles, with the exception of Judas, were filled from above with the radiant Light of the Heavenly Kingdom of the Father, and irradiated from below with the spiritual warmth of the Kingdom of the Mother. These two spiritual qualities, borne by the bread and wine, met and fused in their hearts. In this way, through the Holy Communion, the Kingdom of the Heart, the New Jerusalem, arises—between the Kingdom of the Father in Heaven and the Kingdom of the Mother within the Earth. This is the new paradise, the Kingdom of the Son.

TAT: O father, what was the heavenly configuration at this event?

HERMES: My son, the positions of the Sun and planets in the starry signs on the evening of the Last Supper were more or less identical with those at the crucifixion on the next afternoon. Only the Moon's position differed somewhat. At the crucifixion the Moon was at 12° Libra, more or less exactly Full Moon, opposite the Sun at 14° Aries. At the time of the Last Supper, the Moon was at 2° Libra, on its way towards becoming full. Everything was building up towards the Full Moon. And in the intervening time, as the Moon made its way from 2° Libra to 12° Libra, the trial and passion of Our Lord took place. This will be the subject of our next discourse.

TAT: O father, you spoke of the participation of the exoteric church in the Mass and of the esoteric church in the Grail Mystery. Having discussed the deeper significance of the Mass, can you speak now concerning the Grail Mystery?

HERMES: The Grail Mystery comprises the cosmic side of the mystery of communion. Jesus Christ gave all the apostles the task of celebrating the Holy Communion, in his memory, until the end of the world. But Peter became especially emphasized with respect to this task. For, Jesus Christ, after his resurrection, instructed him with the words: "Feed my sheep." The celebration of the sacrament of Holy Communion is the primary task of the Church of Peter. Over and beyond this task, however, there is on a spiritual level the equivalent of Holy Communion on Earth; this is cosmic communion, in which spiritual beings and human beings who have crossed the threshold participate. An example of cosmic communion was referred to in an earlier discourse; this is the sanctification of the New Moon and the sanctification of the Full Moon, the latter in memory of the Mystery of Golgotha and the words from the cross, and the former in memory of the raising of Lazarus and the I AM sayings. Here the sequence of New and Full Moons may be followed through the starry signs of the zodiac during the course of the year. In fact, the passage of the Sun through the twelve signs of the zodiac, in the space of one year, offers an archetype for the cosmic communion. Here it is a matter of twelve different "cosmic streams" which nourish and sustain the human being on a spiritual level. Just as the human being cannot live on Earth without air, which is needed to breathe in order to stay alive, so on a spiritual level the human being is dependent on the cosmic nourishment taken in from the twelve starry signs of the zodiac. Without thoughts, for example, the human being would perish spiritually, and it is especially the cosmic stream from the starry sign of Aries which nourishes the human being with thoughts. The archetypal thought is that of God—the Father, the Creator—and the cosmic stream of nourishment from Aries can be raised to consciousness by taking God as the point of departure for all thought activity. On the other hand, materialistic thinkers cut themselves off from the real essence of the cosmic stream of Aries. The connection can be found again by imbuing thought with morality.

Secondly, the human being depends spiritually on speech, and the cosmic stream of nourishment underlying speech emanates from the starry sign of Taurus. The point of departure for entering into the stream of speech is the I AM; everything depends on how the human being says "I Am." The true way of saying "I Am," which enables the Taurean stream of nourishment to be found, is from below to above, in consciousness that the true "I" is spiritually rooted in the Godhead. The false way, which works to block the human being off from the essential substance of the cosmic stream of Taurus, is to say "I Am" as if being at the center of existence. This way of saying "I Am" is that of self-assertion. According to the way in which human beings speak "I Am," their whole way of speaking is indicated, and also their relationship to the stream of nourishment belonging to the starry sign of Taurus. When this relationship develops in the right way, speech acquires a moral content and becomes a power in itself, instead of merely bringing thoughts to expression.

TAT: O father, can you elucidate further why Aries is connected with thought and Taurus with speech?

HERMES: My son, viewed cosmically each of the zodiacal signs has its own mode of speech and its own line of thought, so all the zodiacal signs have both a "thought aspect" and a "speech aspect." But when we look at the structural relationship of the human being to the zodiacal signs, the human head—the organ of thought—corresponds to Aries, and the human larynx—the organ of speech—corresponds to Taurus. In terms of this structural relationship, each part of the human being corresponds to a particular zodiacal sign; each bodily part is the organ of some spiritual activity—thought, speech, memory, etc.—and according to this activity receives nourishment from the cosmic stream emanating from the corresponding zodiacal sign. For example, the cosmic stream from Aries, relating to the head, activates thinking, and that from Taurus, corresponding to the larynx, supports speech.

Now, the cosmic stream from Gemini is that of *being*, meaning the relationship with other beings. Whereas Taurus is connected with speaking the "I Am," Gemini is bound up with the "you." The twins of Gemini relate archetypally to *twin souls*—for example, in paradise: Adam and Eve. It is only when human beings can truly say "you" to another that they are able to experience true being. They break through the barrier of loneliness by learning to say "you." Eve was created for Adam because God saw that it was not good for Adam to be alone. Adam learned the transition from the experience of saying "I" to that of saying "you." Thereby he entered into the stream of being. Without learning to say "you," however, he would have remained locked up within himself, cut off from the stream of being. Being is the third cosmic stream of nourishment, after thought and speech. Without contact with other beings, we would perish spiritually. By allowing moral depth in human relationships to grow, the right relationship with the stream of nourishment from Gemini is found.

The fourth stream is that of memory. This is connected with the starry sign of Cancer. Here it is a help if we consider the hieroglyph of this zodiacal sign, which consists of two interlocking spirals. One spiral leads back into the past, the other into the future. Memory is the faculty which connects us with the past, out of which the pathway into the future is indicated, in that memory provides the basis for resolves concerning the future. Memory sustains the human being—all the memories accumulated during earthly life, the most important being childhood memories. Here parental love plays a major role for the way in which human beings take up their path in life. And on a higher level, memory extends back through all incarnations to the *childhood* of humankind in paradise. Here divine love is all-important, the blessing of the Divinity—the Father and the

Mother—which was bestowed on each human being at the beginning of its cycle of earthly incarnations. Through love of the Father and Mother, this higher memory can be awakened, leading into the cosmic stream of nourishment belonging to Cancer. Then memory becomes imbued with moral warmth, instead of merely photographically reproducing impressions.

The fifth stream of cosmic nourishment is that of the starry sign of Leo. In the microcosm the heart corresponds to Leo. The heart is the organ of warmth—moral warmth, sympathy toward others. And the cosmic stream emanating from the starry sign of Leo is warmth, which is received in the best way by becoming open to others.

Then comes the sixth stream of nourishment, that of the starry sign of Virgo. This spiritual nourishment is of the nature of air and it comes to expression in the spiritual-moral atmosphere that surrounds a person. This *moral air* is breathed in not only through prayer and meditation, but also through tolerance and open-mindedness. In the human being the region of the diaphragm and solar plexus corresponds to Virgo. On the physical level the function of breathing is regulated from here, and the corresponding spiritual function is the breathing in of moral air. Accordingly human beings *build their houses.* If they are narrow-minded, for example, they live in a narrowly confined orbit of interests, in a *stuffy atmosphere.* To break out of this they need to broaden their horizons and take an interest in everything around—as it were, *opening the windows* and *letting in new air.*

Proceeding further, the seventh stream of cosmic nourishment, that of Libra, is of the nature of light. The essence of this light is joy, which arises through thankfulness and gratitude toward life. Without it, the heart would darken.

But there is also the dark joy of self-satisfaction, for example, through satisfying greed. Self-satisfaction also comes to expression in the pursuit of pleasure, where often a natural joy can be taken to extremes. Something of the light of joy, for example, can be experienced through the simple fact of the Sun shining. But to spend hour after hour lying in the sun would be to take this natural joy to an extreme. The light of joy arises spontaneously in connection with many of life's experiences, especially when these are experienced in a mood of humble gratitude; but if this joyousness is deliberately pursued for its own sake, a state of imbalance arises. In order to find the stream of nourishment from Libra in the right way, it is a question of balance and harmony, not going to extremes.

The eighth stream of cosmic nourishment proceeds from the sign of Scorpio. This is the cosmic stream of life force. The secret of finding access to this cosmic stream is the practice of silence. Through becoming inwardly quiet and still, an inflow of life force may take place.

Emanating from the ninth zodiacal sign, Sagittarius, is the cosmic stream of nourishment that can be termed *ego force*. This is a kind of inner spiritual fire. It manifests itself as a stimulating force, kindling enthusiasm, and arises especially within the seeker after truth.

From the tenth zodiacal sign, Capricorn, comes the cosmic stream of nourishment that may be termed *sweetness of soul*. This is a stream of conciliatory spirit, calming and at the same time ennobling the feelings, arising especially within human beings who purify their wishes through moral discipline.

The eleventh stream of cosmic nourishment, that of Aquarius, may be termed the *elixir of life*. It is refreshing and strengthening. If taken up in the right way, through moderation and the striving for spiritual harmony, it brings with it the power of healing.

Lastly, the twelfth stream of cosmic nourishment, that of Pisces, can be termed the *bread of life*. It bestows inner substance, such that the organs of the physical body become capable of taking up spiritual life. The physical body is emphasized especially in the early stages (childhood) of life and also towards the end of life (old age). In order to consciously take up the cosmic stream of nourishment of Pisces, the forces of youthfulness (life) and maturity (death) have to be brought into inner balance. The symbol for this is the cord connecting the two fishes swimming in opposite directions.

These twelve streams of cosmic nourishment from the twelve signs of the zodiac compose the Tree of Life. By meditatively following the passage of the Sun through the zodiacal signs in the course of the year, a start can be made on the path of consciously taking up the cosmic communion of the Grail Mystery, communion from the Tree of Life. This may be included in the petition, "Give us this day our daily bread," as the spiritual counterpart to communion by way of the Holy Sacrament.

TAT: Thank you, O father, for this discourse on the Last Supper and the Grail Mystery.

CLOSING INVOCATION

A Discourse of Hermes to Asclepius

Gethsemane Night

OPENING INVOCATION

ASCLEPIUS: After leaving the Coenaculum, Jesus and the eleven disciples went towards the Mount of Olives, to the Garden of Gethsemane. O thrice-greatest one, what took place there?

HERMES: It was late in the evening of Thursday, April 2, A.D. 33, that Jesus and the apostles made their way towards the Garden of Gethsemane. The Moon, almost full, was visible above in the starry sign of Libra. Jesus was deeply troubled, and spoke of approaching danger. When they reached Gethsemane, he said to the apostles: "Remain here while I go to pray." Taking Peter, James and John with him, he entered the Garden of Olives at the foot of the Mount of Olives. He was filled with an indescribable sadness, and sensed temptation approaching. Then he said to the three apostles: "Remain here and keep awake, and pray that you do not fall into temptation." After this he left them and went a short distance to a small cave, which he went into, and knelt down to pray. Here began the fourth temptation, following on from the three temptations in the wilderness, which Jesus had overcome at the start of his ministry during the forty days in A.D. 29 as the Sun was passing through Scorpio and the first decan of Sagittarius. Now, almost 3½ years later, the Sun was in Aries and the Moon—not quite full—was opposite in Libra.

The three temptations in the wilderness had been aimed at the thinking, feeling and will of the Son of man. Now the fourth temptation was directed to the human self of Jesus, the temptation for him to act in his own name instead of the name of God. Having overcome the three temptations, having carried out his work of redemption—teaching and healing—during the last 3½ years, the moment for the fulfillment of his mission had arrived. But in order for the sacrifice of the Lamb of God to occur in complete freedom, the human self of Jesus—independently of the Holy Trinity—had to decide whether or not to take the final step.

On this night of temptation in Gethsemane the Sun was at 13½° Aries, at the same place in the zodiac (14° Aries) as on the night of the transfiguration, April 3/4, A.D. 31, two years previously. As on the night of the transfiguration on Mt. Tabor, Jesus was accompanied by Peter, James and John, the apostles, who represented faith, hope and love. But whereas on Mt. Tabor the three apostles had beheld the glory of the light of the Kingdom of the Father, which radiated from Jesus so that he shone like the Sun, on the night of Gethsemane they saw Jesus subject to such temptation that he sweated blood. On the summit of Mt. Tabor CHRIST, the Son of God, had manifested himself to the disciples in all his radiant glory as divine love; now, at the foot of the Mount of Olives, the three apostles were witness to the human self of Jesus subject to indescribable suffering, which he bore, however, through the purely human love of his heart, his divinity having *retired,* as it were, back into the Holy Trinity. Jesus on the night of Gethsemane, revealed the boundless love of his pure humanity, untainted by sin, in the resolve to sacrifice himself by taking all the world's sin and suffering upon himself.

As he knelt and prayed, he was faced with wave upon wave of the most loathsome scenes portraying the depths of guilt and sin in the world since the Fall of Adam. At the same time this was accompanied by the mocking voice of the Evil One, who taunted Jesus, depicting his deeds of love as completely worthless. Jesus, shocked on the one hand by the abominableness and sheer volume of sin and on the other hand by the unspeakable ingratitude shown by human beings towards God, cast himself down in fear and trembling, and prayed: "Abba, Father! If it be possible, let this cup pass from me. My Father, all things are possible with thee, remove this cup from me; nevertheless not my will, but thine, be done." His will and the will of the Father were one, as he offered himself up in love for the sake of humankind, but he was shaken to the core in the face of death and the onslaught of temptation from the depths of hell.

Covered in sweat, Jesus rose from prayer and made his way from the cave to the three apostles. However, through anxiety and sheer exhaustion they had fallen asleep. He called out: "Simon, are you asleep? Could you not keep awake one hour with me?" They awoke and were deeply shocked at his appearance. John asked: "Master! What has happened to you? Shall I call the other disciples? Shall we flee?" Jesus replied: "Even if I were to live, teach and heal for another thirty-three years, it would not suffice to accomplish what I have to do by tomorrow. Do not call the other eight. I left them behind, because they would not be able to see me in such misery without taking offense. They would fall into temptation, forget almost everything, and lose their faith in me. You, however, have seen the Son of man transfigured; so you may also see him in his darkest hour, wholly forsaken. But watch and pray, so that you do not fall into temptation. The spirit is willing, but the flesh is weak."

Then Jesus returned to the cave, leaving the three apostles, who, inwardly troubled and downcast, began to pray. Jesus also prayed, and a new struggle broke out within him. For, he now bore and felt the burden of the sins of the whole world, and he beheld in vision the immeasurable torment connected with bearing this burden. He began to sweat blood. He also beheld the future, the ingratitude and terrible misdeeds of human beings, whose debts of guilt and the punishment thereof he had taken upon himself. The voice of the Evil One called to him: "Behold! For such ingratitude you want to suffer?" The deepest source of grief for Jesus in this Gethsemane night was to behold the future destiny of his church, the bride upon which he was about to bestow his blood of redemption, his water of purification, and his spirit, nourishing her with the sacred sacrament. For, he saw the future schisms, heresies and further *falls into sin* on account of the vice and disobedience of future Christians, and the abominable sacrileges, committed in his name, that would be perpetrated. Sweating blood, he made his way again to Peter, James and John. He told them that he would be taken captive in one hour's time, that he would be judged, mistreated, mocked, scourged, and killed in an awful way. He bid them to console his mother, and also Mary Magdalena. Meanwhile the other eight apostles, who had remained behind in the Garden of Gethsemane, were tempted and plagued with worry: "What shall we do if he is killed? We have forsaken and abandoned everything; and now we are poor and a mockery to the world; we have depended upon him completely, and how is it that he is now so weak and powerless that he is unable to console us at all?"

Jesus, however, had returned to his cave to pray. Now he beheld everything that would take place: Judas' betrayal, the flight of the disciples, the mock trial before Annas and Caiaphas, Peter's denial, Pilate's judgment, Herod's mocking words, the scourging and crowning with thorns, the death sentence, the carrying of the cross, the crucifixion. Jesus sank down under the weight of these visions of his approaching path of suffering, but he took all upon himself out of love for humankind. In complete freedom he drank the cup of suffering, and he became inwardly strengthened. He then emerged from his cave and went again to Peter, James and John, saying: "This is no time for sleep, for the hour has arrived for the Son of man to be delivered into the hands of sinners. Arise! Let us go. Behold, the betrayer is near. It would have been better for him if he had never been born!" The three apostles jumped to their feet, and Peter said: "Master, I shall call the others. We shall defend you!" Jesus, however, pointed to the approaching group of armed men and said: "Let us go towards them; without resisting I shall deliver myself into the hands of the enemy." Going up to Judas and the armed men, Jesus asked: "Who are you seeking?" One of the armed men replied: "Jesus of Nazareth." To which Jesus answered: "I am he." Then turning to Judas, he raised his hand and asked: "Friend, why have you come?" Judas muttered something about having done some business, and Jesus then said words to the effect that it would have been better for him not to have been born. Judas went up to Jesus and kissed him, saying: "Hail, Master!" This was the sign to the armed men, which Judas had arranged with them beforehand, as to how he would identify Jesus of Nazareth to them. Jesus responded: "Judas, would you betray the Son of man with a kiss?"

ASCLEPIUS: What was the cosmic background to this betrayal of Jesus by Judas?

HERMES: First we need to understand what had led Judas to this step, and then we can look at the cosmic situation. All along Judas had envisaged the Kingdom spoken of by Jesus as an earthly kingdom. But he saw, as time went by, no sign of this being realized. Instead, he experienced the increasing attacks by the Pharisees on Jesus and his followers. He became tired of the life of roaming around and, on account of the persecutions of the Pharisees, he was ill at ease in his role as a disciple. Thus he turned to the Pharisees, whom he saw as holding the reigns of power, with his offer of betrayal, thinking that he would get out of the situation and at the same time earn some money. However, he did not think of the consequences of his action for the Lord, that this would mean Jesus being sentenced to death. He was possessed by the thought of the money that he would receive from the betrayal, and here he was goaded on by the Evil One.

The relationship of Pluto to the working of the evil has been spoken of already, in connection with the temptations in the wilderness, where it was pointed out that the culmination of the temptations—the encounter with the Evil One—was signified macrocosmically by the conjunction in

Sagittarius between Pluto and the Sun. Now, at the time of the Lord's betrayal, Pluto was at 17° Sagittarius, transiting the zodiacal position where the Sun (16° Sagittarius) had been at the birth of Jesus of Nazareth. At the same time, Pluto was in opposition to Jupiter (17° Gemini). At the moment when Judas came to betray Jesus with a kiss—it was about half an hour before midnight—Pluto was rising in the East and Jupiter was setting in the West. This symbolized that the Evil One was now asserting himself, and that the divine wisdom, represented by Jupiter, had to recede in the face of the power of evil. On a higher level, however, divine wisdom was becoming fulfilled through the help of the working of evil, as this had taken hold of Judas. For, it was precisely through Judas' betrayal that the will of the Father that his only-begotten Son be sacrificed for the sake of humankind, was able to be fulfilled. Judas' deed was necessary for the fulfillment of the divine plan leading to the death on the cross on Golgotha. God's *beholding* of the betrayal, and of Jesus willingly giving himself into the hands of his enemies, was indicated at this moment by the position of the Moon (4° Libra), almost full, high in the heavens above the Mount of Olives, culminating at its highest position at the moment of the betrayal. For, the Moon and the Sun can be thought of as the eyes of God, of the beings of the divine world, and thus the almost Full Moon, high above the Garden of Gethsemane, signified the *eye of God* witnessing the fulfillment of divine will. With the kiss of Judas, Jesus was delivered into the hands of those seeking to kill him. This denoted the beginning of his path of suffering, the Lord's Passion, leading to his death. However, it is customary to designate the washing of the feet as the first stage of the Passion, since the washing of the feet portrays the divine will at the outset of the Passion—the will of God to serve humankind, the higher pouring itself out in service of the lower, in an act of self-sacrifice. It was this divine will that was strengthened and confirmed in the hour of Jesus' temptation that Gethsemane night, following which the will to sacrifice himself became stronger every step of the way along the path of the Passion, culminating in the ultimate deed of sacrifice on the cross.

ASCLEPIUS: Indeed, O Hermes, great are the divine mysteries surrounding the path of the Son of man.

CLOSING INVOCATION

A Discourse of Hermes to King Ammon

The Stages of the Passion

OPENING INVOCATION

KING AMMON: It is our wish, O Hermes, to learn more concerning the divine mysteries underlying the stages of the Passion.

HERMES: King Ammon, let us endeavor to become pure in heart and mind that we may begin to approach the mysteries of the Lord's Passion. And if we do so, we shall surely be richly rewarded, for here lies the heart of the Christ Mystery. To begin with, let us look at the sequence of events which began after the Last Supper, when Jesus and the eleven apostles went to Gethsemane. When they arrived there it was about nine o'clock that evening, and the sign of Scorpio was rising in the East, the bright star Antares, the heart of the Scorpio, having just risen above the eastern horizon. There began the Gethsemane night temptation, which we contemplated in the last discourse. Then followed the betrayal—the kiss of Judas—at which time Pluto was rising in the East, in the middle of Sagittarius, and Jupiter, opposite, in the middle of Gemini, was setting in the West. The Moon, almost full, was culminating high overhead.

After the capture of Jesus, he was led from Gethsemane across the Cedron brook, then through the district of Ophel, on the outskirts of Jerusalem, to the palace of Annas on Mt. Zion. Annas presided over the tribunal charged with drawing up accusations against Jesus. It was after midnight when the procession leading Jesus arrived at Annas' palace. Shortly after, Jesus was presented to appear before Annas. The constellation of Capricorn began to rise in the East about a quarter of an hour past midnight. Some two hours later, Aquarius began its ascent in the East, and at half-past two that morning the planet Neptune (3° Aquarius) rose across the horizon. During this time, accusations by Annas and others were brought against Jesus, who was then led to be tried by the high priest Caiaphas at the courtroom on Mt. Zion. The mock trial by Caiaphas of the innocent Son of man thus took place under the cosmic aspect of Neptune rising in the East in Aquarius. Just as the betrayal of Jesus by Judas' kiss coincided with Pluto's ascending in the East, the mock trial by Caiaphas was connected with the ascent of Neptune in the East some three hours later. It was a mock trial, as Caiaphas had determined in advance that it would be expedient for one man—Jesus—to die for the people.

The trial of Jesus by Caiaphas lasted during the time of Aquarius rising and also the rising of Pisces, until Venus (25° Pisces) rose across the eastern horizon. The main charge brought against Jesus was that he held himself to be a king. But there were many other charges as well, one of them being that he and the disciples had already eaten the Passover lamb that evening, instead of waiting for the Sabbath to commence. Nicodemus and Joseph of Arimathea were summoned by Caiaphas to account for themselves, as they were the owners of the Coenaculum on Mt. Zion, where the Last

THE STAGES OF THE PASSION

Supper had taken place. They explained, bringing forward documents in support of their argument, that according to an ancient custom, the Galileans were allowed to eat the Passover one evening earlier—one of the reasons for this custom being that, in the event of large crowds flocking to the temple, there was a risk that preparation for the feast might not be concluded at the appointed time.

Throughout the trial, Jesus remained silent, even while the most blatant lies were being raised as accusations against him. Among the crowd witnessing all this were the apostles Peter and John. Eventually Caiaphas, infuriated at the indescribable patience shown by Jesus through it all, called out: "Do you have nothing to say to these testimonies? I command you in the name of the living God to tell us whether you are Christ, the Messiah, the Son of God Almighty!" Jesus replied, his voice sublimely magnificent, the voice of the Eternal Word: "I am! You have said it! And I tell you, soon you will see the Son of man sitting to the right of His Majesty and coming in the clouds of heaven!" At these words pandemonium broke loose. Caiaphas called out: "He has blasphemed! What need do we have of further witnesses! Now you have heard the blasphemy yourselves, what do you think?" The crowd responded: "He deserves to die! He deserves to die!"

At this moment of triumph of darkness over the light, the apostle John was inwardly filled with the thought of the Mother of Jesus. Looking again towards Jesus, sending his thoughts to him, saying inwardly, "Master, you know why I am leaving," he left the courthouse and hurried off to seek the Blessed Virgin. Peter, however, stayed in the courthouse. Filled with fear and pain, he drew near to the fireplace, to warm himself.

The high priest Caiaphas said to the rough and ready men guarding Jesus: "I deliver this king unto you; render to this blasphemer the honors due to him," and withdrew into an adjoining room. Thus he left Jesus at the mercy of these brutal men, who beat, kicked and mistreated Jesus in the most despicable, inhuman way. Eventually they lead him off to the dungeon, where they continued their abominable mistreatment, all the time mocking the Lord contemptuously.

Peter, standing at the fireplace, could hardly conceal his grief and sorrow. He warmed himself, for the cold of the night made itself felt, although now dawn was approaching. It was almost a quarter to five. In the East the planet Venus (25° Pisces) was rising in the Fishes. A woman came up to the fireplace, voicing her contempt for Jesus and the disciples. Spotting Peter, she said to him: "You are also one of the Galilean's disciples." Peter was thrown into confusion. Fearing that he might also be mistreated by the crowd, he replied: "Woman, I do not know him. I don't know what you mean. I don't understand you."

He withdrew from the fireplace. At that moment a cock crowed outside. As Peter made his way through the throng, another woman said to those standing around her: "This man, also, was with Jesus of Nazareth." Some of the people then said: "Aren't you also one of his disciples?" Confused and frightened, Peter spoke out emphatically: "Truly, I am not! I do not know this man!"

Hurrying to the outer court of the building, Peter wept, full of sorrow and concern for Jesus. Restless, driven by love for his Master, he soon returned to the courtroom, where Jesus, with a straw crown on his head, was being dragged around and mocked by the crowd. Jesus looked towards Peter, his solemn gaze warning him. Peter, smitten with pain, returned to the fireplace. Someone approached and said: "Truly, you also belong to his followers. You are from Galilee, judging from the way you speak." Peter backed away. Just in that moment a brother of Malchus, whose ear Peter had cut with his sword that night at Gethsemane, came up and said: "What! Didn't I see you with them in the garden on the Mount of Olives? Aren't you the one who wounded my brother's ear?"

Peter, quite beside himself, in desperation began to curse, swearing that he did not know this man at all. He ran out again towards the outer court. In that instant the cock crowed a second time, just as Jesus was being led out of the courtroom to the dungeon. Jesus turned towards Peter with a pitiable and sorrowful gaze, and Peter suddenly remembered the words of the Lord: "Before the cock crows twice, you will deny me three times." In his grief and anxiety, Peter had completely forgotten his boasting words on the Mount of Olives earlier that night, that he would sooner die together with his Master rather than deny him. Jesus' gaze smote him to the depths of his being, and he became aware of the full intensity of his guilt.

In the meantime, John had hurried to the Blessed Virgin, who was accompanied by Mary Magdalena, Martha, and seven other holy women. He told them of Jesus' terrible suffering and of the jeering crowd that had called out: "He deserves to die!" The Blessed Virgin, who inwardly beheld all that Jesus was undergoing and suffered in spirit with him, asked to be brought closer to her son. John then led the whole group of holy women towards the courthouse. They came to a halt in front of the door leading to the outer court. Filled with unspeakable pain at the suffering of Jesus, the Blessed Virgin longed for the door to open, which she felt separated her from her son. It was at this moment that the cock crowed for the second time, just as Jesus—on the other side of the door—was being led to the dungeon. Then, as if in answer to her prayer, the door opened, and Peter and several others rushed out. Peter was weeping bitterly. The Virgin Mary asked him: "O Simon, how is my son faring?" Peter called out woefully: "O mother, do not speak with me, your son is suffering inhumanly; do not speak with me, they have sentenced him to death, and I have despicably denied him three times." Peter then ran off in the direction of the Mount of Olives. The Blessed Virgin was torn with compassion at this new suffering of Jesus, occasioned by the denial of the same disciple who had recognized him as the Son of the living God. She sank down on her knees.

It was now almost five o'clock that morning. The planet Mercury (19° Pisces), rising in the East, bore witness to the compassion of the Blessed Virgin for the suffering of her son, just as Venus, which had risen a quarter of an hour earlier, had been the cosmic witness to Peter's denial of the Lord.

KING AMMON: It would seem, O thrice-greatest one, that the rising of each planet coincided with a significant moment on the path of suffering of the Lord—the rising of Venus with the cock crowing for the first time, and the rising of Mercury with it crowing a second time.

HERMES: Indeed, honorable King Ammon!

KING AMMON: And what took place as the Sun rose?

THE STAGES OF THE PASSION

HERMES: The Sun (13½°8 Aries) rose in Jerusalem shortly before six o'clock that morning, on this most fateful day in the entire history of the Earth. At daybreak Caiaphas, Annas and the scribes and elders were gathered together in the courtroom in order to pass judgment on Jesus, for according to Jewish law, a valid court sentence could not be made during the hours of darkness. Caiaphas commanded that Jesus be fetched from the dungeon, where he had been for about one hour, to be sentenced. Caiaphas mockingly addressed him: "If you are the Lord's anointed one, the Messiah, tell us!" Jesus raised his head and spoke majestically the words: "If I were to tell you, you would not believe me; and if I were to put a question to you, you would neither answer it nor release me. But hereafter the Son of man will sit at the right hand of God's power." Caiaphas and the others then said scornfully: "So, then, you—you are the Son of God?" Jesus answered with the voice of Eternal Truth: "Yes, it is as you say. I am he." They replied: "What more proof do we need? We ourselves have now heard it from his own mouth." And they commanded him to be sent to Pontius Pilate, to be led there with a chain around his neck, as customary for someone sentenced to death. This, then, was the awful sight to which the Sun bore witness as it rose across Jerusalem that morning: the innocent Son of man being led to Pontius Pilate as a condemned criminal to be sentenced to death.

But this was not the only sight beheld by the Sun that morning. For, as the darkness began to give way to the light, Judas Iscariot became full of despair. He learned of the demand of the court of Caiaphas that Jesus be sentenced to death. In desperation he ran to the temple to return the thirty pieces of silver that he had received. "Take back your money, by means of which you tempted me to hand over the Righteous One; take back your money, set Jesus free; I revoke my contract, I have sinned grievously by betraying innocent blood," he said. The priests replied contemptuously: "What business of ours is it if you have sinned? If you believe that you have sold innocent blood, look to yourself; it is your own affair. We know what we have bought from you, and we found him deserving to die. You have your money, and we want no part of it." Judas, beside himself with despair, flung the money down upon the floor of the temple, and rushed off. In a frenzy he ran to a desolate spot at the foot of the Mount of Scandals, where he took his girdle and hung himself to death from a tree. This was the other dreadful sight that the Sun beheld on rising to the East of Jerusalem that day.

KING AMMON: After the Sun rose, which planet ascended next?

HERMES: After sunrise, there followed the rising of Mars. This coincided with the second stage of the Lord's Passion. But first let us consider what took place in the intervening time. As I said, Jesus was led to the palace of Pontius Pilate around the time of sunrise. To Pitate's question as to whether he was a king, Jesus replied: "It is as you say, yes, I am a king. I was born and I came into this world to bear witness to the truth, and everyone who is of the truth hears my voice." Pilate asked: "Truth? What is truth?" After considering the charges brought against Jesus, Pilate said that he did not find any kind of guilt attached to this man, and added that Jesus should be sent to Herod Antipas.

THE STAGES OF THE PASSION

To Herod's stream of questions, Jesus answered not a single word. He simply stood in silence, with bowed head. Eventually Herod said: "Take this fool away and show this ridiculous king the honor he deserves. For he is more a fool than a criminal."

Caiaphas, Annas and the high priests then commanded Jesus to be led back to the palace of Pontius Pilate. At the same time they gave instructions and promised money to various people, to the end that they should swiftly round up a crowd to gather in front of the palace to create an uproar, demanding the death of Jesus. When Pilate announced that he did not find Jesus guilty, and Herod also had found no guilt in him, and that therefore he planned to let Jesus go free, the crowd began to murmur in protest. Pilate hoped to find a way out of this situation. It was customary prior to the Passover to set free one of the criminals in his charge, according to the desire of the people. Pilate hoped that the crowd would choose Jesus, if he gave them the choice of letting free Jesus or a criminal named Barabbas. But to the question as to whom he should set free, the crowed roared out: "Away with this one, let Barabbas go free!" Pilate then called out: "What shall I do with Jesus, who is meant to be the Christ, the King of the Jews?" The crowd chanted: "Crucify him! Crucify him!" Pilate then set Barabbas free and commanded Jesus to be scourged. It was about quarter-past eight that morning that the scourging of Jesus Christ began, which took place at the whipping pillar on the forum, the great square north of Pilate's palace. It was carried through with terrible brutality, lasting some three quarters of an hour. As the scourging was building up to a climax, around a quarter to nine, Mars (10° Gemini) was rising across the eastern horizon. Thus the red planet was the cosmic witness to this savage and inhuman act.

Immediately after the scourging Jesus was led to the inner court of the guardhouse, above the prison, located not far from the whipping pillar on the forum. Here he was roughly mistreated, beaten and subjected to constant mockery. His few remaining garments were torn off and an old, ripped, bright red soldier's cloak was wrapped around him. To the jeering call of "Hail, king of the Jews," he was crowned with a heavy crown of thorns. It was about quarter-past nine that morning, and Jupiter was rising across the horizon to the East of Jerusalem—the cosmic witness of the crowning with thorns.

KING AMMON: So, just as Mars bore witness to the scourging, the rising of Jupiter coincided with the crowning with thorns?

HERMES: Yes, indeed, King Ammon, and further, the rising of Saturn took place towards the culmination of the next stage of the Passion, the carrying of the cross. This—the fourth stage of the Passion—began shortly after ten o'clock that morning. At ten, Pilate, swayed by the shouting of the crowd of Jews in front of his palace, sentenced Jesus to be nailed to the cross, and commanded that the cross be brought, which had been constructed during the preceding hours especially for his crucifixion. Jesus was forced to carry this heavy cross through the streets of Jerusalem, accompanied by a procession of guards, soldiers and Pharisees. After Jesus fell to the ground three times under the weight of the cross, Simon of Cyrene was compelled to help him carry the cross. But, nevertheless, Jesus fell to the ground again twice before reaching Mt. Calvary. And on the way up Mt. Calvary he fell a sixth time, and then again a seventh time shortly before reaching the summit.

THE STAGES OF THE PASSION

It was while Jesus was carrying the cross up Mt. Calvary that Saturn (18½° Cancer) rose to the East of Jerusalem, to bear witness to this scene. The rising of Saturn took place at about half-past eleven, and Jesus reached the summit at about quarter-to twelve. Thus Saturn was the cosmic witness to the culmination of the carrying of the cross, the fourth stage of the Passion.

KING AMMON: O Hermes, there seems to be a deep cosmic correspondence between the rising of the planets and the stages of the Passion.

HERMES: Truly, King Ammon, this relates to a profound cosmic mystery. For, if we take into consideration only the seven traditional planets, the rising of these seven planets took place in the order of the planets: Moon, Venus, Mercury, Sun, Mars, Jupiter and Saturn; and the rising of each bore witness to a significant moment along the stages of the Passion.

The Moon, having just entered Libra that afternoon, rose about quarter-past five, a little before sunset on the evening of the Last Supper. The Moon then rose ever higher in the East—shining brightly that night, being almost full—and reached culmination at the time of Judas' kiss at the entrance to the Garden of Gethsemane. Thus the ascending Moon, climbing the vault of heaven, bore witness that evening to the Last Supper and the washing of the feet, designated as the first stage of the Passion. But the Passion—the path of suffering of the Lord—actually began with Judas' betrayal, which was sealed with his kiss. So we see that in a special way the Moon was the cosmic witness to the commencement of the Passion.

On the next morning, while still dark, there then took place the rising of Venus, coinciding with the first crowing of the cock at Peter's denial. At the same time John was moved to go and seek out the Blessed Virgin Mary. This was followed shortly after by the rising of Mercury, coinciding with the cock crowing for the second time. At this, Peter, having denied him three times, became aware of his cowardly repudiation of the Lord, and was smitten with pangs of conscience. At the same time, however, the rising of Mercury bore witness to the tender love and compassion of the Blessed Virgin, who came with John to Caiaphas' courthouse in order to be near to her beloved son in his hour of tribulation.

At the rising of the Sun, which followed about one hour later, there took place on the one hand the suicide of Judas, and on the other hand the deliverance of Jesus, condemned—having been judged worthy of death by Caiaphas and the Jews—into the hands of Pontius Pilate. Sunrise thus marked the culmination of the judgment of the Son of man, which began when he was delivered up by the kiss of Judas. This judgment, first at the hands of Annas and then under Caiaphas, was sealed at the break of that day when the Sun began its course of ascent across Jerusalem. In a sense, the first stage of the Passion could be designated as that of judgment of the Son of man, from which the subsequent stages—the scourging, the crowning with thorns, the carrying of the cross, the crucifixion—followed. The judgment began with Judas' kiss at the entrance to the Garden of Gethsemane and ended at sunrise in the courtroom of Caiaphas, at which time Judas committed suicide.

The judgment was then concluded, for neither Herod Antipas nor Pontius Pilate judged Jesus Christ to be guilty.

THE STAGES OF THE PASSION

In fact, Pilate washed his hands and called out to the Jews: "I am innocent of the blood of this just man." It was the crowd of Jews, stirred up at the instigation of Annas and Caiaphas, who called out: "His blood be upon us and our children!" Then it was those who had passed judgment at sunrise that morning who swayed Pilate to pronounce the sentencing of Jesus to death by crucifixion.

Designating this judgment as the first stage of the Passion, the cosmic witness to the judgment of the Jewish people upon the Son of man was the Sun, which rose in the East at the time of the judgment. Similarly, Mars was the cosmic witness to the scourging, Jupiter to the crowning with thorns, and Saturn to the carrying of the cross—these being the second, third and fourth stages of the Passion, respectively. What took place beyond these first four stages belongs to still higher cosmic realms, beyond the planetary spheres extending up to Saturn.

KING AMMON: Thank you for today's discourse, O thrice-greatest one. We look forward to contemplating the higher cosmic mysteries at the next discourse.

CLOSING INVOCATION

A Discourse of Hermes to Tat

The Mystery of Golgotha

OPENING INVOCATION

TAT: Today, O father, will you speak to us concerning the culmination of the Lord's Passion on Golgotha?

HERMES: Indeed, my son, if this be your wish. Here we shall need all our strength of love and devotion, to approach the Mystery of Golgotha. For, what took place on Golgotha was a deed of divine love. To draw close to this is possible only through human love raised up in devotion to the Divine, or through the grace of the Divine coming to meet the human.

The Mystery of Golgotha is comprised, essentially, in the last three stages of the Passion—the stages of crucifixion, entombment and resurrection. In the preceding discourse we considered the stages leading up to the crucifixion, culminating in the carrying of the cross up Mt. Calvary. We saw that the rising of the Sun at the break of day coincided with the conclusion of the judgment passed by the Jewish people on the Son of man. Then there followed on from this judgment the scourging at the time of the rising of Mars, the crowning with thorns at the rising of Jupiter, and the carrying of the cross up Mt. Calvary at the rising of Saturn. What took place then at the summit of the hill, at the place called Golgotha?

First Jesus was nailed to the cross, which signified the most terrible suffering for him. This took place between a quarter-past and half-past twelve. As the cross was raised up, at about half-past twelve, trumpet calls sounded forth from the temple, announcing the commencement of the slaying of the lambs for the Passover festival. In a higher sense it was the beginning of the slaying of the Lamb of God, who sacrificed his life for humankind through his death on the cross. The constellation of Leo (1° Leo) was just beginning to rise in the East as the cross was raised up. This was a heavenly sign of the courage and unfathomable love of Christ, the Lion of Judah, which now began to ray forth from him who hung on the cross. For, with the crucifixion it was the cosmic realm of the zodiac, beyond the sphere of Saturn, which now bore witness. Leo is the zodiacal sign from which the heart is cosmically fashioned, when the human being is on the path of descent into incarnation into a physical body. And now, with the crucifixion, there began a pouring out of cosmic heart forces, and of sublime love. This pouring out of divine love, to which the constellation of Leo bore witness, continued during the time of the rising of Leo.

During the crucifixion Jesus Christ spoke the words or sayings from the cross, referred to in an earlier discourse in connection with the Christian-hermetic meditation of the Sanctification of the Full Moon. These words were his last to humankind while indwelling his physical body. Hence their profound significance for meditation and contemplation.

Hanging there on the holy cross, the crucified Jesus Christ signified the new Tree of Life, raised up for the first time on Earth since the expulsion of humanity from paradise. The blood flowed from his wounds for the regeneration of the Earth and Humankind, for the restoration of a new paradise, the Heavenly Jerusalem—in place of the earthly city of Jerusalem—away from which, facing northwest, his gaze was now directed. Thus he could say to the repentant criminal crucified to his right: "Today you will be with me in paradise." For, on that Good Friday the new paradise began, a new afterlife for all who unite themselves with Christ. And the repentant criminal was the first human being to die in proximity to Christ, to be taken up by Christ, since the New Era denoted by the Mystery of Golgotha began.

To the left of Jesus, the Sun, which stood high in the heavens, had begun to be covered by a reddish cloud formation from about noon onwards. Now it began visibly to darken. This was not an eclipse of the Sun, however, for the Full Moon was on the opposite side of the Earth, and a solar eclipse can only take place around New Moon, when the Moon passes between the Sun and the Earth. The darkening of the Sun was accompanied not only by clouds and Mists, but also by other mysterious signs in the whole world of nature. Around half-past one the heavens became quite dark. Terrified cattle began bellowing, and swarms of birds flew around unusually close to the ground. The darkness had grown to such an extent that it seemed to be night. The jeering, mocking taunts of the Pharisees faded away, and the whole atmosphere around the cross became quite still. This was the situation: God had set up his cross in the wilderness of the world, as the seed of redemption—a sign for all posterity. And it was this situation to which the planet Uranus (20° Leo) bore witness as it rose to the East of Jerusalem at about two o'clock that afternoon.

TAT: What did this signify, O father?

HERMES: My son, this was a cosmic sign of a profound spiritual event connected with Lucifer. For it was through Lucifer that the Fall had taken place. And with the crucifixion Lucifer beheld the Son of God on the cross bearing the consequences of the Fall for humankind and the Earth. He saw the Son of God being crucified on account of that which he, Lucifer, had instigated at the Fall. Lucifer thus beheld the Son of God suffering in his place, for—from the standpoint of cosmic justice—Lucifer should have been on the cross. Beholding this divine act of the innocent Son of God suffering on account of that which he, Lucifer, was guilty, he underwent a profound conversion. This conversion can be conceived of as the beginning of the redemption of Lucifer. For Lucifer at the crucifixion experienced the true nature of humility, as he witnessed the way in which Christ on the cross bore all the injustice directed against him. This experience of humility, sown as a seed within Lucifer, underlies Lucifer's conversion and, ultimately, will surely lead to the complete redemption of this proud being. And the rising of the planet Uranus, which bears a special relationship to the being of Lucifer, was the cosmic sign of the sowing of the seed of his redemption through the beholding of the crucifixion.

TAT: And now, O father, how was it with the further stages of the Mystery of Golgotha?

HERMES: My son, after ascending through the planetary spheres in connection with the earlier stages of the Passion—the scourging (Mars), the crowning with thorns (Jupiter), and the carrying of the cross up Mt. Calvary (Saturn)—having reached Golgotha the cosmic significance of the crucifixion extended beyond the planetary spheres to the realm of the zodiac. And, as the crucifixion began, with the raising up of the cross, it was the sign of Leo which began to ascend across the eastern horizon. The crucifixion on Golgotha took place under the cosmic aspect of Leo rising, and the rising of Leo continued until shortly before three o'clock that afternoon. The sign of Virgo began to ascend, and with this the darkness started to recede. A new phase in the Mystery of Golgotha commenced, connected with the very foundations of existence. The Sun was still shrouded with red mist, but the Sun's rays began to break through here and there. And now Jesus Christ spoke his last words from the cross. He bowed down his head and gave up his spirit. At this moment, it was just after three o'clock, an earthquake rent a gaping hole in the ground between Jesus' cross and that of the criminal crucified to his left. It was fulfilled! And this was God's sign of the fulfillment of Christ's ministry for humanity and the sign of the start of his deed of love for the Earth.

The soul—the Spirit Being—of the Son of man departed from his body and descended into the womb of the Earth. Thus began the next stage of the Passion—the descent into hell, also designated as the entombment—which followed on from the crucifixion. This new stage of the Passion, the sixth, commenced shortly after the zodiacal sign of Virgo began its ascent in the East.

THE MYSTERY OF GOLGOTHA

TAT: What does this signify, O father?

HERMES: Now we approach one of the deepest aspects of the Mystery of Golgotha, my son. For, with the descent into hell, Christ descended to the Mother, to the heart of Mother Earth. This is the deeper significance of this sixth stage of the Passion. And it was under the sign of the Virgin that this descent commenced. It was a fulfillment of the Messiah's words to the Pharisees concerning the sign of the prophet Jonah: "For as Jonas was three days and three nights in the belly of the whale, so will the Son of man be three days and three nights in the heart of the Earth."

You see, my son, Christ was not only the Son of the Father, he was also the Son of the Mother. He came from the Kingdom of the Father and bore testimony, during the 3½ years of his ministry, to the Father. But his ministry was concluded with his last words from the cross. Then began his descent to the Mother, to bring about a reunification. Through the Son, Christ, the Father was reunited again with the Mother, after they had become separated through the Fall. For the Fall signified not only the falling away of humankind from the Divine, but also the Fall of nature, the Mother, as well. In paradise the Kingdom of the Father interpenetrated that of Mother Nature—this was the Garden of Eden, in which humankind dwelt. But with the Fall of humankind, nature fell too. The Mother descended into the darkness of the underworld, becoming separated from the Kingdom of Light of the Father. This was nature's tragedy, and it was to the heart of Mother Nature, towards the center of the Earth that Christ now descended. Having brought the seed of redemption to humankind during the 3½ years of his ministry, now he turned to the Mother, to the kingdom of nature, to bring redemption also here, to implant his spirit as a seed within the womb of the Earth. It was towards this task that Christ turned, as the sign of Virgo began to rise in the East on the afternoon of Good Friday. For, Virgo is connected with the womb, with the sowing of the seed of new impulses within the womb of creation.

TAT: This is indeed a profound mystery, O father, one which it is scarcely possible to comprehend.

HERMES: My son, through deep and concentrated meditation, carried out over a period of time, it is possible to begin to penetrate this profound mystery. The key is to consider the descent into hell in relation to the ascent into heaven, the ascension. After descending into the bowels of the Earth, to the Mother, there began the ascent to the Father. Just as the sixth stage of the Passion is bound up with the Mother, so the seventh stage, the resurrection, is connected with the Father. And this seventh stage began with Christ's ascent, his return from the heart of the Earth. This was the miracle effected by the Father: the raising up of the Son. And so the miracle of the resurrection took place at the break of day on Easter Sunday morning—the miracle of the birth of the Risen One from the womb of the Earth. But the resurrection on Easter Sunday morning was only the conclusion of the first stage of ascent to the Father. This is indicated in Christ's words to Mary Magdalena that morning: "Do not touch me, for I have not yet ascended to the Father; but go to my brethren and say to them, I am ascending to my Father and your Father, to my God and your God."

THE MYSTERY OF GOLGOTHA

TAT: The further ascent, O father, then took place at the ascension?

HERMES: Yes, my son. From the resurrection on Easter Sunday morning to the ascension forty days later, the Risen One remained—in his resurrection body—in the company of the apostles and disciples. It was only on Ascension Day that he began to withdraw from the Earth, beginning his path of ascent through the planetary spheres back towards the Kingdom of the Father. Thus, on Ascension Day, the cosmic ascent to the Father began with the Risen One withdrawing from the earthly realm first into the Moon sphere, which is the realm of the Angels, and then subsequently into the higher planetary spheres.

However, in a sense this ascension began already during the night from Easter Saturday to Easter Sunday, after the completion of the descent into hell. From this standpoint, the last three stages of the Passion are: crucifixion, descent into hell, and ascent to heaven—each following consecutively one after the other. We have, therefore, the crucifixion of the Son as the Lamb of God, the true Passover lamb, followed by the descent of the Son to the Mother, in turn followed by the ascent of the Son to the Father. Descent to the Mother and ascent to the Father are the essence—looked at from a cosmic standpoint—of the last two stages of the Passion, comprising the heart of the Mystery of Golgotha. The significance of these two stages goes beyond even the zodiacal sphere, to the very foundations of existence provided by the Mother in the depths and the Father in the heights of heaven.

The path taken by the Son of man shows the way for each human being, *to cosmic sonship*—to become a son both of the Father and of the Mother of existence. This entails ascent and descent—to have the courage to descend into hell to find the Mother, the reward being the ascent, the raising up by the Father, towards the kingdom of heaven.

Jesus Christ has shown us the way—both the path of descent and that of ascent. He is the Tree of Life. And just as every tree strives on the one hand up towards the light and on the other hand, with its roots, down towards the hidden depths, so it is with the Tree of Life, Jesus Christ. The roots of this Tree extend down to the Mother, to the heart of the Earth, and the trunk and branches of this Tree reach up to the Kingdom of Light of the Father. We tend to forget the roots of trees, as they are concealed beneath the Earth, but without them, no tree could live. In the same way, we tend to overlook Christ's descent into the underworld, and focus solely upon his resurrection and cosmic ascension.

TAT: But, nevertheless, O father, it is true to say that the resurrection and ascension are events of overwhelming significance.

HERMES: Yes, my son. For, the moment of resurrection was that of the birth of the Risen One. It took place shortly before six o'clock on the morning of Easter Sunday. At this moment, then, the heavenly configuration was the *birth horoscope,* so to speak, of the Risen One. The Sun was rising across the eastern horizon and was located in the middle of Aries, at $15\frac{1}{2}°$ Aries. The Ascendant being a little above the Sun, as it was dawn, was also in the star-sign of Aries. This location of the Sun and Ascendant in the middle of Aries in the horoscope of the Risen One indicates him as the Lamb of God—the Lamb being symbolized by the Ram (Aries). Interestingly, at the start of the cosmic ascension forty days later, at midday on Thursday, May 14, A.D. 33, the Moon was situated at 15° Aries, at exactly the location where the Sun had been at the moment of the resurrection.

The positions of the planets at the resurrection were similar to those on Good Friday, as less than two days had elapsed. Only the position of the Moon was significantly different, having moved from 12° Libra at the climax of the crucifixion to $1\frac{1}{2}°$ Scorpio at the moment of resurrection. This position of the Moon entering Scorpio at the resurrection points to the beginning of the transformation of the Scorpion, through the Christ Impulse, to become the Dove of the Holy Spirit. For, when the forces of Scorpio are taken hold of by the human being and raised up, transformed in the light of Christ, they become forces of the Holy Spirit, symbolized by the Dove. This is a profound, holy mystery.

TAT: Indeed, O father, our hearts are longing for knowledge of these cosmic mysteries.

CLOSING INVOCATION

A Discourse of Hermes to King Ammon

The Forty Days After the Mystery of Golgotha

OPENING INVOCATION

KING AMMON: Hermes, the Mystery of Golgotha signified the beginning of a New Era. What took place during the first days of this New Era?

HERMES: King Ammon, as the birth of the Risen One took place at the resurrection, and as the Risen One signifies the ideal and evolutionary aim for all human beings, the planetary configuration for the moment of the resurrection is of eternal significance. In Christian hermetic astrology it is referred to as the Horoscope of Eternity. And just as the days following birth are astrologically significant, so the days following the birth of the Risen One are of profound significance in a cosmic sense. In the case of the Risen One, it was a period of forty days. During these forty days the Risen One manifested himself to the apostles and disciples on a number of occasions. These forty days from the resurrection to the ascension therefore deserve special consideration, for it is a matter here of the mysteries of Christ's body: that is, his resurrection body, this being his transformed physical body.

In fact, we may distinguish between four phases of Christ's activity on Earth, each phase being connected with one of four aspects of the Christ Mystery. What, then, are these four phases?

Just as the moment of the resurrection signified the birth of the Risen One, the moment of the baptism was, analogously, Christ's conception. From the time of the baptism onwards, up until the moment of his death on the cross, Christ was active on Earth as a teacher and healer. Even his last words from the cross were words of teaching communicating profound mysteries. But this phase—from the baptism to the crucifixion—had two sides to it: a *day side* and a *night side*.

Something of the "day side" is reported to us in the four Gospels. But what actually is revealed to us here?

At the moment of a person's death, his body of life forces (etheric body) separates from the physical body, leaving the latter as a corpse. All the experiences of an individual during the days from birth until death are inscribed into the etheric body, and now, indwelling the etheric body, the human being in the period immediately following death beholds a panorama of these daily life experiences. This panorama or *flashback* of all the experiences undergone during life is often reported by people on the brink of death or who have died and returned to life. But how was this in the case of Jesus Christ?

From the birth of Jesus to the Mystery of Golgotha was a period of $33\frac{1}{3}$ years, and all the experiences undergone during the days lived through during these $33\frac{1}{3}$ years were inscribed into his etheric body. Of special significance were the last $3\frac{1}{2}$ years of these $33\frac{1}{3}$ years, as the time of Christ's activity—his ministry. At the Mystery of

Golgotha, with the release of the etheric body, something remarkable took place. For, Jesus Christ did not then behold the panorama of his life, as is normally the case. Instead, he offered up his etheric body to his community of disciples and followers, as a source from which they could draw strength and support. And it was especially four disciples who came into a deeper relationship with this etheric body: Matthew, Mark, Luke and John. What they wrote down as the four Gospels was drawn from the etheric body of Jesus Christ.

This etheric body, with its rhythm of $33\frac{1}{3}$ years which has been active since the Mystery of Golgotha, is the source of the Eternal Gospel, parts of which were revealed to Matthew, Mark, Luke and John. Apart from these four, others, later in history, came into contact with this etheric body. For example, St. Augustine, whose teaching was imbued with a remarkable power. What was the source of the spiritual strength of Augustine's teaching? It arose through Augustine's deep inner relationship with the etheric body of Jesus Christ.

Later still, the blessed seer was able, through her profound connection with Christ's etheric body, to reveal far more of the Eternal Gospel than had been possible for the four evangelists. And the initiate, too, communicated many more of the hidden mysteries of the Eternal Gospel, which he referred to as the *Fifth Gospel.*

The etheric body of Jesus Christ will remain preserved as a source of living inspiration and contact with the Christ Impulse—as the source of the Eternal Gospel, containing all the *day experiences* undergone during the $33\frac{1}{3}$ years. But how is it with regard to the *night experiences*, this being the other side of Christ's life?

Whereas the human beings's *day experiences* are inscribed into the etheric body, the *night experiences* are undergone in the astral body. For, every night during sleep the human self, indwelling the astral body, separates from the physical and etheric bodies. In this sense sleep is the *brother* of death, the difference being that at death the etheric body together with the astral body and self separates from the physical body, leaving the latter behind as a corpse; whereas at the moment of falling asleep the etheric body remains united with the physical body and only the astral body and self separate themselves off. But what takes place during the period between falling asleep and waking?

The human being, indwelling the astral body, then experiences each night the moral consequences of thoughts, words and deeds from the preceding day. If during the day a man had lost his temper and said unkind words to someone, at night he experiences the effect of his unkind words—in such a way that he himself undergoes the suffering and discomfort inflicted upon the other person. These *night experiences* are undergone in the reverse order of the *day experiences*. Essentially the former are a kind of *moral review*, in the light of conscience, and in reverse order, of the latter. Each night a cosmic-spiritual judgment of the *day experiences* takes place.

KING AMMON: And in the case of Jesus Christ? What was the content of his *night experiences?*

HERMES: Jesus Christ, as the spiritual light, the DIVINE CONSCIENCE of the world, did not undergo judgment of his daily thoughts, words and deeds. Rather, he was, and is, the source of judgment. His nightly experiences, indwelling his astral body, entailed divine judgment.

KING AMMON: Can you explain this further, O Hermes?

HERMES: Yes, King Ammon; here again it is a help to consider the human being's inner experiences. As referred to already, at the moment of death of the human, the self, astral body and etheric body separate from the physical body. Initially, for a period of a few days, the human being experiences the panorama of the *day experiences,* as inscribed into the etheric body. After this period, indwelling the etheric body, the self and astral body separate from the etheric body. The human being then indwells the astral body, and here a new experience sets in, known in esotericism as *kamaloca.* This experience of kamaloca constitutes the reliving, within the astral body, of the entire sequence of *night experiences.* This signifies a living through, in reverse order, of the moral consequences of all the thoughts, words and deeds of the entire incarnation, this being the *night* side of the *day* experiences from birth to death. Kamaloca could be described as the divine judgment of the earthly incarnation, this being the content of the astral body.

In the case of Christ, however, the content of his astral body was, and is, divine judgment of the world and humankind. And after his death he did not live through this, as he offered up his astral body, bestowing it upon the world, as the eternal divine judgment. The content of Christ's astral body is the Eternal Apocalypse, a fragment of which was revealed to St. John and was recorded by him as the Apocalypse, or Book of Revelation. And just as access to the Eternal Gospel is gained through entering into contact with Christ's etheric body, access to the Eternal Apocalypse is acquired by way of coming into connection with Christ's astral body.

KING AMMON: How may this be attained, O Hermes?

HERMES: Essentially it is a question of communion, of two different kinds of communion with Christ, one with his etheric body, leading to contemplation of the Eternal Gospel, and one with his astral body, leading to revelation of the Eternal Apocalypse. Meditative reading of the four Gospels is a good preparation for the first kind of communion. Similarly, meditative reading of the Apocalypse of St. John helps to prepare the way for the second kind of communion.

KING AMMON: Are these two kinds of communion related to the communion of bread and wine?

HERMES: There are, in fact, several different kinds of communion with Christ, of which four may be considered primary. These are: communion with his etheric body; communion with his astral body; communion with his Self, his Spirit; and communion with his physical body, that is, his resurrection body. The latter two come to expression in the communion of wine and bread. For wine is the substance that—in its nature—relates to the self, and bread to the physical body. Wine is related to the *fire* principle of the self, and bread to the *earth* principle of the physical body. In between the *fire* principle of the self and the *earth* principle of the physical body are the *air* and the *water* principles of the astral and etheric bodies.

Just as the two kinds of communion we have discussed so far—the communion with Christ's etheric body (Eternal Gospel) and with his astral body (Eternal Apocalypse)—

have their source in the *day* and *night* experiences of the biography of Jesus Christ, so do the other two kinds of communion also have their source in the life of Jesus Christ. The source of the communion with the Self of Jesus Christ is to be found in the descent into hell, that is, the descent to the Mother. This is the archetype of the wine communion indicated by Jesus Christ's words: "I am the true vine." The true vine extends down, with its roots, to the Kingdom of the Mother, and it was the deed of the Self of Christ, after the crucifixion, to descend down to the Mother.

It was this archetype, also, which prevailed in the Grail mysteries, where Parsival, who became king of the Grail, sought his mother. Something of the mystery of Christ's descent to the Mother in the underworld was known of in the Grail mysteries. And the training of the knights of the Grail, to fearlessly combat evil, echoed the archetype of Christ's descent into hell. It was thus the wine communion—communion with the Self, the Spirit of Christ—which formed the central content of the Grail mysteries. The central meaning of the Grail mysteries can therefore be expressed in the words of St. Paul: "Not I, but Christ in me."

KING AMMON: And what of the communion with Christ's resurrection body?

HERMES: This, King Ammon, has its source in the forty days from the resurrection to the ascension. This is the deeper meaning of this period of Christ's activity. And it is to this that we shall now turn our attention. In these forty days we find the archetype of bread communion, understood as communion with Christ's physical body, his resurrection body. This came to expression in the experience of the two disciples, Luke and Cleophas, who traveled from Jerusalem to Emmaus on the day after the resurrection. While Luke and Cleophas went on their way, discussing all that had taken place during the preceding days, they were joined by a third person, who accompanied them to Emmaus. This third person interpreted to them the words of Moses and the prophets concerning Christ. It was towards evening on Easter Monday—April 6, A.D. 33—when they arrived at Emmaus, and the three went together to a guest house, where they were served with food. As the third person took the bread, blessed it and broke it into small pieces, Luke and Cleophas recognized him to be the Lord. Almost beside themselves with joy, Luke and Cleophas each received a small piece of bread placed directly into their mouths by the hand of the Risen One, as in receiving the Holy Sacrament. Then Jesus Christ disappeared from before them. The deeper significance of this receiving of the bread directly from the hand of the Risen One was the communion with his resurrection body. And the words of Jesus Christ, "I am the bread of life," summarize this experience of the communion with the bread, the communion with him in his resurrection body.

KING AMMON: Was there a special cosmic configuration at this event at Emmaus?

HERMES: As referred to in the last discourse, at the resurrection at dawn on Easter Sunday morning, the Moon had just entered Scorpio ($1\frac{1}{2}°$ Scorpio). That evening the apostles, without Thomas, were gathered together at the

Coenaculum, together with the holy women and a number of disciples. There they ate a meal together, at the end of which Peter broke bread, blessed it, and let it circulate together with a large cup of wine, so that all ate of the bread and drank of the wine. Although Peter blessed the bread, this was not a sacrament, but an agape, a love-feast. Peter said that it was their wish all to be one, as the bread they were eating and the wine they were drinking. Afterwards they stood and sang Psalms. At the time of this love-feast (agape), the Moon had progressed further through Scorpio and was placed at about 9° Scorpio. By late afternoon the next day, it had progressed further still, and at the bread communion of Luke and Cleophas in Emmaus it was at about 20° Scorpio.

Immediately following this appearance of the Risen One in Emmaus, Luke and Cleophas hurried back to Jerusalem. They went to the Coenaculum where the ten apostles (without Thomas) and many disciples, and the Blessed Virgin Mary, Mary Cleophas and Mary Magdalena were joined together in prayer in the hall of the Last Supper. Interrupting the prayer, Luke and Cleophas joyfully related their experience in Emmaus. Scarcely had the praying resumed, when Jesus Christ entered through closed doors, passed through their midst, and stood under the lamp. After showing them his wounds, Jesus asked for food. Peter brought him a piece of fish and some honey, which the Lord blessed. Then he ate, and gave of this food to some of those standing around him. Afterwards he taught. While he did so, light flowed from his mouth and from his wounds, streaming into them. The apostles received the power to forgive sins, to baptize, to heal, and to lay on hands. Jesus also instructed them concerning the

Holy Sacrament and its veneration, saying that this should take place following the close of Sabbath. After having taught, Jesus disappeared before their eyes. The Moon was now at about 22° Scorpio.

Thus we see that the first appearances of the Risen One after his resurrection—to Mary Magdalena in the Garden of the Holy Sepulcher, to Luke and Cleophas in Emmaus, and to the ten apostles and the others in the hall of the Last Supper—all took place as the Moon was traversing Scorpio. Since the Scorpion symbolizes death, the sting of death, the significance of these first appearances points to the transformation and overcoming of death through resurrection. In the words of St. Paul: "O death, where is thy sting!" Cosmically expressed, it indicates the beginning of the metamorphosis—through the Christ Impulse—from the Scorpion to the Dove.

KING AMMON: But why, O Hermes, should the Moon be of such significance with regard to the manifestations of the Risen One during the time after the resurrection?

HERMES: From the resurrection to the ascension, although Jesus Christ manifested himself on Earth on numerous occasions, he was no longer an *earthly citizen* but a *citizen of the cosmos*. And as the Moon is the cosmic body that stands closest to the Earth, it was especially the movements of the Moon with which the activity of Jesus Christ harmonized. During these forty days the Moon passed almost 1½ times around the zodiac. At the resurrection it started out at the beginning of Scorpio, and at the ascension—midday on May 14, A.D. 33—it was in the middle of Aries. If it had progressed through Aries to the beginning of Taurus, it would have completed exactly 1½ orbits. But the final position of the Moon at 15° Aries, at the ascension, was the goal towards which the activity of the Risen One was directed—15° Aries being the Sun's position in the zodiac at the resurrection. As the Moon reached this point in the middle of Aries and the ascension began, the Risen One departed from the earthly sphere, that of humankind, into the Moon sphere, that of the Angels. The whole period of forty days was a time during which Jesus Christ indwelt the Earth's aura—between the Earth and the Moon sphere—before ascending into the Moon sphere at the ascension. From this, the significance of the Moon during the forty days is clearly evident.

The indwelling of the Earth's aura during the forty days after the resurrection corresponds to the human being's indwelling of the etheric body for the first few days after death, and the ascension into the Moon sphere, by analogy, corresponds to the subsequent commencement of kamaloca—the indwelling of the astral body—in the human being's afterlife. However, in the case of Jesus Christ the situation was completely different, because of his having offered up his etheric and astral bodies. The forty days was a time in which Christ indwelt his resurrection body—his transformed physical body—offering this, too, to his disciples and followers: this being the archetype of *bread communion.*

KING AMMON: O thrice greatest one, can you say more concerning further appearances of the Risen One during the forty days?

THE FORTY DAYS AFTER GOLGOTHA

HERMES: Yes, King Ammon. Let us recall that on the Monday evening after Easter Sunday, when Jesus Christ appeared to the apostles, Thomas was not present, having gone to a little place in Samaria. At Jesus' bidding, after this appearance, the ten apostles also went to Samaria, to the town of Thanath-Silo. There they preached the resurrection and healed the sick. Thomas came to Thanath-Silo, and the ten told him of Jesus' appearance to them, but Thomas replied that he would believe it only if he could touch the Lord's wounds.

On Friday, April 10, A.D. 33, before daybreak the apostles left Thanath-Silo and returned to Jerusalem for the Sabbath, which they celebrated together at the Coenaculum. After the close of the Sabbath on Saturday evening, April 11, the apostles took a meal, a love-feast (agape), for the second time. Afterwards they stood and sang Psalms together, and knelt and prayed. During a brief pause, the Risen One entered, resplendent with light. He greeted them with the words: "Peace be with you!" Thomas drew back, frightened at the sight of the Lord. Yet Jesus took hold of Thomas' hands and laid them in his wounds, at which Thomas exclaimed: "My Lord and God!" Then the Lord requested something to eat, as he had done at the previous appearance in the hall of the Last Supper. Again he was given some fish, which he blessed and from which he ate and gave to the others. There then followed a special blessing of Peter. Peter knelt before the Lord, who placed a morsel of food in his mouth, at which Peter received some special power. Jesus also breathed on Peter, pouring strength into his ears and mouth. Then the Lord laid his hands on Peter and invested him with power over the others. After this a special mantle, which John was holding on his arm, and which had been prepared beforehand, was placed upon Peter. Jesus said that all the strength and power which he had imparted to him would remain within him by virtue of the mantle, which he should wear whenever he wanted to make use of this power. Jesus also spoke of the coming of the Holy Spirit, and of a great baptism in connection with this event. Peter then addressed all, speaking with a new force, by virtue of that which the Lord had imparted to him. During this discourse of Peter's, the Risen One disappeared from the room, having said beforehand to Peter that they should go to Tiberius and fish upon the Sea of Galilee.

KING AMMON: Was there a special heavenly configuration at the time of this appearance of Jesus Christ to the eleven apostles?

HERMES: Indeed, King Ammon! That evening the Moon was at the tail end of the Goat (29° Capricorn) in conjunction with Neptune (3½° Aquarius). The Moon entered Aquarius shortly before midnight, and was in the same part of the zodiac as the hermetic conjunction between Mercury (3° Aquarius) and Neptune (1½° Aquarius). At the same time, Mercury was hermetically square to Venus (5° Scorpio). The hermetic conjunction between Mercury and Neptune was particularly striking, as at the ascension thirty-three days later, Mercury and Neptune were hermetically exactly in opposition to one another. The hermetic alignment of the Sun, Mercury and Neptune was thus prominent two times during the forty days, the alignment on the evening of the second love-feast (agape) being emphasized by the conjunction with the Moon.

KING AMMON: And following on from the second agape, O Hermes, what took place then?

HERMES: Following the instructions of the Lord, the apostles and disciples traveled northward from Jerusalem in the direction of the Sea of Galilee, in separate groups. Peter went with the apostles Thomas, James and John, accompanied by the disciples Nathanael, John Mark and Silas, to Tiberius, arriving there on Tuesday, April 14, A.D. 33. Taking a boat from a fishery there, they set out to fish, traveling northeast across the Sea of Galilee throughout the night. Towards dawn they arrived at the northeastern shore, but, despite having repeatedly cast the net, they had not caught any fish. As they were tired, they wanted to cast anchor. Just then a man appeared on the shore and called to them: "Children, have you any fish?" They answered: "No!" He called out that they should cast the net into the water again. They did so, and caught a miraculous haul of 153 fish. John then recognized the man to be Jesus, and cried out: "It is the Lord!" When the apostles and disciples got out on land, they saw a fire burning, with a fish cooking, and also bread and honey cakes were there. The Risen One said that they should come and eat, and together they ate of the cooked fish, the bread, and the honey cakes. After the meal they walked up and down together along the shore. As they walked, Jesus asked Peter three times whether he loved him, and each time as Peter answered affirmatively, Jesus bid him: "Feed my sheep!" This indicates the task of Peter as the spiritual leader of the Church of Peter to ensure that the sacraments—above all Holy Communion—continue to be celebrated for all time. And then Jesus spoke with John. However, Peter asked the Lord, indicating John:

"And what will become of him?" To which the Risen One replied: "If it is my will that he remain until I come, what is that to you?" In these words Jesus Christ indicated the task of the Church of John: to wait until the second coming. Implicit here is that the real task of the Church of John begins only with the second coming.

KING AMMON: O Hermes, at this appearance of Jesus Christ was there again a significant heavenly configuration?

HERMES: At this manifestation of the Risen One, at dawn on Wednesday, April 15, A.D. 33, the Sun was in the middle of the third decan of Aries (25° Aries), having progressed there from the middle of Aries at the resurrection. Moreover, the Sun—hermetically—was square to Saturn (25½° Cancer). The Moon was in the middle of Pisces (17° Pisces), visible as a thin waning crescent above the eastern horizon in the morning twilight, approaching conjunction with Venus (23½° Pisces). The actual conjunction took place later that day. But at dawn there was a striking planetary configuration involving the Moon. For the Moon was at right angles ("square") to Mars (17° Gemini) and Jupiter (19° Gemini), which were drawing into conjunction in the Twins. At the same time, Mars was in exact opposition to Pluto (17° Sagittarius), and therefore the Moon was also square to Pluto.

Here something very interesting is indicated from an astrological point of view. For, often the square aspect is thought of as something ominous. However, looked at in relation to the Christ Impulse—as in the example of this manifestation at the Sea of Galilee—it can be seen to be, at least potentially, something of the highest good. At this appearance of the Risen One there took place an intimate communion, in the eating together of the fish, bread and honey cakes, through which the disciples and apostles, especially Peter, were endowed with new strength. And at the same time Christ communicated to the two leading apostles—the head (Peter) and the heart (John) of his church—something concerning their respective tasks. So this *ominous configuration* of Mars conjunct Jupiter in opposition to Pluto and square the Moon was actually an occasion of supreme good.

KING AMMON: Is it true, therefore, to say, O Hermes, that all that which is potentially negative may, through the Christ Impulse, be turned to something good?

HERMES: Indeed, King Ammon! This becomes clear if we look at the next appearance of the Risen One to the apostles and disciples. After conversing on the shore of the Sea of Galilee with Peter and John, the Lord disappeared before their eyes. Peter, John and the five others gathered up the fish from their miraculous haul, loaded them into their boat, and set sail back to Tiberius, arriving there that afternoon. After a meal they traveled southward to Thebez in northern Samaria, and arrived there around the break of day. After taking some refreshment and resting awhile, Peter told the many disciples gathered together of the miraculous haul of fish and of the meal with the Lord. He taught in the synagogue at Thebez, and then healed the sick in the name of Jesus Christ. Early that afternoon Peter and the apostles and disciples, accompanied by many other people, left Thebez and traveled several hours in a northerly direction to a small mountain in Galilee, arriving there around dusk. Here they met up with the other apostles and a great many disciples, and all the holy women, with the exception of the Blessed Virgin Mary and Veronica. Many people had come together from far and wide, as news had spread of the coming of the apostles and of the death and resurrection of Jesus Christ. Some five hundred people were gathered together. After taking something to eat, Peter and the newly arrived disciples went up onto the mountain, which was relatively flat and able to accommodate several hundred people. It was now exactly two weeks since the Thursday evening on which the Last Supper had taken place, and there was a strong mood of expectation among the people there.

Peter addressed the crowd, speaking of the suffering and resurrection and appearances of the Lord. Then the Risen One approached, a radiant figure, and passed through the middle of the crowd. Peter moved aside, and the Lord took his place. He spoke of the persecution which would befall his followers, but also of the eternal reward in heaven. He told the apostles and disciples that they should remain in Jerusalem and, after the coming of the Holy Spirit, should baptize in the name of the Father, the Son and the Holy Spirit. They should establish a community in Jerusalem, and also in other places. Then Jesus disappeared from their midst.

KING AMMON: Can you tell us, O Hermes, of the heavenly configuration at the time of this appearance of the Risen One to the five hundred?

HERMES: Yes, King Ammon; again the Moon was significantly placed. It had crossed through its node ($7\frac{1}{2}°$ Aries) that day, and on that Thursday evening, April 16, A.D. 33, it was at about 11° Aries, in conjunction with Mercury (11½° Aries). Hermetically there was an opposition between Mercury (24½° Aquarius) and Uranus (23° Leo); this was a repetition of the hermetic opposition between Mercury and Uranus on the afternoon of Monday, February 12, A.D. 31, when Jesus healed the Syrophoenecian woman and her daughter. Thus, Mercury was doubly emphasized at this appearance of the Risen One to the five hundred—geocentrically, by virtue of being in conjunction with the Moon, and heliocentrically, because of the opposition to Uranus. This time it was not so much the healing aspect of Mercury as the teaching aspect which came to expression.

KING AMMON: O Hermes, what took place after this appearance to the five hundred?

HERMES: On Friday, April 17, A.D. 33, the apostles traveled back from Galilee to Thanath-Silo in Samaria, where they remained for the Sabbath, healing the sick. After the close of the Sabbath, they journeyed back to Bethany, where the Blessed Virgin Mary was staying. Arriving in Bethany on Sunday, April 19, A.D. 33, that evening the apostles and disciples and holy women joined together for a love-feast (agape) in Lazarus' house. This was the third agape since the resurrection, the first having been held on the Sunday evening of the day of the resurrection, two weeks previously, and the second on the Saturday evening, one week previously, on which occasion the Lord had appeared to all eleven apostles, and Thomas had laid his hands in the Lord's wounds.

A few days later a fourth love-feast (agape) took place, this time in the Coenaculum, and later that evening, shortly after midnight, the Blessed Virgin Mary received the Holy Sacrament from Peter. By now Mars and Jupiter were close together—in conjunction in Gemini—Mars having overtaken Jupiter on Monday, April 20, A.D. 33. At the time of this event of Mary's first communion, three weeks had elapsed since the Last Supper. As Mary received the Holy Sacrament, Jesus appeared to her, but was not seen by the others. Afterwards she retired to her room to pray and towards dawn the Lord appeared to her again and spoke with her. He gave her power over the church, a protective force, such that light flowed from him into her.

During the following days, leading up to the ascension, Jesus appeared several times to the apostles and disciples. Thus, on the morning of Thursday, April 30, A.D. 33, before daybreak, he appeared suddenly in their midst as they were praying and singing together in the Coenaculum. The Moon was at 3° Libra, where it had been on the evening of the Last Supper, and Mercury was in superior conjunction with the Sun (10° Taurus). On the following Sunday, May 3, A.D. 33, around midday, as Peter, John, James the Lesser, Thomas and some other apostles were approaching the Mount of Olives on their way from Bethany to Jerusalem, the Lord appeared in their midst and spoke with them, accompanying them part of the way, before he disappeared again. This was at the Full Moon; the Sun was at 13° Taurus and the Full Moon, opposite, was at 14° Scorpio, in conjunction with Antares (15° Scorpio).

In the last days immediately preceding the ascension, the Risen One was almost continuously in the company of the apostles, dining with them, praying with them, and teaching them. As they were gathered together at Lazarus' house in Bethany on Wednesday, May 13, A.D. 33, the day before the ascension, the Lord took leave of Lazarus. He blessed some bread and gave it to him to eat. Lazarus then remained behind in Bethany, while Jesus, the apostles and disciples and holy women made their way from Bethany to Jerusalem, taking the same route that he had taken on the occasion of his triumphant entry into Jerusalem.

Shortly after sunset they arrived at a house, where a meal had been prepared. Here there took place another love-feast (agape), this time at which Jesus blessed the bread and wine which were passed around after the meal. Jesus taught. Then he went with the eleven apostles and Mary to the hall of the Last Supper, where they celebrated the Holy Sacrament, exactly as on the evening of the Last Supper. The other disciples and holy women remained in other parts of the Coenaculum. They prayed and sang together throughout the night.

Next morning, before leaving the Coenaculum, Jesus presented the Blessed Virgin Mary to the apostles and disciples as their advocate and as the center of the community. Around dawn they left the Coenaculum. They visited various places in the city; all the while Jesus taught them. As the Sun climbed higher, towards midday, he proceeded to the Mount of Olives and ascended to the top, becoming more and more radiant with light as he went. The light issuing forth from him grew and grew in intensity, becoming more radiant than the midday Sun. And before the eyes of the apostles and the crowd assembled there, Jesus Christ disappeared into the radiant light. Two Angels then appeared from the rays of light and, in resounding tones, said: "Men of Galilee, why do you stand looking up to heaven?

This Jesus, who was taken up from you into heaven, will come again in the same way as you saw him go into heaven." Thereupon the two Angels disappeared.

KING AMMON: Undoubtedly, O Hermes, this was a special cosmic moment, this start of the Lord's ascent through the planetary spheres to the Kingdom of the Father.

HERMES: Indeed, King Ammon! Forty days had elapsed since the resurrection, so the Sun had progressed from the middle of Aries to the latter part of Taurus (23° Taurus), towards the horns of the Bull. And the Moon had traversed the zodiac almost $1\frac{1}{2}$ times, to reach the middle of Aries (15° Aries), where the Sun had stood at the resurrection. Venus ($8\frac{1}{2}°$ Aries) stood in the Moon's node ($6\frac{1}{2}°$ Aries), signifying an outpouring of love. Hermetically, Mercury (1° Leo) was exactly opposite Neptune (1° Aquarius) at this moment of the Lord's departure from the apostles, whereas at dawn on Tuesday, January 13, A.D. 33, as Jesus—after his journey to the three kings—met up with the apostles at Jacob's well, having not seen them for $5\frac{1}{2}$ months, Mercury and Neptune had been hermetically exactly in conjunction. As at the ascension, also at the wedding at Cana Mercury was hermetically opposite Neptune. And at the ascension Mars ($28\frac{1}{2}°$ Cancer) and Saturn ($26\frac{1}{2}°$ Cancer) were in conjunction, viewed hermetically.

KING AMMON: Profound indeed, O Hermes, are the cosmic mysteries relating to the God-Man!

HERMES: And these mysteries, King Ammon, are the content of our daily meditation on the path of Christian hermetic astrology.

KING AMMON: Thank you, O thrice-greatest one, for leading us towards a contemplation of the mysteries of the forty days from the resurrection to the ascension.

CLOSING INVOCATION

A Discourse of Hermes to Tat

The Whitsun Mystery

OPENING INVOCATION

TAT: O father, can you relate to us something concerning the period after the ascension?

HERMES: My son, it is good if we now contemplate the great event that took place ten days after the ascension: the Whitsun event, at which, as promised by Christ, the Holy Spirit was sent to the apostles.

In the days following the ascension, the eleven apostles, and also the Blessed Virgin Mary, spent most of the time together in prayer and worship in the hall of the Last Supper in the Coenaculum. Thus, to a certain extent, they withdrew in seclusion from the other disciples and holy women. A few days after the ascension, Matthias was chosen as the twelfth apostle, to fill the gap left by Judas. In order to be in a position to grasp the Whitsun Mystery, the descent of the Holy Spirit, we need to focus our attention especially on the Blessed Virgin Mary. As referred to in the last discourse, on the morning of the ascension, before leaving the Coenaculum, Jesus Christ presented the Blessed Virgin Mary as the central figure of the community. What was the spiritual background to this?

THE WHITSUN MYSTERY

With this, his last act at the end of the forty days after the resurrection, Christ was preparing the way for the coming of the Holy Spirit at Whitsun. For, the Holy Spirit has to be seen especially in connection with the feminine side of existence, the Eternal Feminine. Not that the Holy Spirit is to be thought of as being feminine, but in its manifestation it is to be seen in connection with the Eternal Feminine. Thus, for example, the Holy Spirit is referred to as the "Comforter," and this is essentially a feminine quality or activity.

TAT: O father, when you speak of the Eternal Feminine, do you mean some kind of goddess?

HERMES: In a certain sense, my son. But in order to grasp this more clearly, let us consider the religion of our Egyptian forefathers. They worshipped Osiris and Isis as the Father and Mother of cosmic and human existence. The Osiris of our Egyptian forefathers is none other than the Being whom we call Christ, who took on flesh in Jesus at the baptism in the Jordan. Thus, in pre-Christian times the Egyptians worshipped Christ—under the name of Osiris—as a Cosmic Being, that is, a Being indwelling the cosmos, prior to the Incarnation. In this sense our Egyptian forefathers can be thought of as *pre-Christian Christians*.

However, they worshipped not only Osiris, but also Isis. The goddess Isis was just as real to them as the god Osiris. Like Osiris, she was a Cosmic Being. But whereas Osiris was likened spiritually to the Sun, Isis was likened spiritually to the Moon. She was seen to reflect the warmth, light and goodness of Osiris, as the Moon reflects the warmth, light and power of the Sun.

We may draw nearer towards an understanding of Isis if we consider the teaching of King Solomon concerning Sophia, the Divine Wisdom. For, the Isis of the Egyptians was the Sophia of the people of Israel. And according to Solomon, Sophia spoke: "The Lord created me at the beginning of his works." In other words, Isis-Sophia, the Divine Wisdom, was the first created Being, the first Being to issue forth from the matrix of the Holy Trinity. Here it is important to note that whereas the Holy Trinity is God, Isis-Sophia, the Divine Wisdom, is a created Being. Thus, we must clearly distinguish between the Logos, the Second Person of the Trinity, and Sophia. As stated by St. John: "All things came into being through the Logos." However, in order for all things to come into being, just as an architect needs a plan before he builds, so the Logos created all with the help of a *plan*—the Divine Wisdom, Sophia.

Logos and Sophia—or Osiris and Isis—were both active in the work of creation. But whereas the Logos, Christ, is an uncreated Being, Sophia is a created Being. Bearing this distinction in mind, just as Christ maybe designated *God*, being the second person of the Holy Trinity, so Isis-Sophia can be called a *goddess* at the pinnacle of creation, being the first created being to issue forth from the Holy Trinity.

TAT: Is it true to say, O father, that the Eternal Feminine is identical with Isis-Sophia, the Divine Wisdom?

HERMES: My son, here we touch upon deep mysteries, which I shall speak of in a later discourse. For, there is a threefold aspect to the Eternal Feminine, and these three aspects compose the counterpart to the Holy Trinity. That is, we may speak of the Eternal Feminine as comprising *Mother, Daughter, and Holy Soul,* as the counterpart to the Father, the Son and the Holy Spirit. Each of these three belonging to the Eternal Feminine is the created aspect corresponding to the uncreated Holy Trinity of Father, Son and Holy Spirit. In the act of the creation, the Father aspect of the creation is the Mother, the Son aspect is the Daughter, and the Holy Spirit aspect is the Holy Soul. Therefore, strictly speaking, it is the Daughter aspect of the Eternal Feminine which is identical with Isis-Sophia, the Divine Wisdom. For, Sophia is the counterpart of the Logos.

TAT: Now I begin to understand, O father, why Osiris and Isis were always seen together—as husband and wife, or as brother and sister.

HERMES: Indeed, my son. Or, to use the language of the Book of Revelation: the Lamb and His Bride. Christ and Sophia are to be seen together, and may be likened to the Spiritual Sun and the Spiritual Moon. Now, just as Christ took on flesh in Jesus at the baptism in the Jordan, so, in a certain sense, Sophia took on flesh in Mary at Whitsun. This belongs to the Whitsun Mystery, the Mystery of Pentecost. And the descent of the Holy Spirit, as the *feminine pole* within the Holy Trinity, was made possible through the incorporation of the Sophia—the Daughter aspect of the Eternal Feminine—in Mary. Just as, from the baptism onwards, a new Being—God and man, Jesus Christ—exists, so, since the Whitsun event, a new Being—*goddess* and woman, Mary Sophia—exists. The entire life of Mary up to the Whitsun event was a preparation for the incarnation of Sophia, just as the life of

Jesus up to the baptism was a preparation for the Incarnation of Christ. In this sense Mary Sophia may be seen as the counterpart to Jesus Christ, and we can understand why, as his last act on the morning of his ascension, Jesus Christ presented the Blessed Virgin Mary to the apostles and disciples as the center of the community.

TAT: O father, what then took place at Whitsun?

HERMES: Before we consider the Whitsun event itself, let us review the period in the Blessed Virgin's life leading up to Whitsun. After the crucifixion, she was present as the body of the Lord was taken down from the cross, and she accompanied Nicodemus and Joseph of Arimathea as they took it to be laid in a sepulcher in a garden belonging to Joseph of Arimathea. Afterwards, the Sabbath was approaching, and Mary and the other holy women and John went to Mt. Calvary to pray. Then they went to the Coenaculum, where they celebrated the Sabbath and remained in prayer and mourning. That night John accompanied the Blessed Virgin Mary and some of the holy women through the streets of Jerusalem to places that were sacred to her because of Jesus, and she also paid a visit to the temple. Mary and the others returned to the Coenaculum before the break of day, and remained there praying and mourning till the close of Sabbath.

That Saturday evening an Angel instructed her to go to the "Nicodemus portal" in the town wall, through which they had entered upon returning from the Garden of the Holy Sepulcher. Mary went there alone in the dark. It was about nine o'clock. There Jesus appeared to her, accompanied by the souls of the patriarchs, to whom he said, indicating the Blessed Virgin: "Mary, my mother." After speaking these words he disappeared, and Mary returned, full of joy, to the Coenaculum.

Shortly after, around eleven o'clock that night, the Blessed Virgin left the Coenaculum again. Walking alone through the streets, she went to Pilate's palace and from there she retraced the path taken by Jesus as he had carried the cross to Mt. Calvary. At each place along the route where Jesus had fallen under the weight of the cross, or where something had happened to him, she knelt down and kissed the ground. She was radiant and glowing with love, filled with loving devotion for Jesus Christ. It was past midnight when she completed the way of the cross to the top of Mt. Calvary, where she remained in prayer. Jesus appeared to her again and proclaimed to her that he had been down to hell and that he would now arise in his transfigured body. He was accompanied by Angels and a host of redeemed souls. Then he proceeded along the way of the cross, pointing out to the accompanying host of Angels and redeemed souls all the brutality he had suffered on the way. Mary beheld all this in spirit, and prayed and contemplated the way of the cross in loving devotion. Thus began the practice of contemplation of the way of the cross.

Jesus, radiant and surrounded by many figures of light, proceeded to the Holy Sepulcher. There he united spiritually with his body, penetrating it with glorious light, and then rose up in his transfigured body. At that moment the earth quaked and a whirling wind swept through the sepulcher, swirling the linen cloths from the corpse into a pile on the ground, while the remains of the corpse disappeared into the ground opened up by the earthquake and then closed again.

It was approaching dawn at this moment of the resurrection, the first rays of sunlight lightening up the eastern horizon. At this very moment the Risen One appeared to the Blessed Virgin on Mt. Calvary. He was gloriously radiant and he showed her his wounds, which shone like suns. She sank to the ground and kissed his feet. Then he disappeared.

TAT: So, O father, the Blessed Virgin Mary was the first person to whom the Risen One appeared?

HERMES: Indeed, my son! First the Lord appeared to her on Easter Saturday night upon his return from the descent into hell, which had lasted some thirty hours, and then he appeared to her at the first light of day on Easter Sunday morning, in his transfigured body, as the Risen One.
    Shortly after, in the dawn twilight, the Risen One then appeared to Mary Magdalena in the Garden of the Holy Sepulcher. Magdalena had gone there with three other holy women—Mary Cleophas, Joanna Chuza, and Salome of Jerusalem—but the other women, frightened at the sight of the soldiers numbed by the earthquake and lying on the ground, had not entered the garden. When Magdalena rejoined the other holy women, she told them that she had seen the Lord and then hurried off back towards the Coenaculum. Close to the Garden of the Holy Sepulcher Jesus then appeared to the three holy women and said: "Greetings!"
    In the meantime Peter and John had been to the sepulcher and seen that the body of the Lord was no longer there. Quite beside themselves, they ran back towards the

Coenaculum. On the way the Lord appeared to them, and also, close to the Coenaculum, to James the Lesser and Judas Thaddeus, who had left the Coenaculum in order to follow Peter and John to the Holy Sepulcher.

These first appearances of the Risen One on Easter Sunday morning were followed by those on the next day to Luke and Cleophas on the way to Emmaus, and then, that Monday evening, to the ten apostles (without Thomas), as we discussed in the last discourse. Here in this discourse, it is a matter of considering the Blessed Virgin Mary, who was the first person to whom Jesus appeared, and who inaugurated the practice of contemplation of the way of the cross.

TAT: O father, after the Blessed Virgin Mary, was Mary Magdalena the second person to whom the Lord appeared?

HERMES: My son, Mary Magdalena was indeed the second person to whom the Lord appeared as the Risen One, in his transfigured body, after the resurrection at dawn on Easter Sunday. But already on Easter Saturday night, after returning from the descent into hell, shortly after appearing to the Blessed Virgin Mary at the Nicodemus portal, Jesus appeared to Joseph of Arimathea. On Friday night after the crucifixion, after having celebrated the Sabbath with the others in the Coenaculum, as Joseph of Arimathea was on his way home, he was seized suddenly by a group of soldiers, at the command of Caiaphas, and was locked in a cell in a tower in the town wall. Caiaphas intended to let Joseph of Arimathea starve to death, and not to say anything about his disappearance. However, on Easter Saturday night, some twenty-four hours after he was imprisoned, while he was sunk deep in prayer, Jesus appeared as a radiant figure to Joseph of Arimathea in his cell, and helped him to escape. That same night he fled from Jerusalem to his home town, Arimathea.

TAT: So, father, the Blessed Virgin Mary and Joseph of Arimathea were specially graced by the appearance of the Lord already on Easter Saturday night.

HERMES: Indeed, my son, both were favored by the Lord in a special way. The Blessed Virgin Mary initiated the practice of contemplation of the way of the cross, and Joseph of Arimathea was the founding figure of the spiritual stream associated with the mysteries of the Holy Grail. We can gain some idea of the central mystery of the Holy Grail if we contemplate the Last Supper and also the event of Mary receiving the Holy Communion for the first time, which took place three weeks after the Last Supper. For, when she received the Holy Sacrament from Peter, it remained present in her heart. From this moment in time onwards, she was devoted to the God-Man sacramentally present in her heart. She became the tabernacle of the holy sacrament, and practiced the prayer of eternal devotion.

TAT: And her role at the Whitsun event itself?

HERMES: My son, this was the next decisive step, the culmination in her life, the incarnation—or, better, the *incorporation*—of the Sophia in the Blessed Virgin Mary. But first let us consider the Whitsun festival itself. What is the background to this festival?

The people of Israel traditionally celebrate the Feast of Weeks (Pentecost) on the fiftieth day after the Passover. The two main days of the Passover festival are Nisan 15 and Nisan 16. Adding fifty days leads us to Sivan 6 and Sivan 7. In the year of the Mystery of Golgotha—A.D. 33—Sivan 5 coincided with the Sabbath, so Sivan 6 began on Saturday evening after the close of the Sabbath. Historically this meant that Sivan 6—Pentecost (the fiftieth day)—began on the evening of Saturday, May 23, A.D. 33. In addition to celebrating the offering of the first fruits of the wheat harvest, the Jewish Pentecost commemorates the giving of the Law to Moses on Mt. Sinai.

At the first appearance of the Risen One to the ten apostles (without Thomas) in the Coenaculum, he had instructed them concerning the veneration of the Holy Sacrament, saying that this should occur following the close of Sabbath. In accordance with this instruction, on the evening of Saturday, May 23, A.D. 33, the twelve apostles (with Matthias) were together with the Blessed Virgin Mary in the hall of the Last Supper, and Peter blessed and broke the bread and divided it among them. They all experienced a wonderful warmth of depth and inwardness upon receiving the Holy Sacrament. They remained together in prayer, and this wonderful inner mood grew and grew in intensity. This mood seemed to be present not just in the apostles, but in the whole of nature.

In the hall of the Last Supper a sublime peace and stillness emanated from the Blessed Virgin, who stood in prayer with her arms folded across her breast. This peace and stillness permeated the apostles and spread out throughout the entire house, enveloping the other disciples and holy women who were there. This radiant peace was a sign of the incorporation of the Sophia Being into Mary that was now taking place. Just as Moses many, many centuries before had received the revelation of the Law on Mt. Sinai at Pentecost, so now at this Pentecost festival in A.D. 33 a sublime revelation—the descent of Sophia to unite with Mary—was taking place on Mt. Zion, in the Coenaculum. By dawn on Sunday, May 24, A.D. 33 the spiritual union between Sophia and Mary was more or less complete, and into the aura of heavenly peace pervading the atmosphere of the Coenaculum the Holy Spirit descended.

TAT: Can you help us, O father, to picture this event more clearly?

HERMES: My son, we can picture on the one hand the earthly figure of the Blessed Virgin, enveloped in the quiet stillness of prayer, as the spiritual center of the group of apostles; on the other hand, overshadowing her the sublime presence of the Sophia, enveloping the whole group of apostles. The Sophia, as the crown of the creation, we can imagine crowned with twelve stars, and above her the Holy Trinity, from the womb of which the Sophia had been born at the beginning of time. Proceeding from the Trinity, the Holy Spirit descended, via Sophia, upon all those gathered together that morning, as day was breaking. Like a radiant Sun, and with a sound like a great rushing wind, came this descent of the Third Person of the Godhead. It penetrated into and pervaded not only the Blessed Virgin and the twelve apostles, but also all the disciples and holy women gathered together in the Coenaculum that Pentecost. In ecstasy they experienced this pouring out of the Divine Fire of the Holy Spirit into their inner beings. Filled with intoxicating joy and a new inner certainty, all were deeply moved. Alone the Blessed Virgin Mary, the spiritual center of all, remained still, tranquilly peaceful, whilst the apostles, disciples and holy women embraced one another joyfully. She was now no longer just a human being, for the Divine Sophia was indwelling her. This was the *birth* of Mary Sophia.

TAT: O father, what was the heavenly configuration at this event?

HERMES: My son, the Sun had just entered the Twins (2½° Gemini), and the Moon (23½° Leo) was in conjunction with Uranus (20° Leo). Moreover, Mercury (25° Gemini) was in conjunction with Jupiter (26½° Gemini). Hermetically, Mars (2½° Leo) was in opposition to Neptune (1½° Aquarius), just as at the ascension Mercury—hermetically—had been opposite Neptune.

This configuration signified not only the "birth" of Mary Sophia but also the birth of the church—the community of Christians. For, on that same day the apostles and disciples—after receiving the blessing of the Virgin Mary—went to the Pool of Bethesda and began to baptize the people gathered there, many of whom had come to Jerusalem to celebrate Pentecost. By the time the Sun set that evening they had baptized some three thousand people, who had been inwardly moved by the outpouring of the Holy Spirit through the apostles and disciples.

TAT: O father, is it true to say that just as the Horoscope of Eternity—the horoscope of the birth of the Risen One at dawn on Easter Sunday—signified the birth of the Spiritual Sun, so the horoscope of the *birth* of Mary Sophia at dawn seven weeks later, on Whit Sunday, signified the birth of the Spiritual Moon?

HERMES: Indeed, my son, this is a true image. For, just as our Egyptian forefathers worshipped Osiris and Isis as the Spiritual Sun and Spiritual Moon, so the incarnation of these two Beings—Christ and Sophia—into Jesus and Mary, signified their births on Earth at Easter and Whitsun.

TAT: Thank you, O father, for this discourse on the Whitsun Mystery.

CLOSING INVOCATION

A Discourse of Hermes to Asclepius

The Christ Impulse in History

OPENING INVOCATION

ASCLEPIUS: Having spoken, O thrice-greatest one, on the events following from the Mystery of Golgotha, can you shed light on the historical consequences of this central event in the history of the Earth and humankind?

HERMES: Noble Asclepius, this theme is of great importance, and today we shall endeavor to encompass it in our discourse. First let us contemplate something of significance in the life of Jesus Christ. From the moment of birth—shortly before midnight on December 6 in 2 B.C.—to the moment of the resurrection was a period of exactly $33\frac{1}{3}$ years less about $1\frac{1}{2}$ days. With the life of Jesus Christ this period of $33\frac{1}{3}$ years was inscribed into the Earth's aura. Ever since then it has repeated itself as a new rhythm—over and above the various planetary rhythms—active in history.

For example, after nine repetitions of this rhythm, following on from the resurrection, the year A.D. 333 was arrived at. This denoted a turning point in the history of Christianity, which came to expression outwardly on the one hand in the Council of Nicea in 325 and on the other hand in the death of Constantine the Great in 337. The year A.D. 333 lies between these two dates, and corresponds to a profound inner transition in the unfolding of the Christ Impulse.

ASCLEPIUS: How, O Hermes, may this inner transition be characterized?

HERMES: Up until A.D. 333 the unfolding of the Christ Impulse was carried very much by the spiritual wave of this Impulse emanating from the Mystery of Golgotha. To use an image: When a stone is dropped in the water, the ripples proceed outward in concentric waves. As spoken of in a previous discourse, the movement underlying the Mystery of Golgotha was twofold—that of descent and ascent: descent to the Mother, and ascent to the Father. However, the movement of descent was, on the whole, overlooked, and it was the movement of ascent—coming to expression in the resurrection and the ascension—which was the focus of attention: the path of ascent of Christ to the Father. Analogously, an image for this would be a stone moving from the depths of a lake up to the surface, breaking through the surface and setting up concentric ripples, and then proceeding further, upwards through the air. Up until the year 333 this movement of the Christ Being in the vertical still lived, by way of transmission and inner experience, in the souls of many Christians. But from 333 onwards it was increasingly the expansion of Christianity horizontally in the world which became the focus of attention, the primary concern of numerous Christians. Here, in a sense, a kind of reversal in man's understanding of the Christ Impulse took place. How may this be understood?

We may come to an understanding of the change, in A.D. 333, in the direction of humanity's relationship to the Christ Impulse, if we contemplate the fourth and fifth miracles of Jesus Christ, as described by the apostle John. These were the feeding of the five thousand and the walking on the water. After the miraculous feeding of five thousand people with five loaves and two fishes, the people wanted to proclaim Jesus their king, but he withdrew by himself. The people did not understand that he did not want to be a king on Earth, that the kingdom he was speaking of was the kingdom of heaven. It was only the twelve disciples who understood him, and they set sail that night by boat across the Sea of Galilee. There arose a great storm which threatened to capsize the boat, and it was then that Jesus appeared to them, walking on the water. This miracle serves as an image of the relationship of Christ to his disciples in the course of history, accompanying them, as the Good Shepherd, across the waters of historical time. Now, in comparing the two miracles, we see that Christ came as the Bread of Life for all (the five thousand), but that he in no way intended to become a king proclaimed by the five thousand. Only the twelve disciples understood that he had come not as a king but as a shepherd of souls, to reveal the heavenly kingdom. And in the case of Judas, his subsequent betrayal of Jesus shows that he had not truly understood this, or that he had forgotten this. For, his betrayal took place largely because he could see no signs of an earthly kingdom being established by Jesus. But Judas was replaced by a disciple who did understand Jesus' true *kingship*.

In the ratio five thousand to twelve is expressed the division of Christianity into two groups—those who, like the five thousand want to make Jesus a king, and those who, like the twelve, recognize him as the shepherd of souls. After the resurrection and ascension of Jesus Christ, it was the twelve who, especially from Whitsun onwards, became the bearers of the Christ Impulse. Through them something of the true nature of the Christ Impulse was transmitted to others who became Christians. But this true understanding deriving from the original Impulse was weaker as time went on, and by A.D. 333 the attitude of the five thousand began to gain the upper hand. The vertical movement underlying the original Christ Impulse became increasingly replaced by the horizontal movement of wanting an expansion of Christianity on Earth. This latter tendency is exemplified clearly by Constantine the Great. Thus, during his lifetime Christianity began to undergo a tremendous expansion in the world, but this was at the expense of the vertical element, the *heights* and *depths* of the Christ Impulse. Of course, there have always been those *true disciples* of Christ who have been inwardly true to the vertical element of the Mystery of Golgotha, but these have remained few in relation to the majority.

ASCLEPIUS: Is it true to say, O Hermes, that in the first period of Christianity, up to 333, the vertical element predominated, whereas from 333 onwards the horizontal element prevailed and has continued to prevail up to the present time?

HERMES: By and large, Asclepius, this is true. Of course, it is a matter of tendencies rather than sudden developments. Moreover, in recent times a new development has entered, which has brought with it a re-opening of the vertical dimension of the Christ Impulse. This has to do with the second coming of Christ.

ASCLEPIUS: Is it possible for you to say more concerning this event, O Hermes?

HERMES: Yes, Asclepius. But first we need to have a mode of counting time, with respect to the $33\frac{1}{3}$-year rhythm of the life of Jesus Christ. This rhythm began with the life of Christ at the beginning of the Christian era. This was the first cycle, which lasted from the hour of birth, shortly before midnight on December 6, 2 B.C., until the resurrection at sunrise on April 5, A.D. 33. This was almost exactly $33\frac{1}{3}$ years. In fact, it was $33\frac{1}{3}$ years less $1\frac{1}{2}$ days—this is the precise rhythm of Christ's life, which was inscribed into the Earth's aura with the first cycle. Since then this rhythm has repeated itself again and again, just like the rhythm of a planet—for example, the Saturn rhythm of $29\frac{1}{2}$ years. But whereas the planetary rhythms are externally visible phenomena, whereby the return of a planet to conjunction with a fixed star can be observed, the $33\frac{1}{3}$-year rhythm of Christ's life is not externally visible. This rhythm can be brought to consciousness, however, as an inner, spiritual rhythm, by attuning oneself to the life of Jesus Christ.

In A.D. 333, the tenth cycle of the $33\frac{1}{3}$-year rhythm was concluded, if we count the $33\frac{1}{3}$-year life of Jesus Christ as the first cycle. Thus, the new direction in the unfolding of Christianity, which began with the conversion of the emperor Constantine the Great at the battle of Milvian Bridge in 312, commenced during the tenth cycle. This conversion took place, according to the report of Constantine to Eusebius, because shortly before the battle Constantine had had a vision of a cross of light superimposed on the Sun with the inscription "In hoc signo vinces" above it.

Constantine recognized the cross as the sign of the Christians, and on account of the promise proclaimed by the inscription, "In this sign you shall conquer," he had the sign of the cross inscribed on his troops' shields before the battle. His victory in this battle at the Milvian Bridge Constantine attributed to the protection of the Christian God, and so he converted to Christianity. However, with the second coming of Jesus Christ the sign is not the cross but the rose-cross, where the black cross is encircled by a garland of seven roses. The seven roses signify the seven stages of the Passion, and it is in this sign of the rose-cross that those who seek Christ in his second coming will triumph. But this entails a battle with evil.

ASCLEPIUS: How does this battle manifest itself, O Hermes?

HERMES: A clear manifestation of the confrontation with the evil powers seeking to oppose Christ's second coming came to expression in the twentieth century. The onset of the second coming in the human realm, looked at from one point of view, can be dated to the twentieth century. The precise onset, according to this viewpoint, coincided with the start of the fifty-ninth cycle of the $33\frac{1}{3}$-year period. This was on the day of the first Full Moon in 1933, on January 11. The Sun ($27\frac{1}{2}°$ Sagittarius) was in opposition to Pluto ($28\frac{1}{2}°$ Gemini), and in turn the Full Moon ($27\frac{1}{2}°$ Gemini) was in conjunction with Pluto. We may recall that at the resurrection Jupiter, hermetically, was at $27\frac{1}{2}°$ Gemini. Further, on the night of the birth of Jesus (radiant star), as beheld by the three magi in the stars, the Full Moon (13° Virgo) was in conjunction with Pluto

(14° Virgo). This configuration of the Full Moon in conjunction with Pluto in opposition to the Sun, which was present on the night of the birth of Jesus and also at the onset of the New Age in 1933, indicates a confrontation with evil. For Jesus the attack of the powers of evil, through the medium of Herod the Great, resulted in the massacre of the innocents. At the onset of the return of Jesus Christ, in spiritual form, in 1933, the onslaught of evil, personified in the leader of the Third Reich, led to a repetition of the massacre of the innocents on a widespread scale—the holocaust of the Jews.

The New Age that began with the onset of the second coming in 1933 was opposed by the setting up of an evil impulse on Earth in the shape of the Third Reich, the *third kingdom*—this being a false kingdom. The sign of the Third Reich was the swastika, which became set up in place of the cross. This sign of the swastika opposed that of the rose-cross. For, the rose-cross arises through the garland of roses being placed around the cross, and if the cross is nullified or replaced by another symbol, then it cannot be raised up. The flowering of the roses around the cross depends upon the existence of the cross.

Now, with the first coming the cross was set up in the world. With the second coming it is a matter of the rose-cross being set up—not, however, in the physical world, but in the Earth's aura—in the etheric or life world. This is the world in which the forces of growth and decay are at work, active in the whole of nature, and also in the human being. Here the roses are an appropriate symbol, being the most beautiful gifts of the world of nature.

The setting up of the rose-cross in the etheric world, as the sign of the second coming of Christ, was undertaken during the fifty-eighth cycle in preparation for the onset of the second coming at the beginning of the fifty-ninth cycle in 1933. The fifty-eighth cycle began on September 12, 1899. Of course, the beginning of a cycle simultaneously denotes the end of the preceding cycle. And the end of a cycle means a repetition, on an inner level, of the Mystery of Golgotha. It was at this time in 1899 that one human being, the initiate referred to already in previous discourses, underwent an inner experience of the Mystery of Golgotha. As a consequence of this experience, which may be likened to that of Paul on the road to Damascus, the initiate devoted himself fully and completely to the Christ Impulse. But whereas Paul proclaimed Christianity under the sign of the cross, the initiate became a herald of Christianity under the sign of the rose-cross. He became active from the beginning of the twentieth century, and from 1910 onwards he began to proclaim the imminent approach of the onset of the second coming in 1933. He himself did not live to witness the fulfillment of his prophecy of the advent of the second coming in the human realm in 1933. For he died in 1925. But by the time of his death, the foundations of a new Christianity—under the sign of the rose-cross—had been established, at least, on the level of thought.

In fact, as with the founding of the people of Israel, where a threefold process of foundation took place through Abraham, Isaac and Jacob, so with the Christianity of the New Age, arising in the twentieth century, three distinct steps or phases are evident: from thought to word to love. These phases correspond to the stages of development of the human being on the spiritual path. For, first the two-petalled lotus, the organ of thought, has to be developed; this is the center whose physical correlation is the pituitary gland, located above and between the eyes. After the development of the thought center, a *descent* has to take place in order to make possible the development of the 16-petalled lotus flower, the organ of the word, whose center of location, looked at in relation to the physical body, is the larynx. Lastly, a further *descent* has to take place (in reality it is an ascent of consciousness) in order to bring about the development of the 12-petalled lotus flower, the organ of love, bound up with the heart.

Analogous to this path of development on the microcosmic level, the stages of unfolding of the Christianity of the second coming, under the sign of the rose-cross, comprise three phases: the first, during the first third of the twentieth century, on the level of thought; the second, during the second third of the twentieth century, on the level of the word; and the third, during the last third of the twentieth century, on the level of the heart. Only at the end of these three phases, at the end of the twentieth century, is the development from thought to word to love complete. In this sense the entire twentieth century is connected with the onset of the New Age, the age of the second coming.

During the first quarter of the twentieth century, the initiate became a vehicle for the new revelation of Jesus Christ, under the sign of the rose-cross. At that time, Christ was on his path of descent from the cosmos towards the Earth, or on the path towards the onset of the second coming in the human realm. The preparation made by the initiate was on the level of thought. Thus during the first third of the twentieth century the New Age began on a cosmic level, and preparation for the second coming in the human realm was made by the initiate during the first quarter of the twentieth century. Already by 1910, having become aware of the path of descent of Jesus Christ towards the Earth, the initiate was able to proclaim with certainty that the second coming would begin in 1933.

ASCLEPIUS: But then opposition arose?

HERMES: Indeed, Asclepius, and it was exactly in 1933 that this opposition, under the sign of the swastika, began to come to full expression. Right down to the last detail it is possible to see that this opposition was the polar opposite of the new Christianity seeking to come to birth under the sign of the rose-cross. For, it was especially in Germany that the preparation for the new Christianity had been made, and it was precisely in Germany in 1933 that the masses chose an earthly leader and the promise of an earthly kingdom in place of the heavenly guidance of the Good Shepherd into the mysteries of his heavenly kingdom. This earthly leader came to power on January 30, 1933, just nineteen days after the start on January 11, 1933, of the new $33\frac{1}{3}$-year cycle of the life of Jesus Christ in the New Age.

Remembering that the period of the ministry, the crowning period of Christ's life, lasted for $3\frac{1}{2}$ years, the last $3\frac{1}{2}$ years of each $33\frac{1}{3}$-year cycle are of overriding significance. And it was exactly during the $3\frac{1}{2}$ years preceding January 1933 that the temptation of the *will to power* presented itself, this being the first of the three temptations in the wilderness.

Similarly, during the last $3\frac{1}{2}$ years of the fifty-ninth cycle—that is, the $3\frac{1}{2}$ years preceding May 11, 1966—a new temptation arose: the second of the three temptations in the wilderness. This second temptation, summarized in the words, *Cast yourself down from the pinnacle of the temple,* presented itself to humankind in the form of the drug epidemic. For, to "cast oneself down from the pinnacle of the temple" means to plunge down from the clear light of thought and conscience into subconscious depths. And taking drugs is a most effective way of accomplishing this.

The drug culture arose in opposition to the new Christ Impulse that sought to make itself felt at that time as a worldwide impulse of peace and love. Of course, there are other manifestations of the second temptation in addition to drug taking, but in each case it is always a matter of forsaking the light of thought and conscience. And this temptation, like that of the will to power, works on further. Moreover, the last $3\frac{1}{2}$ years of the sixtieth cycle—that is, the $3\frac{1}{2}$ years preceding September 8, 1999—entail a new temptation: the third of the three temptations in the wilderness. This is the temptation of *turning stones into bread*, meaning the substitution of the mechanical for the living. This temptation is connected with the development of technology. But, at the same time as presenting a new temptation, each such $3\frac{1}{2}$-year period opens up a new aspect of the Christ Impulse in its unfolding in the age of the second coming, and therefore contains the greatest possible blessing for humankind.

ASCLEPIUS: It would seem, O Hermes, that everything is building up to a climax at the end of the twentieth century.

HERMES: Undoubtedly, Asclepius, for this signifies the completion of the sixtieth cycle, on September 8, 1999. This date lies close to another important date—January 1,

2000—on which the Sun will return for the 2000th time to 16° Sagittarius, where it was located at the birth of Jesus of Nazareth. It is towards this great event, denoting the start of a new millennium, that everything is building up. And all the trials and temptations of humankind in the twentieth century are the birth pangs leading towards this momentous point in time. With the descent of Christ in his second coming, the vertical dimension has been reopened and renewed. For, the deeper significance of the second coming lies in this descent of Christ from the Father to the Mother. Whereas at the first coming Christ opened the path to the Father—"No one comes to the Father, but by me"—with the second coming he is opening the path to the Mother. But now, Asclepius, it is time to close this discourse for today.

ASCLEPIUS: Thank you, O Hermes, for these words that shed new light on the unfolding of the Christ Impulse.

CLOSING INVOCATION

A Discourse of Hermes to King Ammon

The Most Holy Trinosophia

OPENING INVOCATION

KING AMMON: In the last discourse, O Hermes, you spoke of Jesus Christ—through his second coming—opening up the path to the Mother. Can you tell us more concerning this mystery?

HERMES: Yes, King Ammon, herewith we approach the *holy of holies,* a sacred mystery, which we may best comprehend when we direct our hearts and minds to the relationship between the Holy Trinity and the creation. Who was the first created being of the creation? This was the Divine Sophia, the wisdom of creation, of whom Solomon spoke. As Solomon said, she was there from the beginning, and she has set up her seven pillars—these being the seven pillars, or stages, of the temple of creation. Just as an architect, before building a house, draws up a plan, so Sophia was created at the beginning as the wisdom or plan of the creation.

Looking at Sophia in relation to the Holy Trinity, three aspects emerge. Like the Holy Trinity, Sophia is three in one. She is the *Most Holy Trinosophia.* The first aspect of Sophia, as the feminine counterpart to the Father, is the Mother. She is the Mother of everything living. All the beings of nature live between the Father above and the Mother below. Thus, all plants and trees strive on the one hand up towards the Kingdom of Light of the Father and on the other hand down, via their roots, down towards the Kingdom of the Mother in the depths.

The Mother was known to the Greeks as Demeter, but she and her kingdom—the lost kingdom of Shamballa—have fallen away from human consciousness. Just as the Father is approachable only through the light of consciousness, so the Mother is approachable only through the warmth of morality—morally awakened will. It is deeds, moral deeds, that bring the human being into connection with the Mother.

The second aspect of Sophia, as the feminine counterpart to the Son, is the Daughter. She is the cosmic wisdom who appeared to the apostle John in his great vision as "a woman clothed with the Sun, with the Moon under her feet, and on her head a crown of twelve stars." As the counterpart of Christ, she mediates between the Son and humankind, revealing herself especially in the wisdom underlying the great religions and spiritual movements. With the descent of Christ from cosmic realms towards his second coming, she—the Divine Sophia, as the Daughter, the cosmic wisdom—mediated between Christ and the initiate in his teaching work during the first quarter of the twentieth century. Through him there took place, to an unprecedented extent, an unveiling of the Sophia, revealing the seven pillars of her temple, the seven stages of the creation. She was known to the Greeks as Persephone, and there is a deep relationship between the Mother and the Daughter, between Demeter and Persephone. Thus, with the second coming and the descent of Christ to the

Mother, the unveiling of the Daughter is not only on behalf of humankind but also to the purpose of helping the Mother, that is, for the salvation of Mother Earth.

Lastly, the third aspect of the Most Holy Trinosophia, as the feminine counterpart to the Holy Spirit, is the Holy Soul. Just as the Holy Spirit leads people together to form spiritual communities, so the Holy Soul is the soul of community. She brings peace and harmony into the relationship between people in groups, and works as a power of inspiration. For example, after the death of John the Baptist, by which time the Twelve had been called together by the Lord, the Holy Soul worked as an inspiring being of the Twelve, as a *group soul* of the apostles. As another example, the Greeks of Athens worshipped the Holy Soul as *Athena*, as the protecting goddess of the people of Athens, bestowing wisdom and strength upon her subjects.

The Most Holy Trinosophia—the Eternal Feminine—comprises, therefore: Mother, Daughter and Holy Soul, and is the feminine counterpart to the Holy Trinity. And the mystery of the second coming is deeply bound up with the Most Holy Trinosophia. Just as at the first coming Christ came as the revealer of the Holy Trinity—Father, Son, Holy Spirit—with the second coming he is awakening to consciousness the Most Holy Trinosophia. During the path of the cosmic descent of Christ, especially in the period from 1900 to 1925, it was the Daughter aspect that was unveiled—in the weaving of the Divine Sophia between Christ and the initiate. This unveiling would have continued until the completion of Christ's cosmic descent in 1932/1933, if it had not been for the untimely death of the initiate in 1925. Since 1933 the Eternal Feminine—especially the Mother aspect, in the deep concern for

Mother Earth, but also the Holy Soul aspect, in the awakening to community—has been coming more and more to the foreground in human consciousness. All of this is a sign of the second coming, of Christ's descent to the Mother, and the opening up through Christ of the path to the Most Holy Trinosophia.

KING AMMON: How is it possible to understand Christ's path of descent to the Mother?

HERMES: Here there is another cosmic rhythm to be taken into consideration, over and above the $33\frac{1}{3}$-year rhythm. This is the 12-year rhythm of Jupiter. Of special importance is Jupiter's passage through Leo. We need only recall that it was during the rising of Leo that the crucifixion took place, to see that Leo has a special relationship with the Christ Impulse. And at the onset of the second coming in the human realm, on January 11, 1933, Jupiter was at the tailend of Leo, having passed through this constellation during the preceding six months.

With regard to the descent to the Mother in the underworld, we may recall that this began originally at the culmination of the crucifixion on Good Friday, as the sign of the Virgin began to ascend. The earthquake, which split open the ground next to the cross, took place immediately following the sounding forth of Jesus' last words in his hour of death. This moment of death, coinciding with the earthquake, occurred as $2\frac{1}{2}°$ Virgo was rising. And on the morning of August 6, 1945, as an atomic bomb rent open the Earth at Hiroshima, Jupiter was at $2\frac{1}{2}°$ Virgo. This terrible event coincided closely with the opening up of the first sub-earthly realm leading into the underworld. The gates of hell were opened—this was the significance of the Hiroshima bomb. This coincided closely with the beginning of Christ's descent into the underworld, one Jupiter cycle after the onset of the second coming in 1933. During the Jupiter cycle from 1933 to 1945, Jesus Christ was seeking to become active in the human kingdom, but was opposed by the evil powers that gained hold under the sign of the swastika, and there took place a fearful conflict between good and evil in the human kingdom.

As referred to in the last discourse, this conflict was an opposition, on the part of the powers of evil, to Christ's second coming. The path of descent of Christ in his second coming may be followed in connection with the 12-year cycle of Jupiter. For, the passage of Christ through each cosmic realm took place during a cycle of Jupiter, each new cycle beginning with Jupiter's entrance into Leo. The path of descent of Christ from the cosmic sphere of the Sun began with the entrance of Jupiter into Leo in 1861. This coincided with the birth of the initiate. This descent of Christ from the Sun sphere took place during the course of six Jupiter cycles, extending from 1861 to 1932. During each Jupiter cycle Christ, on his path of descent, traversed a particular cosmic sphere. For example, during the Jupiter cycle from 1920 to 1932 he passed through the sphere of the Moon, which is the cosmic sphere of the Angels, just as the Earth is the domain of humankind. This descent of Christ from cosmic realms was mirrored on Earth in the life of the initiate, especially in his teaching activity during the first quarter of the twentieth century.

However, at the same time as Christ was descending from above, this descent was mirrored by an ascent from the interior of the Earth of the powers of evil. And just as a human being, the initiate, was especially a vehicle for the descent of Christ, so one human being became a vehicle for the ascent of those evil powers. This human being became the leader of the Third Reich, proclaimed in 1933, as the counter impulse to the second coming of Jesus Christ, the onset of which in the human kingdom commenced during Jupiter's passage through Leo in 1932/1933. There then ensued, during the Jupiter cycle from 1933 to 1945, the conflict in the human kingdom between the powers of good and the powers of evil, which ended with the vanquishing of the Third Reich in 1945, at the end of the great war. This conflict signified a repetition of the way of the Passion for Christ, this time not on the physical plane of existence but on the life plane, in the etheric realm, involving the whole Earth.

The repetition of the stages of the Passion, for Jesus Christ in his second coming, can be followed from 1933 onwards through the judgment, the scourging, the crowning with thorns, the carrying of the cross, and then the crucifixion, signified by the great war from 1939 to 1945. On a cosmic level the great war signified a repetition of the Mystery of Golgotha, with the crucifixion taking place in the etheric realm interpenetrating the physical plane. This culminated with the Earth being rent apart by the explosion of an atomic bomb at Hiroshima on August 6, 1945, just as on Good Friday in A.D. 33 at the end of the crucifixion, the Earth was rent open by an earthquake.

It should not be imagined, however, that the conflict with evil stopped here. The explosion of the atomic bomb at Hiroshima in 1945 signified that the conflict, which from 1932/1933 up until then had been fought out in the human realm, had begun to become transposed to the sub-earthly spheres within the Earth. For, each sub-earthly sphere is the domain of a particular kind of evil, and on the path of Christ's descent into the underworld a confrontation with the evil at work there, in each sphere, is taking place.

In all there are nine sub-earthly spheres, each the domain of a particular kind of evil. For example, the sixth sub-earthly sphere, known as the *fire earth*, is the realm of evil passions. From this realm there works up continuously into the human subconscious the fire of passion, which, when it takes hold of someone, can corrupt him completely, driving him to acts of bestial lust. Each sub-earthly sphere is the source of an evil impulse working up into the subconscious life of human beings. It is into this underworld of evil, known traditionally as *hell*, that Christ—in his second coming—has descended, beginning in 1945. On his path of descent he is bringing a counter impulse of good to counteract the evil in each sub-earthly sphere. Thus, the counter impulse to the fire of passion in the sixth sub-earthy sphere is purity, as this comes to expression in the sixth Beatitude: "Blessed are the pure in heart, for they shall see God." In fact, each Beatitude contains the impulse of good counteracting the evil working from the corresponding sub-earthly sphere. Hence meditation on the nine Beatitudes leads us into connection with the essence of the Christ Impulse now unfolding on Christ's path of descent through the nine sub-earthly spheres, on his path of descent to the Mother.

KING AMMON: How may we conceive of the Kingdom of the Mother in relation to the hell of the nine sub-earthly spheres?

HERMES: Righteous King Ammon, here we approach a deep mystery connected with the interior of the Earth. As a help to penetrating this mystery, let us consider the Pythagorean teaching concerning the *counter Earth*. The counter Earth of the Pythagoreans is identical with hell, the nine sub-earthly spheres. In the Pythagorean teaching the counter Earth is placed between humankind and the *central hearth* around which the universe rotates. The central hearth is the Kingdom of the Mother, known in the East as *Shamballa*. In the astronomical system of Philolaus, who was a Pythagorean, the central hearth is at the center of the universe, and the various heavenly bodies rotate around it, in the order: counter Earth, Earth, Moon, Sun and planets. The central hearth was envisaged to be the center of the creative force of life. If we do not take the astronomical system of Philolaus literally, but interpret it as an imaginative picture, we can begin to gain a feeling for the relationship between the Earth, the sub-earthly spheres, and the Kingdom of the Mother. That the latter is a center of creative life force is indicated to us by the fact that trees and everything in the plant kingdom strive—via the roots—down towards the *central hearth*, at the same time as striving up towards the heavens. And every human being, too, is placed between the Father in the heights and the Mother in the depths. And it is through the Son being born within the human being, that the path is found on the one hand to the Father in heaven and on the other hand to the Mother in the underworld. It is especially the latter path now, through the onset of the second coming in the twentieth century, that is being opened up.

KING AMMON: So it could be said, O Hermes, that in the course of the twentieth century the gates of hell are being opened?

HERMES: Indeed, King Ammon. Just as a conflict between good and evil took place on the surface of the Earth, in the human kingdom, between 1933 and 1945, so in each successive sub-earthly sphere of the nine spheres leading to the Kingdom of the Mother at the heart of the Earth's interior—a confrontation with evil is taking place. This constitutes Christ's descent to the Mother, which will be followed by his ascent. Through this descent the gates of the successive spheres of hell, the nine spheres of the underworld, are being opened. This path of descent, which took place originally in a matter of hours, immediately following the death on the cross, will last until around the year 2040 in the twenty-first century. Thereafter will follow the ascent, which will be completed during the course of the twenty-second century, by 2133/2134. From then onwards the Earth and humankind will experience the resurrection and the forty days leading up to the ascension. This will be a time of the greatest blessing for nature—from the twenty-second century to the forty-third century—corresponding to the historical period of the forty days between the resurrection and the ascension. And just as after the ascension there took place the Whitsun event, and therewith the great impulse for the spread of Christianity, so in the future historical period after the forty-third century there will be a great new impulse, culminating in the incarnation of the Maitreya Buddha towards the end of the Aquarian age, leading over into the age of Capricorn.

KING AMMON: So, O Hermes, the age of the second coming, lasting from the twentieth century to the end of the age of Aquarius, mirrors on a large historical scale the first coming?

HERMES: Truly, King Ammon, this is so. That which took place in a few hours on Golgotha—the nailing to the cross and the crucifixion—was enacted during the years of the great war, from 1939 to 1945. And that which followed on from the crucifixion—the descent into hell and the subsequent ascent—is now taking place, in the postwar period, and will last until the twenty-second century. It is now, in this period of time since the great war, that Christ is opening up the path to the Mother, on his path of descent to the heart of the Earth. There is no other way of coming to the Mother, but through Jesus Christ. But the opening up of this path entails the confrontation with evil, and it is here that each human being is called upon to participate—to embark on a path of moral development, and thus to be able to overcome the trials and temptations of the evil powers that are now, with the opening of the gates of hell, making themselves ever more strongly felt among humankind on Earth.

KING AMMON: How would you describe such a path of moral development, O Hermes?

HERMES: As spoken of in the previous discourse, honorable King Ammon, it is under the sign of the rose-cross that the spiritual path is to be found that leads to Jesus Christ in his second coming. For, the rose-cross is the symbol of Christ in his second coming—the garland of seven roses around the cross signifying the seven stages of the Passion. And just as the first stage of the Passion—the judgment—took place at sunrise on Good Friday, so in the inner being of humans, dawn of the second coming is signified by the arising of the inner spiritual Sun of the light of conscience. In place of the false judgment made by Caiaphas and the Jewish people two thousand years ago, the second coming is bringing with it the possibility of a moral awakening—the awakening of conscience—entailing the possibility of true judgment in the light of the inner Sun of conscience.

And just as the scourging took place on Good Friday with the rising of Mars, whereby Christ was cruelly beaten, so in his second coming he is bringing the inner courage of Mars. This courage he is able to bestow—not as a *beating*, but through *inner touching* of those who, in the depths of despair, are seeking a new way forward. This is Christ's way of returning the scourging that he received unjustly at human hands.

At the third stage of the Passion, the crowning with thorns, Jupiter rose on that Good Friday morning. With the second coming Jesus Christ is bringing the inner power of initiative needed for the taking up of tasks. Christ's way of returning the humiliating crowning with thorns is the crowning of human beings with tasks, the fulfillment of deeds of love, for which initiative and insight are needed, these being Jupiter's gifts.

And at the carrying of the cross up Mt. Calvary, Saturn rose in the East towards midday on Good Friday. Now, with the second coming Jesus Christ is bestowing the Saturn quality of inner strength to bear the trials of destiny. He is bringing healing into the realm of destiny, helping human beings to shoulder their cross of destiny, saying: "Come unto me all who are heavy laden and I will give you strength of soul, for my yoke is easy and my burden is light." This is his way of returning the heavy load that was placed upon his shoulders by human hands.

At the crucifixion on Good Friday Jesus Christ took upon himself the destiny of all human beings, the whole of humankind. And on the path of moral awakening through the stages of the Passion now being opened up through the second coming, Jesus Christ is bestowing the inner strength needed not just to bear one's own destiny but also the destiny of others. This entails insight into the destiny of others, such as that yielded up by way of the gift of karmic clairvoyance. It is with this gift that Christ is repaying the crucifixion that he suffered at the hands of men. This stage goes beyond the planetary sphere of Saturn; it corresponds to the zodiacal sphere.

The next two stages of the Passion go beyond the zodiac to the very foundations of existence—to the Father and Mother. The sixth stage, the descent into hell—often designated as the laying in the grave or the entombment—leads to the Mother. Human beings who attain this stage on the path of moral development unite themselves not only with the destiny of other human beings but, through Christ, with the whole of nature. This possibility is now being opened up by Christ, through his second coming, in a new way. But here the gifts of the preceding five stages are needed in order for the soul to take the step of consciously uniting itself with the Earth right down to its core, descending into the underworld in order to participate in Christ's work of confronting and overcoming the powers of evil. For, this is the path of redemption of the Earth and nature.

Lastly, the seventh stage—the resurrection and ascension to the Father—transcends all human comprehension. Here it is a matter of a miracle performed by the Father. It is with this miracle that the path of moral development culminates—the path being opened by Christ through his second coming. This path through the stages of the Passion is the garland of roses bestowed by the Divine on the human soul—the first five roses being bestowed as gifts by Christ, the sixth by the Mother, and the seventh by the Father.

This path is preceded by three stages of pupilship, corresponding to the Moon, Venus and Mercury, whereby the essence of these three stages may be summarized as *hope, love* and *faith*—these being the essential prerequisites for embarking on the stages of the Passion.

Thus, filled with faith, hope and love—under the sign of the rose-cross, in which sign we shall conquer—we may take the path of moral development being opened up by Jesus Christ through his second coming. This path is connected with the mysteries of the Most Holy Trinosophia. And one aspect of the unveiling of the Sophianic mysteries now taking place is Astro-Sophia—the wisdom of the stars. It is to the sublime Astro-Sophia that Christian hermetic astrology aspires.

KING AMMON: Thank you, O Hermes, for leading us to a deeper comprehension of these holy mysteries.

HERMES: Noble King Ammon, all that we have spoken of in these discourses can be taken as the subject of meditation on the path of Christian hermetic astrology leading to astrosophy. We began by contemplating the spiritual stream founded by "radiant star," which culminated with the three magi and the star of the magi. This spiritual stream was founded in expectation of the coming of the Messiah. Now, in this New Age of the second coming, a continuation—in metamorphosed form—of this ancient spiritual stream of star wisdom is arising. This continuation of the spiritual stream of the magi has the task of looking to the second coming of Jesus Christ, in accordance with Christ's words that with his second coming there will be *signs in the heavens*. The path of Christian hermetic astrology looks to the heavenly signs, much as the magi did two thousand years ago, but with the difference that now these signs may be read in relation to the heavenly configurations which prevailed during the earthly life of Jesus Christ two thousand years ago. A start on this path has been made in these discourses, but it is only a start. Further progress can be made through deep and profound meditation on the various cosmic relationships we have described in connection with Christ's life. In so doing, we may feel that we are following in the footsteps of the magi, as modern magi, with our hearts full of love and devotion to the Lord and his Blessed Mother, bearing our *gifts* of thought, word and deed, to be placed in the service of the Risen One and the Blessed Virgin Mary. In this mood, then, through grace, we may be favored by their Divine Presence. But we must actively seek them, going towards them, following their star, as the magi did long ago—following not in a physical sense, but inwardly, spiritually, while contemplating the hermetic and geocentric planetary configurations. As Jesus Christ said: "Watch and wait!" Let us actively watch—looking to the heavens not just outwardly, but also inwardly, contemplatively—and let us actively wait in expectation of the possibility of visitations from the Risen One and Mary Sophia. This, then, is Christian hermetic astrology, as a Christian metamorphosis of the ancient hermetic astrology such as the magi cultivated and, earlier still, the priests of ancient Egypt practiced.

KING AMMON: May your words, O Hermes, serve as a guiding beacon to us on our path towards a new wisdom of the stars.

CLOSING INVOCATION

HERMES: Encircling spirits in the North, West, South and East—servants of the sublime Sun Spirit CHRIST—in sacred devotion to the Holy Sacrifice on Golgotha we direct our will, feeling, thought and all our love toward thee for the fulfillment of the Great Work.

(turning to the North): Holy Uriel, thou who bears the memory of the Golden Age of Saturn, whence streams the foundation of human will, pray strengthen the will of all who humbly seek to unite themselves with Christ and His Mission.

(turning to the West): Holy Raphael, thou who embodies the power of the Age of the Sun, whence flows the spiritual stream underlying feeling, may thou imbue human feeling with never-ending devotion to the Christ Being and His Healing Work of Redemption.

(turning to the South): Holy Gabriel, thou who carries the spirit-light of the Age of the Moon, whence radiates the fount underlying the life of thought, help illumine our thinking that it be raised to knowledge of the cosmic mystery of the Logos who is the Salvation of humankind and the Earth.

CLOSING INVOCATION

(turning to the East):   Holy Michael, thou who guards the Evolution of the Earth, during which the Mystery of Golgotha took place, whence comes the inner spirit-birth of the true Self of the human being, may thy radiant Being guide this Self in freedom and love along the path of human existence which receives its meaning alone through Christ.

Encircling spirits of the North, West, South and East—hear our prayer!

TAT, ASCLEPIUS, KING AMMON: Christ graciously hear us!

HERMES: Go forth in peace!

Sun Chronicle

The following Sun Chronicle is based on the Sun's sidereal position at important events in (or connected with) the life of Christ. With the help of this Sun Chronicle it is possible to follow, during the course of the year, the dates of commemoration of these Christ events. Here it should be noted that it is a matter of the *cosmic commemoration*, that is, when the Sun returns to the same location in the sidereal zodiac as at the particular Christ event under consideration. For example, as Jesus of Nazareth was born, shortly before midnight on the night December 6/7, 2 B.C., the Sun was located at 16° Sagittarius in the sidereal zodiac. Owing to the precession of the equinoxes, at the present time the Sun returns to 16° Sagittarius on January 1 each year. Thus, January 1 is the date of the *cosmic commemoration* of the birth of Jesus of Nazareth, whereas December 6 is the historical date.

In Cosmic Christianity, arising now in the New Age, the age of the second coming, it is the cosmic aspect of the life of Christ which is of central importance. Therefore it is a matter of the dates of "cosmic commemoration" of the Christ events, rather than the historical dates. Of course, the latter are also important. Indeed, without the historical dates it would not be possible to find the corresponding dates of *cosmic commemoration*.

The following Sun Chronicle is based on material presented in the author's books *Chronicle of the Living Christ* and *The Horoscopes of Jesus Christ and the Blessed Virgin*

Mary. Usually two consecutive calendar days are given for the date of cosmic commemoration, since—owing to the occurrence of leap years—the date may shift one day in the calendar.

Sun Chronicle of the Christ Events

Sun's sidereal longitude	Present date of Sun's arrival at this longitude	Christ Event	Historical Date
9° Aries	Apr 23/24	Beginning of teaching in the temple	Mar 29, 30 A.D.
10° Aries	Apr 24/25	Visitation of Mary to Elizabeth	Mar 30, 2 B.C.
12° Aries	Apr 27	Mary Magdalena anointed the Messiah	Apr 1, 33 A.D.
13½° Aries	Apr 28/29	Last Supper/Gethsemane Night	Apr 2, 33 A.D.
14° Aries	Apr 29	The Transfiguration	Apr 3/4, 31 A.D.
14° Aries	Apr 29	The Crucifixion	Apr 3, 33 A.D.
14½° Aries	Apr 29/30	Union of the two Jesus children	Apr 3, 12 A.D.
15½° Aries	Apr 30/May 1	The Resurrection	Apr 5, 33 A.D.
16° Aries	May 1	First Passover (with Lazarus)	Apr 5, 30 A.D.
16½° Aries	May 1/2	Drove out money lenders from Temple	Apr 6, 30 A.D.
16½° Aries	May 1/2	Appearance to the two disciples: Emmaus	Apr 6, 33 A.D.
19° Aries	May 4	Conversation with Nicodemus	Apr 8/9, 30 A.D.
22° Aries	May 7	Appearance to the eleven apostles	Apr 11, 33 A.D.
25° Aries	May 10	Appearance to the seven: Sea of Galilee	Apr 15, 33 A.D.
27° Aries	May 12	Appearance to the five hundred	Apr 16, 33 A.D.
3° Taurus	May 18	First communion of the Virgin Mary	Apr 23, 33 A.D.
23° Taurus	Jun 8	The Ascension	May 14, 33 A.D.
2½° Gemini	Jun 18	Whitsun (Pentecost)	May 24, 33 A.D.
12½° Gemini	Jun 28/29	Birth of John the Baptist	Jun 3/4, 2 B.C.
14° Gemini	Jun 30	Death of Solomon Jesus ("radiant star")	Jun 4/5, 12 A.D.
16° Gemini	Jul 2	Conception of Solomon Jesus	Jun 7, 7 B.C.
21° Gemini	Jul 7/8	Healing of ten lepers (Lk. 17:11-19)	Jun 12, 32 A.D.
21° Gemini	Jul 7/8	Raising of a girl (7) from the dead	Jun 12, 32 A.D.

Sun Chronicle of the Christ Events

Sun's sidereal longitude	Present date of Sun's arrival at this longitude	Christ Event	Historical Date
25° Cancer	Aug 12	Birth of Nathan Mary (Mary of Nazareth)	Jul 17, 17 B.C.
25° Cancer	Aug 12	Herod imprisoned John the Baptist	Jul 17, 30 A.D.
2½° Leo	Aug 20	Conversation at Jacob's well	Jul 26, 30 A.D.
3° Leo	Aug 20/21	Raising of Lazarus from the dead	Jul 26, 32 A.D.
10½° Leo	Aug 28	Healing of the nobleman's son	Aug 3, 30 A.D.
12½° Leo	Aug 30	Death of Nathan Mary	Aug 4/5, 12 A.D.
19½° Leo	Sep 6/7	Pharisees sought to kill Jesus	Aug 12, 30 A.D.
22½° Leo	Sep 9/10	Death of Solomon Mary in Ephesus	Aug 15, 44 A.D.
26° Leo	Sep 13	Healing of Peter's mother-in-law	Aug 19, 30 A.D.
9° Virgo	Sep 26/27	Raising of Nazor from the dead	Sep 1, 32 A.D.
10° Virgo	Sep 27/28	Bestowal of gift of healing	Sep 2, 30 A.D.
12° Virgo	Sep 29/30	Healing of Mara the adulteress	Sep 4, 30 A.D.
16° Virgo	Oct 3/4	Birth of Solomon Mary (Blessed Virgin Mary)	Sep 7/8, 21 B.C.
17° Virgo	Oct 4/5	Conception of John the Baptist	Sep 9, 3 B.C.
29° Virgo	Oct 17	Visit to the two surviving kings	Sep 21, 32 A.D.
0½° Libra	Oct 18/19	Baptism in the Jordan	Sep 23, 29 A.D.
1° Libra	Oct 19	Raising of child (3) from the dead	Sep 23, 30 A.D.
14° Libra	Nov 1	Healing of the blind youth Manahem	Oct 6, 30 A.D.
29° Libra	Nov 16	Start of 40-day fast in the desert	Oct 21, 29 A.D.
1° Scorpio	Nov 18	Bartholomew became a disciple	Oct 23, 30 A.D.
1½° Scorpio	Nov 18/19	Judas Iscariot became a disciple	Oct 24, 30 A.D.
2° Scorpio	Nov 19	Conception of Nathan Mary	Oct 25, 18 B.C.
7° Scorpio	Nov 23/24	Thomas became a disciple	Oct 29, 30 A.D.

Sun Chronicle of the Christ Events

Sun's sidereal longitude	Present date of Sun's arrival at this longitude	Christ Event	Historical Date
15° Scorpio	Dec 1/2	Healing of Jephte, son of Achias	Nov 6, 30 A.D.
17° Scorpio	Dec 3/4	First conversion of Mary Magdalena	Nov 8, 30 A.D.
19° Scorpio	Dec 5/6	Healing of slave of Roman centurion	Nov 10, 30 A.D.
22° Scorpio	Dec 8/9	Raising of youth of Nain	Nov 13, 30 A.D.
27° Scorpio	Dec 13/14	First raising of Salome from the dead	Nov 18, 30 A.D.
28½° Scorpio	Dec 15	Summons of Matthew (12th disciple)	Nov 19, 30 A.D.
7½° Sagittarius	Dec 23/24	Commencement of Sermon on the Mount	Nov 28, 30 A.D.
9½° Sagittarius	Dec 25/26	End of 40-day fast in the desert	Nov 30, 29 A.D.
10½° Sagittarius	Dec 26/27	Second raising of Salome from the dead	Dec 1, 30 A.D.
13½° Sagittarius	Dec 29/30	Bestowal of gift of healing	Dec 4, 30 A.D.
16° Sagittarius	Jan 1	Birth of Nathan Jesus	Dec 6/7, 2 B.C.
17° Sagittarius	Jan 2	First walking on the water	Dec 8, 30 A.D.
17½° Sagittarius	Jan 2/3	Conception of Solomon Mary	Dec 8, 22 B.C.
19½° Sagittarius	Jan 4/5	Sending out of the disciples to teach	Dec 10, 30 A.D.
29° Sagittarius	Jan 14	Meeting with Peter (Jn. 1:42)	Dec 19, 29 A.D.
4° Capricorn	Jan 18/19	Summons of Philip (Jn. 1:43)	Dec 24, 29 A.D.
6° Capricorn	Jan 20/21	Adoration of the magi	Dec 26, 6 B.C.
6° Capricorn	Jan 20/21	Second conversion of Mary Magdalena	Dec 26, 30 A.D.
8° Capricorn	Jan 22/23	Wedding at Cana	Dec 28, 29 A.D.
11° Capricorn	Jan 25/26	Raising of a man from the dead	Dec 31, 29 A.D.
14½° Capricorn	Jan 29	Beheading of John the Baptist	Jan 3/4, 31 A.D.
20° Capricorn	Feb 3/4	Conversation of Jesus with Mary	Jan 8/9, 30 A.D.
24° Capricorn	Feb 7/8	Arrival from Egypt at Jacob's well	Jan 13, 33 A.D.

Sun Chronicle of the Christ Events

Sun's sidereal longitude	Present date of Sun's arrival at this longitude	Christ Event	Historical Date
24½° Capricorn	Feb 8	Arrival at place of baptism (Here Jesus Christ—through the disciples Andrew and Saturnin began to baptize people.)	Jan 13, 30 A.D.
26° Capricorn	Feb 9/10	Presentation in the Temple (Nathan)	Jan 15, 1 B.C.
0½° Aquarius	Feb 14	Healing of the paralysed man (Jn. 5)	Jan 19, 31 A.D.
10½° Aquarius	Feb 23/24	Feeding of the five thousand	Jan 29, 31 A.D.
11° Aquarius	Feb 24	Second walking on the water	Jan 30, 31 A.D.
19½° Aquarius	Mar 4/5	Raising of a girl (16) from the dead	Feb 7, 30 A.D.
24½° Aquarius	Mar 9/10	Healing of woman and daughter (Mt. 15)	Feb 12, 31 A.D.
15½° Pisces	Mar 30/31	Birth of Solomon Jesus	Mar 5, 6 B.C.
16° Pisces	Mar 31	Conception of Nathan Jesus	Mar 6, 2 B.C.
25° Pisces	Apr 9	Feeding of the four thousand	Mar 15, 31 A.D.
28½° Pisces	Apr 12/13	Peter received keys of the kingdom	Mar 19, 31 A.D.
29° Pisces	Apr 13	Meeting with Jerusalem disciples	Mar 19, 30 A.D.
29° Pisces	Apr 13	Triumphant entry into Jerusalem	Mar 19, 33 A.D.

Annotated Bibliography

For the reader interested in exploring in more depth the basis of Christian Hermetic Astrology, and Christian Hermeticism in general, the following books, representing only a selection, are warmly recommended to the reader as a starting point for his or her investigations.

Emmerich, Anne Catherine. *The Life of Jesus Christ.* 4 vols. Rockford, Illinois: Tan Books, 1979.

___. *The Life of the Blessed Virgin Mary.* Rockford, Illinois: Tan Books, 1970.

Hermetica, trans. Walter Scott. 4 vols. London: 1924. Reprint. Boulder, Colorado: Hermes House, 1982.

Meditations on the Tarot, A Journey into Christian Hermeticism, trans. R. Powell. Warwick, New York: Amity House, 1985. Reprint. Rockport, Massachusetts: Element Books, 1991.

Powell, Robert, and Treadgold, Peter. *The Sidereal Zodiac.* Tempe, Arizona: American Federation of Astrologers, 1985.

Powell, Robert. *Chronicle of the Living Christ, The Life and Ministry of Jesus Christ: Foundations of Cosmic Christianity.* Hudson, New York: Anthroposophic Press, 1996.

___. *Hermetic Astrology vol. 1: Astrology and Reincarnation.* Kinsau, Germany: Hermetika, 1987; distributed in the United Kingdom and Europe by Element Books, and in the United States by Anthroposophic Press.

___. *Hermetic Astrology vol. II: Astrological Biography.* Kinsau, Germany: Hermetika, 1989; distributed in the United Kingdom and Europe by Element Books, and in the United States by Anthroposophic Press.

___. *The Zodiac: A Historical Survey.* San Diego, California: Astro Computing Services, 1984.

Steiner, Rudolf. *Christ and the Spiritual World, the Search for the Holy Grail.* London: Rudolf Steiner Press, 1983.

___. *How to Know Higher Worlds: A Modern Path of Initiation.* Hudson, New York: Anthroposophic Press, 1994.

___. *An Outline of Esoteric Science.* Hudson, New York: Anthroposophic Press, 1997.

___. *The Spiritual Hierarchies and the Physical World.* Hudson, New York: Anthroposophic Press, 1996.

ABOUT THE AUTHOR

ROBERT A. POWELL was born in 1947 in Reading, England, and studied mathematics at the University of Sussex, graduating with a Master's degree. At the same time, he developed an interest in astronomy and this, in turn, led him to explore the roots of astrology, the ancient science of the connections between the stars and human beings.

In the mid-seventies, while researching these fields at the British Museum in London, Powell discovered the Rudolf Steiner Bookshop and Library on Museum Street. From that moment on, Steiner's anthroposophy or spiritual science became the esoteric or spiritual context in which he was to work: a path and a guide. Steiner's many works provided the epistemological, cosmological, and Christological foundations he sought to continue his work. But Steiner's influence, though essential, was not the only one in these formative years. For, through Steiner, he was led to the work of both the astrosophist Willi Sucher (1902-1985) and the Russian anthroposophist, hermetic sophiologist, and (in his later years) Roman Catholic, Valentin Tomberg (1900-1973).

From 1978 to 1982, Powell, while continuing his research, was in Dornach, Switzerland, at the Goetheanum, where he completed a eurythmy training. Since graduating from eurythmy school, still continuing to study, research, and lecture on themes arising from the practice of esoteric Christianity and astrology, Robert Powell has lived and worked as a eurythmist and movement therapist at the Sophia Foundation in Kinsau, Germany.

www.ingramcontent.com/pod-product-compliance
Lightning Source LLC
Chambersburg PA
CBHW020943230426
43666CB00005B/136